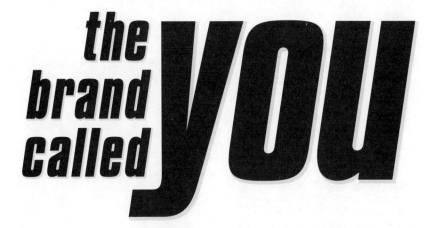

the brand called you

The Ultimate Brand-Building and Business Development Handbook to Transform Anyone into an Indispensable Personal Brand

peter montoya

with tim vandehey

PERSONAL
BRANDING
PRESS

FIRST EDITION PUBLISHED 2003

1 2 3 4 5 6 7 8 9 0   DOC/DOC   0 9 8 7 6 5 4 3 2 1

ISBN 0-9674506-5-9   Price: $24.95

Library of Congress Control Number: 2002109520

Montoya, Peter.
   The brand called you: the ultimate brand building and business development handbook to transform anyone into an indispensable personal brand / Peter Montoya with Tim Vandehey. -- 1st ed.
   p. cm.
   Includes index.
   LCCN 2002109520
   ISBN 0-9674506-5-9

   1. Brand name products--Marketing. 2. Success in business.   3. Entrepreneurship. I. Vandehey, Tim. II. Title.

HD69.B7M65 2003   658.8'27
                             QBI02-200716

Personal Branding Press

Printed and bound by Vaughan Printing

Peter Montoya's books are available at special quantity discounts to use as premiums and sales promotions, or for use in corporate training programs. For more information, please contact us at www.petermontoya.com. or (866) 288-9300

Book Designed by Andrew Rea
Author Photography by Robert Randall
Copyedited by Ginger Sprinkle Perez & Eric Eberwein

To My Loving Wife

Table of Contents

Foreword ix

Introduction 1

Part One: What Is Personal Branding?

1. Why Build a Personal Brand?
   or, How to Have Your Competitors
   Working for You in Five Years 11

2. What Are Selling, Marketing and Branding? 23

3. How Personal Branding Works 35

Part Two: What's Your Brand?

4. Building the Brand Your Business Needs 51

5. Putting the "Personal" in Your Personal Brand 61

Part Three: Branding Strategies

6. Specialize or Sink 75

7. Positioning: Drive a Stake in the Ground 89

8. Branding Channels:
   Many Ways to Get Your Message to
   Your Target Market 103

9. Customer Service:
   Back Up Your Brand with Great Performance 125

Part Four: Power Tools for Your Personal Brand

10. Personal Brochures:
    The One Tool You Can't Live Without 139

11. Personal Logo:
    Name, Slogan and Icon 151

12. Personal Web Sites:
    "Dot Com" Your Brand 165

13. Personal Postcards:
    Direct Mail that Actually Works 179

14. Public Relations, or
    Creating the Credibility Advertising Can't 197

15. Networking and the Beauty of Referrals 209

16. Still More Tools:
    Advertising, Catalogs, CD-ROMs 221

Part Five: Establishing Your Personal Brand in 12 Months

17. Write Your One-Year Branding and Marketing Plan 233

18. Maintaining and Defending Your Brand 255

19. Things to Know, Mistakes to Avoid 269

    Index 275

    Glossary 279

Foreword

What does it mean to consider yourself a brand?

This is not a trivial question. Many people casually assume they are brands, and then go about living their business lives as if brands don't really matter.

Even companies make the same, casual mistake. When you consider your brand, start with your name. If you don't have a good brand name, what can you do about it? You could change it.

When Ralph Lifshitz wanted to become a famous designer, he didn't start by working 24 hours a day designing clothes. The first thing he did was to change his name to Ralph Lauren.

Would you do that? You might say you would, but my experience with hundreds of people suggests just the opposite. In five decades of consulting, I have never worked with an individual who has taken my advice about changing their name.

Ralph could have read this book by Peter Montoya a dozen times, but he wouldn't have gotten anywhere as a designer unless he first got rid of the Lifshitz. In our 1981 book, *Positioning: The Battle for Your Mind*, we wrote: "The name is the hook that hangs the brand on the product ladder in the prospect's mind. In the positioning era, the single most important marketing decision you can make is what to name the product."

When Xerox wanted to get into mainframe computers, the company spent billions trying to build a better product, but they didn't take the first step toward building a better brand, which was making sure the name was right. Xerox meant copier; how could the Xerox name also mean mainframe computer?

When IBM wanted to get into personal computers, the company spent billions trying to build a better product, but they didn't take the first step toward building a better brand. IBM meant mainframe computers; how could the IBM name also mean personal computer?

Many people (and most companies) talk about "branding" until they are blue in the face, but they don't really believe it. They really believe they are going to be successful because they are going to build a better person (or a better product or service), not because they are going to build a better brand.

Don't counter-punch, either. That is, don't look for examples that prove the opposite point of view. Montoya's book, along with most business books, is based on studying what works and what doesn't work... most of the time. (Nothing in business will work 100 percent of the time.)

As a result, you can always find an example that will prove any point you want to prove. It's been my experience that most business people decide what they want to do first, and then look for an example or two that will prove the validity of their decision.

(As far as names are concerned, I'll give you one you can use to justify your own bad name. When Jerome Monroe Smucker started selling apple butter in northeastern Ohio in 1897, he could have used a better name, but didn't. Today, the J.M Smucker name dominates the jelly and jam business.)

Does that mean a Smucker-type name will work for you? Probably not. Just because a 100-to-1 shot once won the Kentucky Derby doesn't mean that's the way to bet. Life is a gamble, but life is more likely to go your way when the odds are in your favor.

What's a brand anyhow? It's not necessarily a better product or person, although it may be. A brand is a name that stands for something in the mind of the prospect.

Branding seeks to create a better perception, not a better product. So your role is to make the changes necessary to create a better perception. Most people don't want to do that. They want to work harder to create a better individual (read: product). Sometimes they get lucky, most times they don't.

When you ask most people what they are good at, they usually reply, "I'm good with people, I'm a good planner and organizer and I'm good at strategic thinking." Translation: "I'm good at everything." Is that any way to build a brand?

What's a Chevrolet? A Chevrolet is a large, small, cheap, expensive car or truck.

Is that anyway to build a brand? Of course not. Chevrolet keeps losing market share to its major competitor, Ford.

The principles for creating a Personal Brand are spelled out in great detail in *The Brand Called You*. It's not enough to understand what those principles are. What you need more than anything else is the flexibility of mind to actually adopt and use the principles.

How do you build a brand? You create a better perception in the mind.

You need to seriously ask yourself, "Am I trying to create a better person or am I trying to create a better perception?" When the smoke clears away, most people are focused on creating a better person. And then they spend the rest of their life going around asking themselves, why doesn't someone recognize my terrific abilities?

That's your job. The world doesn't care about you. Your prospects don't care about you. Your customers don't care about you. They care about themselves, and if they give you a minor thought once in awhile, consider yourself lucky.

Only you care about you. And only you are in a position to do something about it. So if you want to be rich and famous, read this book.

But it won't do one bit of good unless you have the flexibility of mind to recognize the difference between creating a better person and creating a better brand.

Your brand lives or dies, not in your mind, but in the minds of your prospects. If you recognize this fact, you are halfway along on the road to success.

Have a pleasant journey.

Al Ries
Atlanta, GA
Winter, 2003

Introduction

Congratulations. You've started your own business and lived to tell the tale. No matter how long you've been in business, simply lasting beyond your first year is an impressive achievement. But this book is about doing more than that; it's about getting out of survival mode and turning your business into a consistent profit center. It's about reaching the potential you know your business has. Most of all, it's about your branding being as strong as your skills, and making more money than you ever thought possible.

Have you asked yourself these questions?

- Why am I flush with cash one month and struggling the next?
- Why do competitors with less ability consistently get more business than I do?
- Why am I so dependent on one or two clients?
- Why do I never seem to reach my income goals?
- When does it get easier?
- How do I balance my Personal Brand and Company Brand?
- What the hell is branding anyway?
- Why am I the best-kept secret in my community?

They Don't Care About Your Business

We all face the same dilemma: whether you're a CPA or a graphic designer, a computer consultant or a real estate agent, when you start your own company, you don't have any perspective. You know you're good at what you do, and it's natural to think other people—prospective clients—will automatically see the value you offer. So, you get an office, print business cards, perhaps take out a Yellow Pages ad, and then sit back and wait for the business to roll in. And wait...and wait...

Of course, it's not that easy. While it's understandable to think the rest of the world will find your work as fascinating as you do, that's a dangerous fallacy. You must tell prospects why they should choose you over someone else. In fact, from this point on, follow Personal Branding Rule No. 1:

Always assume the world is utterly indifferent to your business, no matter how good you are. Your task is to grab customers by the hand and make them care.

Personal Branding Is the Answer

This book is about changing the rules. It's designed to be the definitive training manual and sourcebook on Personal Branding—the process that takes your skills, personality and unique characteristics and packages them into a powerful identity that lifts you above the crowd of anonymous competitors. Personal Branding is the most powerful success and business-building tool ever devised. Because Personal Branding is a natural aspect of how people evaluate one another, you don't need a master's degree in marketing to put it to work. All you need is some essential information and guidance...precisely what you'll get in these pages.

How Tiger, Schwab and Oprah Have Done It

Personal Branding lets you control how other people perceive you. That's powerful mojo for your business. In essence, you're influencing how others think of you. You're telling them what you stand for—but in a way that's so organic and unobtrusive, they think they've developed that perception all by themselves. That's the beauty of Personal Branding. When done right, it's irresistible, yet it flies under the radar of 90 percent of your target market, so their sales resistance doesn't kick into action.

The subtlety and power of Personal Branding has led to one of its greatest misconceptions: that it's only for wealthy stars with agents and publicity machines. Not true. After all, how do you think Tiger Woods, Oprah Winfrey, Charles Schwab and others like them—one-person industries worth millions—got famous in the first place? They built their Personal Brands back when they weren't famous. What they had was a vision of where they wanted to go, and an instinctive understanding that to get there, they had to come to represent something clear and beneficial in people's minds.

The Brand Called You pulls back the curtain to teach you the same methods used by Martha Stewart, Larry King, Bob Vila and others to make themselves household names. The strategies and ideas are exactly the same…minus the paid staffs and huge advertising agencies. What they and their promoters know, you'll know…and you'll learn the secrets to making Personal Branding work.

Branding Gives People Irresistible Reasons to Work with You

You are your business. Period. Clients choose you not because you have a cool business card or a snazzy office, but because something about you engenders trust and makes them decide to do business with you. Clients choose to work with *you*.

Your business depends entirely on your personal involvement, on your ability to hunt down new clients. If you want to grow, you've got to spend more time making sales calls or placing ads or servicing customers, until there simply aren't enough hours in the day. What's worse, competitors who spend more money on marketing usually get more business, even if your products or service are superior. You scramble, working long days, making big money one month and struggling the next, wondering if your old job is still available.

But once you create a powerful, compelling Personal Brand, business comes to you instead of vice versa. A Personal Brand acts as a "proxy self" for you with prospects and decision-makers. It creates perceptions of positive value in the minds of your target audience, and gives them reasons to work with you. Even when you're not around, it keeps you in people's minds, tells them how you create value, and puts you in the running for business. It makes you a player.

Here's one of the best reasons for spending the time and money to build an unforgettable Personal Brand: once you establish your brand and a sustainable business model, you can scale back your hours or even sell your business. Many successful companies—Famous Amos, Dale Carnegie, Walt Disney Company, Mary Kay—are still built around great Personal Brands, even though their founders are no longer involved with the companies…or no longer alive.

Who Needs a Personal Brand?

Any business built around the ideas, skills, passions and leadership of an individual can benefit from a powerful Personal Brand custom-crafted for that person. It doesn't have to be a one-person business, just one in which the identity of a single man or woman is synonymous with the company. Three categories of business need Personal Branding:

1. **Independent Service Professionals**
   Actors, agents, architects, artists, athletes, attorneys, authors, caterers, chiropractors, consultants, CPAs, dentists, financial advisors, engineers, fashion designers, graphic designers, interior designers, insurance professionals, media personalities, mortgage brokers, musicians, network marketers, physicians, photographers, real estate professionals, therapists, travel agents, speakers, trainers, stockbrokers, wedding planners, wholesalers and writers.

2. **Personal Service Businesses**
   Owners of gyms, tanning salons, auto shops, cleaners, bakeries, appliance repair shops, computer repair shops, print shops, child care, tailors and seamstresses, painters, gardeners, and more.

3. **Value-Adding Product Sellers**
   Personal Branding is equally well-suited for owners of product-based businesses: Auto dealers, bookstores, book publishers, record stores, specialty furniture makers, collectibles companies, specialty retail, gourmet food stores and so on.

Make Your Personal Brand Your Company Brand

So, the eternal question surfaces: If you have a small company, do you develop a Company Brand, or make your Personal Brand your Company Brand? The answer is easy: your Personal Brand should be your Company Brand, without exception. Personal Brands are 100 times easier for people to relate to, because they represent real individuals, not company names that could be hiding virtually anything.

Is this the right direction for you? To find out, answer these simple questions:

- Whom do you trust more—corporations or people?

- Who is more likely to do the right thing—corporations or people?

- Who is more likely to be accountable for their actions—corporations or people?

From our experience, most will answer "people" to all the questions above. We believe and trust people far more than corporations. Corporations are big, uncaring, and have unbending policies that roll over their clients. If you don't like the way a company does business, too bad.

Go somewhere else. There's not much concern about losing your business.

People, on the other hand, care more because they have more at stake. When a person names his company after himself, his personal reputation is on the line. If he loses your business, that is only the beginning of his problems—he also risks losing your respect.

Your Company Brand and Personal Brand, in most circumstances, should be one and the same. A Personal Brand more compelling, easy for your clients to understand, and ultimately will lead to a far more powerful brand.

What You'll Learn

This is a Personal Branding master class. Read it carefully, cover to cover, and you'll learn what it's taken professional marketers years to absorb. You'll develop skills and gain insights that will transform how you market yourself, pursue new business, deal with current clients, and portray yourself in the business community:

- How and why Personal Brands work

- Where a Personal Brand fits into your marketing strategy

- How to make yourself and your personality the center of your branding

- How to create Personal Branding tools and materials that actually work

- How to attract clients instead of chasing them down like a bloodhound

- How to pick the right name for your business

- How to choose the right conduits for getting your message to your target market

- How to determine the right target market

- Why specialists are 100 times more successful than generalists

- Why visibility is more important than ability

- How to balance your personal life and Personal Brand

A Sense of Purpose

In writing this book, we've interviewed hundreds of successful entrepreneurs, professionals and business owners. Over the months, we began to notice a common thread running through 90 percent of the interviews: the truly successful people who had built great brands that helped them dominate their region or niche brought a true sense of purpose to their work.

These folks aren't crusaders. They want to make a living like everyone else. But most of them have approached their businesses from day one with higher goals in mind: to educate, serve the community, help people become financially sound, and so on. They love what they do, and it's not just about the money. That genuine passion shines like a beacon as part of their Personal Brands.

Do you have a sense of purpose for your business? Are you doing what you love? Before you jump into creating a Personal Brand, ask yourself if you can bring that passion to it. If you can, you'll be many steps ahead in crafting a brand that feels real and connects with your prospects. You don't need a sense of purpose to succeed, but why would you want to spend 20 years doing something you don't love?

It's a Commitment

Personal Branding demands total commitment, or it won't work. You've got to be willing to step outside business as usual, to focus on brand-building instead of selling or advertising. You must dedicate a certain block of hours each month to activities that grow your Personal Brand. You need to become your own brand strategist, not a reactive businessman or woman who tries one marketing idea for three months, then another.

Personal Branding takes time—six to nine months to create your brand, create your branding tools, and get your message out to your target market. It's not a quick fix. But, if you stay focused and keep your eyes on the long-term goals, Personal Branding will change your business—and your life—forever.

Your Personal Branding Bible

Our promise to you: you'll find everything you need to know about creating, maintaining, marketing, and targeting your Personal Brand between these covers. *The Brand Called You* was written with the business owner and service professional in mind, designed as an easy-to-use reference you can come back to again and again—for a refresher course, to bone up on ideas for your Web site, or to get inspired to take your Personal Brand in a new direction.

You're in good hands. We've pioneered the concept and methods of Personal Branding, held sold-out branding seminars throughout the country, and worked with hundreds of professionals to help them craft and launch great Personal Brands that brought them wealth and success. We publish the only magazine devoted to Personal Branding and run the only advertising agency in the world solely devoted to the subject. Everything in this book is proven to work in the field, under any conditions.

Ready to get started?

Peter Montoya

Tim Vandehey

April 2003

the brand called you

Part One:
What Is Personal Branding?

Why Build a Personal Brand?

or, How to Have Your Competitors Working for You in Five Years

You already know it's a different world—one in which 40-year job security is a distant memory. These days, there's no loyalty in corporations; you're as apt to be laid off at the first economic hiccup as you are to be promoted. That's probably one of the reasons you struck out on your own and started a business. And now, whether it's just you or you have a small office and a few employees, here's a new question: How do you create your own security?

Before you answer that, answer this: How many people actually know you, as opposed to knowing your reputation? Whether you're a dentist or a caterer, a freelance writer or a clothing designer, odds are most of the people in your professional world barely know you, the person, at all. They have expectations, and know your skills, your quirks and your résumé. But what percentage of all those people—clients, vendors, prospects, industry contacts and colleagues—have you actually shared drinks with? Had dinner with? Talked about something besides work with? Twenty percent? Ten percent?

The point is, outside your immediate circle of friends and family, people know you primarily by your personality, reputation and past performance. In a sense, they know you by your Personal Brand.

Now, how do you create your own security? You develop a powerful Personal Brand that influences how potential clients, employees and decision-makers perceive you. Once you do, your Personal Brand will transform the marketing and growth of your business.

What Is a Personal Brand?

Your Personal Brand is the powerful, clear, positive idea that comes to mind whenever other people think of you. It's what you stand for—the values, abilities and actions that others associate with you. It's a professional alter ego designed for the purpose of influencing how others perceive you, and turning that perception into opportunity. It does this by telling your audience three things:

Who you are

What you do

What makes you different, or how you create value for your target market

There are probably many professional contacts who already hold a high opinion of you based on these qualities, and you've never tried to make them feel that way. So, imagine the benefit of *consciously* crafting your Personal Brand to powerfully convey your value to people you want to work with, and who can influence others to work with you. Personal Branding help you do like the song says: "Ac-centuate the Positive."

What a Personal Brand Does

A Personal Brand is all about *influence*. It influences how the people in your target market perceive you. If you've done your homework and know the characteristics that those people find valuable, you'll create perceptions that in turn create a sense of comfort and confidence in talking to you about doing business. To be effective, your Personal Brand must evoke three basic perceptions in the minds of your target market:

1. **You are different.** Differentiation—the ability to be seen as new and original—is the most important aspect of Personal Branding. If you can't be seen as different, you'll be seen as a follower; that makes capturing "market share" much more difficult.

2. **You are superior.** Your brand must encourage the belief that you are among the best at what you do in some way—faster, providing better service, having the latest technology, and so on. Being seen as a leader in your field is critical to gaining the confidence of people who don't know you personally.

3. **You are authentic.** Great Personal Brands are spin-free zones. Your brand must be built on the truth of who you are, what your strength is, and what you love about your work—and it must communicate this to your market. Today's savvy consumer can smell shallow hype like a hound smells a fox.

A Personal Brand Is a Promise

Your Personal Brand tells prospects what they can expect when they deal with you, which is why it's so powerful. It's an implied covenant between a service provider and a client; it's a promise that makes the client believe, "When I buy this, I will be getting that." You see it all the time in consumer products from cars to computers. People buy because a brand makes them feel a certain way; their choices are rarely rational. But the brands create expectations, and if those expectations are met, people buy again. That's "brand loyalty." If the brand doesn't live up to expectations, buyers go somewhere else.

A Personal Brand works the same way. Every minute of every day, it broadcasts information about your character, abilities and performance. It creates expectations in the minds of others of what they'll get when they work with you. If your brand is sending out the right message, telling prospects they will absolutely get what they're looking for when they work with you, they'll beat down your door and burn up your phone lines.

You can see the power of a Personal Brand's promise in the success of Charles Schwab. You'll probably never work directly with Schwab, but his Personal Brand makes us a promise: When we invest using his company, we'll be treated like we're wealthy. Walt Disney's brand reassures us about the experience we'll have when visiting his parks, watching his movies, or buying his products.

Some of Today's Greatest Personal Brands

How do you know a person's brand? If, when you think of him or her, a single idea blocks out everything else, that's a Personal Brand. That's what you're shooting for in your own branding. Some of today's best examples:

Michael Jordan – *The Greatest Basketball Player of All Time*

Jimmy Buffett – *Purveyor of the Margaritaville Lifestyle*

Walter Cronkite – *The Most Trusted Newsman in the Nation*

Madonna – *The Genius at Self-Reinvention and Self-Promotion*

Tom Hanks – *The Everyman of the Big Screen*

Bob Vila – *The Home-Renovation King*

Colin Powell – *Noble Leader and Statesman*

Branding Is as Old as Humanity

The term "Personal Branding" is a modern invention, but the phenomenon of people instantly labeling each other based on reputation and behavior is as old as human interaction. Even within primitive societies, individuals judged each other based on quick impressions, and decided whom to trust based on unreliable emotional contexts.

Today, we all make judgments about other people with only surface information in hand. Consider a cocktail party. You meet someone and in seconds you've made up your mind about his education, his wealth, and his manners. If you get to know him later, you may change your mind about some things, but those quick-flash perceptions will be hard to shake. You've just encountered his personal image, the DNA of his Personal Brand.

So, Personal Branding is a natural, organic part of human society. The difference today is, we've learned the secrets that let *you* determine how others perceive you. What we're basically saying is: *Define your brand, or your brand will define you.*

A Personal Image Is Not a Personal Brand

Everyone has a *personal image*. It's the collection of qualities people identify with you: your sense of humor, your hairstyle, your clothing, your favorite food, your physical characteristics, and so on. Together, these qualities help people form a mental picture of you.

A Personal Brand is different because it is how other people perceive you. On the outside, former President Bill Clinton looks like a noble, attractive and credible statesman. But because of his past actions, most people perceive Clinton very differently—his brand is that of a misguided, has-been politician.

In the best circumstances, a personal image is an accurate reflection of the Personal Brand. Mother Theresa looked like a woman dedicated to lifelong servitude of the poor and indigent, and we think of her as a modern-day saint. There is complete integrity between her personal image and Personal Brand; the personal image is truly an accurate reflection of the Personal Brand.

To Brand, Take Active Steps

Your personal brand also exerts influence in your professional world…and it's not always the kind of influence you're seeking. You've been creating your personal brand *passively*, without any awareness of the process or the consequences. That's all right; 99 percent of people—including your competitors—do the same. But do you really want to be as clueless as your competitors?

Transforming a personal image into a Personal Brand that creates business opportunity means taking *active* control of the process—defining how prospective customers, colleagues and members of the media perceive you. It means cutting and polishing your brand so everyone who comes into contact with it forms the same basic set of words in their mind when they hear your name. It's packaging the things that make you great at what you do, and sending that message out into the world to sparkle.

Imagine being able to shape the opinions of decision-makers in your profession or of the CEOs of top corporations. Imagine being regarded as a uniquely gifted expert offering value that's instantly obvious. Imagine being able to double your fees because demand is so high. Those are the things Personal Branding can do.

It Isn't About Getting Famous

Our culture loves Personal Brands. We celebrate and analyze them in the most public ways possible. We love to rank them, to debate who's fallen from grace and why. And we pay for them, turning icons like Oprah Winfrey or Tiger Woods into multimillionaires.

That explains the many "most powerful" lists published every year, ranking the 100 biggest power brokers in Hollywood, the 100 mightiest names in sports, and so on. But for us, there's a point to these lists. See how many of these names you know:

Time/CNN Global Business Influentials 2002

Richard Barton, *Founder and CEO of Expedia*

Carla Cico, *CEO of Brasil Telecom*

Guerrino de Luca, *CEO of Logitech International*

Hebert Demel, *Chief of Magna Steyr*

Robert Kazutomo Hori, *CEO of Cybird*

David Ji and Ancle Hsu, *Founders of Apex Digital*

Naina Lal Kidwai, *Investment Banking Guru, HSBC*

Eric Kim, *Marketing Chief of Samsung*

Sallie Krawcheck, *CEO of Citi's new Smith Barney unit*

Rob Lawes, *CEO of HIT Entertainment*

Strive Masiyiwa, *Founder of Econet Wireless*

Dee Mellor, *Vice President, GE Medical Systems*

Adebayo Ogunlesi, *CSFB's Global Banking Chief*

Myrtle Potter, *COO of Genentech*

Ginni Rometty, *GM, IBM Business Consulting Services*

These are all very powerful Personal Brands—in their professions. But there's no Bill Gates, no Larry Ellison, no Steve Jobs or Jack Welch. You've probably never heard of most of these people. Personal Branding is all about wielding influence in your profession, not getting famous. Influence changes minds and creates wealth.

What Can Personal Branding Do for Your Business?

Personal Branding works for everyone. It doesn't matter if you're a physician in private practice or an attorney looking for clients, a caterer trying to get the attention of affluent neighbors or a collectibles specialist with your own shop. All business is based on relationships. People work with you not because of your size or reach, but because they know you, your reputation, and your character. *You create the value.*

The Benefits of a Great Personal Brand:

• **More of the right kind of clients**—Do you want more affluent clients? Clients from a certain ethnic group? Clients with the right connections? Building a tailored Personal Brand is the best way to get them to come to you.

• **Increased earning potential**—Your Personal Brand will position you as one of the leaders in your field of expertise. As such, you'll be able to demand higher pay.

• **Consistent flow of business**—Once you're branded, you're no longer anonymous in your field. Your name, expertise and strengths are known. When you're consistently getting your Personal Brand message out, business comes to you in a steady stream, without you having to chase after it.

• **Draws beneficial people**—A powerful Personal Brand creates an "aura" that attracts the people who can benefit you. Look at the Personal Brand of Secretary of State Colin Powell: honest, noble, a leader. In 1996, Powell had no interest in running against Bill Clinton for President, yet he had to beat the Republican nomination off with a stick. He didn't pursue the opportunity; his Personal Brand *attracted* it.

- **"Top-of-mind" status**—When someone thinks about a project or opportunity where you are one of numerous candidates, your name is one of the first that comes to mind.

- **Increased credibility**—If you're well-known, you must be good. That's the logic of the marketplace, and when you have a Personal Brand, it works in your favor. Your ideas and decisions gain weight and clout.

- **Leadership role**—A strong Personal Brand encourages people to put you in charge. Federal Reserve Chairman Alan Greenspan (Personal Brand: Wizard of the Economy) can prop up or torpedo Wall Street with a few well-chosen words.

- **Enhanced prestige**—Prestige can stem from accomplishments, position, knowledge, or even personal style. It gives your actions more weight and increases your financial value.

- **Added perceived value**—A Personal Brand that conveys honesty, knowledge and intelligence will enhance sales as the customer perceives that the relationship with you adds value.

- **Greater recognition**—Recognition is about credit for accomplishments and the opportunities that result. Great Personal Brands are hard to hide, and if your stamp is on a project or product, people will know it.

- **Association with a trend**—A Personal Brand can position you as being part of a hot business methodology or new technology.

What a Personal Brand Won't Do for You

- **Cover up incompetence**—You've got to be good to make your Personal Brand work. If you're second-rate at what you do, it will come out. Not only will a Personal Brand not hide incompetence, it will make the consequences worse.

- **Make you famous**—Fame is an accident, and it's certainly not a ticket to success. Your Personal Brand is about influencing key people in your domain, not fame for fame's sake.

- **Get you to your goals by itself**—On its own, your Personal Brand will not put your goals on your doorstep. You've got to set the right goals, maintain a level of excellence, actively promote your brand, and be consistent.

Some Cold, Hard Facts About Personal Branding

A great brand is the advertiser's Holy Grail. But like Arthur's knights, most of them end up following false leads and never find what they're seeking. That's because building a brand takes knowledge, patience and persistence. As the failed Internet companies who wasted millions on Super Bowl ads can attest, branding doesn't happen overnight.

Here are our Personal Branding Commandments (stone tablets optional):

- **Brands take time to develop.** A smart brander can put the elements of a great brand in place, but it grows at its own pace. You can't rush branding. Oprah Winfrey is a perfect example of growing a brand over time with exposure, sincerity and accomplishment. Oprah spent years acting, doing her talk show and working to help other women before she became a world-famous media mogul, and she did it without rampant self-promotion. Only after she built her empire did she strap into the hype machine. Typically, even the best Personal Branding campaigns take at least six months to show results.

- **Brands grow organically.** The best Personal Brands develop at the grassroots level, as a result of strong communication, a sense of purpose, and the person behind the brand backing up the brand's promise again and again. With the help of judicious PR and consistent public exposure, people start to see that the brand has real value, and the person behind the brand is just as real. You can't force a Personal Brand down someone's throat in this skeptical age; they'll spit it back in your face. To last, your Personal Brand must grow at its own pace. Plant it and let it blossom.

- **Brands are not rational.** Imagine the meeting when ad agency Wieden + Kennedy pitched the slogan "Just do it" to Nike. The tagline has nothing to do with shoes, which is why it has become a classic. Instead of trying to build a brand based on their shoes—a commodity—Nike built it on striving, sweating and sacrificing to be the best. To its credit, Nike focused on hitting customers in the gut.

- **Brands demand consistency and clarity.** In 2001, K-Mart filed for bankruptcy in a move that left market-watchers in shock. As the dust settles and K-Mart reorganizes, one of the biggest factors in its downfall has to be the lack of a consistent, clear brand. What was K-Mart? It had no clear brand, and in the face of brutal competition, that's as bad as having no brand at all.

- **Branding never doesn't work.** Skeptical companies will claim branding doesn't work. This is simply not true. Branding always works—it either attracts new business or drives it away. There's no middle ground to branding; it always produces a result. Will that be the result you want? That depends on how well you know your target market and build your brand.

Is Personal Branding Cynical and Manipulative?

Personal Branding is controversial. In this age, when advertising has permeated every part of daily life, and corporations are seen as being able to commercialize anything, some claim that building Personal Brands dehumanizes us, manipulates human relationships for financial gain, and turns us all into products.

We could not disagree more, and here's why:

- **Personal Branding is already part of human interaction.** Everyone has a Personal Brand. It's an essential part of how we relate to each other, allowing us to make fast judgments of others based on a few clues. So, while the concept may seem sinister and akin to mind control, it's simply part of who we are.

- **Personal Branding is already everywhere.** How do you think Charles Schwab, Stephen Covey, Meg Ryan and Joe Montana have become rich and famous? Personal Branding. It's already in use by celebrities, people who want to turn their names into industries and themselves into moguls. It's accepted by our culture, and the culture's built-in filters have an uncanny knack for rejecting Personal Brands they don't like.

- **Personal Brands must "keep it real" to be successful.** The best Personal Brand always reflects the true character of the person behind it. Slick, shallow, manipulative brands always crash and burn, sooner or later. People respect what's real and Personal Brands built on lies inevitably spiral in an ugly way. Just ask former televangelist Jim Bakker. Your Personal Brand *must* represent who you are, flaws and all.

- **You've got to build a brand you can live with...consistently.** Most people know that strong relationships with clients build strong long-term business. The only way to build those relationships is if your Personal Brand and the person behind it—you—are 100 percent in sync. In our experience, brands that reflect your true passions, goals and purpose are brands you can live with and maintain over your entire career.

Personal Brand Case Study

David Deal
Deal Design Group

Position: Creative, responsive graphic design and marketing
Location: Carlsbad, CA
Business: Advertising and graphic design
Online: dealdesigngroup.com

David Deal took the plunge in 2000, transitioning out of a failing dot-com to launch his own design and advertising business. He began by naming the business after himself (actually, he and his wife, Nancy, also a designer), avoiding a common error of most new businesses: coming up with a fancy name that obscures the value your name has for people who know you. Beginning business with a small in-house staff and a carefully chosen team of independent contractors, Deal has grown steadily and now occupies a new office in Carlsbad, California.

How It Started:
Deal knew he had a name that was memorable, and he'd built a reputation for himself in the corporate world. Starting his agency was simply a matter of leveraging that reputation. Since his wife, Nancy, is also a graphic designer, using the Deal name kept the business all in the family.

Most Important Steps in Building a Personal Brand:
Being in marketing, Deal had an edge from the beginning: He knew to immediately begin using the Deal Design Group name and graphic identity in every type of communication, from business cards and signage to brochures, answering the phones, and so on. Even his outside contractors get their own dealdesigngroup.com e-mail address to maintain the appearance of brand unity.

Biggest Success:
Deal's successes so far include steady expansion as well as landing accounts for several up-and-coming software and financial services firms in the San Diego area.

On Personal Branding and Personal Attention:
"One of the benefits clients get by using us is my personal attention on their work. With some large agencies, the principals may go in and close

the deal, but the work is done by people the client has probably never met. With Deal Design Group, clients know they get me as well as my team. Also, people know what I say is credible. They're talking with the senior principal of the company, and that gives them a level of confidence in what I say."

Advice:

"Don't think of branding as something you do, and then it's done. It's a relationship, like a marriage. There's a way you present yourself to the other person. There are expectations and benefits that are shared, back and forth. Start with ongoing communication and continue to run your business that way. One thing I've learned is a brand isn't something that goes out there and lives on its own. It takes care."

Brandstorming Your Personal Brand:
8 Great Things You Can Do Right Now

1. Talk to colleagues, customers and staff about how they see you.

2. Make a list of your strongest professional traits and skills.

3. Compare your list with what others tell you. How do things differ?

4. List your main competitors and their personal images.

5. List the things that make you different from your competition.

6. Write down the values, interests or traits you share with your customers.

7. Start asking referral clients what the person who referred them said about you.

8. Start a "genius file": Collect the branding materials of the professionals in your area who have great Personal Brands: real estate agents, doctors, financial advisors, etc. Make sure they're not competitors.

Bottom Line No. 1: How Personal Branding Equals More Business
Creating basic name awareness

Situation: You're a real estate agent in a highly competitive market. In this market, you have about 3,000 competitors, all offering basically the same service as you. So, you're anonymous, just another voice on the phone or name on a lawn sign.

Solution: Because you've been through a divorce, you create a Personal Brand as a skilled specialist in handling real estate during divorce settlements. You promote your brand via ads and direct mail throughout an area heavily populated with couples in their 40s, the most common age group for divorce.

Result: Couples in this area get to know you not as another real estate agent, but as a specialist who's been through a divorce and is sensitive to the situations that can arise. You've gone from a large group (generalists) to a small group (specialists). You've given divorcing couples a strong benefit to calling you, and your calls from this target market increase by more than 100 percent within three months.

Brand Surgery: Avoiding Tragic Branding Mistakes
The Patient: Your Company Brand

- Do not create a Company Brand that's separate from your Personal Brand. You are your company.

- Don't give your company a dry, corporate-sounding name. The plague of independent businesses everywhere is they think they must sound like "a company" to be taken seriously. But would you rather work with a monolithic corporation or a person who cares for your needs?

- If you have employees, pass along the personal values that make you love your business to them. They help spread your brand in everything they do, and if they understand your passions, most will reflect them. Get rid of the ones who don't.

- Design your workspace to reflect your Personal Brand, which is your Company Brand. This doesn't have to mean renovating your building (let's be realistic), but it can be as simple as small décor changes, signage or furniture.

- Be specific in communicating the benefits underlying your Company Brand. Everyone offers "great customer service" or "the lowest prices." Use your brand to communicate the unique things you do that create value, from creativity to specialized experience to comfortable chairs.

- Don't make your Company Brand dependent on your direct involvement. If you do, you'll be a slave to your business, with everything dependent on your hands-on participation.

CHAPTER 2

What Are Selling, Marketing and Branding?

Here's a great way to win a few bucks. When you find an ad agency executive at a party, before you introduce yourself, bet a buddy that within five minutes, the word "branding" will leave the executive's lips. You'll score every time.

Branding is the "it" concept of the past few years. During the late, great dot-com boom, you heard of it everywhere, and it's still the Holy Grail of marketers and ad agencies. "Build brand equity" is the goal of every campaign. But how many of these so-called experts really know what branding is? Not many. They use the word to justify the fees they charge people like you.

Well, we're really going to enrage the ad professionals by telling you what branding is, so you don't need them to build your Personal Brand. In fact, in this chapter, we're going to break down the difference between selling, marketing and branding. We'll also show you why, when you've got a strong Personal Brand, selling is the last thing you'll be spending your time doing.

Selling Is Convincing

You've encountered old-fashioned salesmanship at one time or another; it's unavoidable. Whether those infuriating telemarketing calls pull you away from your dinner table or you trade offers and counteroffers with a car salesman, you've experienced the essential truth of selling: it's adversarial. It's sequential, in that one line of questioning leads to another. And it's hard work. Commission salespeople earn every dime they make, because it's a brutal business.

That's the key. Selling is tough and time-consuming, so it makes no sense for you to get the majority of your business through sales tactics. Selling is the act of *creating a need* where one does not exist, or where the need is too small to stimulate action on its own. In sales, you chase a customer who may not want to listen, and you make him listen. It's the business equivalent of capturing and tagging a wild animal. Selling is not about image or finesse. It's arm-wrestling for dollars. You're selling pure benefits and price without a thought of the customer's emotional needs.

Why Sales Should Be the Last Thing You Do

Selling is about applying pressure. A common example is those TV ads for the latest handy-dandy kitchen implement that slices, dices, cultures yogurt, whatever. After the first pitch, the announcer suddenly shouts, "How much would you pay? Don't answer! There's more!" What follows is a new pitch for some other can't-do-without item you get only if you make the initial purchase. That's pressure: bombarding you with "extras" until you're overwhelmed and hand over your Visa number. Never mind that you eat out every night.

Because you're convincing someone to spend money on something they didn't want when you walked in, selling can be alienating. More important, it takes a lot of sales calls to make one sale. If you're a general contractor cold-calling wealthy homeowners in the hopes they want to renovate, how many will you call before you find one willing to meet with you? 50? 100? Sales is like ditch digging: eventually you get the job done, but not without a lot of sweat and time.

That said, selling is essential. No business can operate without it. But it must come at the right point in the business-development process: after your prospect has seen your messages and absorbed your Personal Brand, decided he likes what you have to say, and is sitting across the table, primed to do business. Successful business owners know a strong Personal Brand does the heavy lifting that selling used to do, leaving them more time to service existing clients. When your brand has done its work and your branding has gotten past sales resistance, selling is how you close the deal. In the world of Personal Branding, it's almost never how you open it.

Marketing Is Generating

Marketing is a single term for the collective activities companies use to *generate* business: running ad campaigns, conducting demographic research, buying TV commercial time, and so on. It's also a dirty word these days for consumers tired of mailboxes filled with creditcard offers. Today's non-stop marketing has created a culture of sales resistance, in which consumers bristle with contempt at the first hint of a marketing message.

But strip away the baggage and marketing is as simple as its name: the act of *creating a market* by sending carefully crafted messages to the proper target market, through multiple channels, over the long term. Marketing puts a sales message in front of the potential customer using different means such as radio ads, direct mail and the media.

In a way, marketing is like farming: You're planting the seeds of customer awareness, to be cultivated and harvested later by salespeople. Good marketing sets the stage for selling by letting customers know the product exists and telling them how they should feel about it. Done well, marketing builds awareness, gets past sales resistance, and creates interest.

The Four Levels of Marketing Response

In your own marketing, you're probably doing more selling than you realize, hitting prospects with a direct cost-benefit message: "Here's what I can do for you and what I charge." Such messages are easily ignored, because you're offering the same thing as everyone else. True marketing appeals as much to the emotions as to the intellect; we all make decisions, even on major purchases, as much with our hearts as with our heads. So, as you refine your branding, remember that it produces four levels of response:

1. **Awareness**—When a target market first comes into contact with a marketing message, its members go from being ignorant that the service provider even existed to the knowledge that he or she does. Prospects can't choose you if they don't know you exist.

2. **Affinity**—After multiple exposures to marketing messages, some prospects begin to develop positive feelings toward your Personal Brand, even without knowing much about the product. That's why soft drink commercials are so relentlessly upbeat; the marketers want you to feel good about drinking their soda even when you're not drinking it. Affinity takes time, which is why it's so critical to be persistent in your marketing, even if you see no short-term results.

3. **Understanding**—Eventually, affinity leads to greater investigation. At this point, good marketing helps consumers understand how and why the service provider benefits them or is right for them. You're appealing to the intellect as well as the emotions, giving the prospect the tools to make the right decision.

4. **Value Threshold**—At some point, the prospect flips a mental switch and decides, "This person is offering something of value to me, and I want it.

Branding Is Influencing

Branding happens before marketing or selling; it's their source. Without a strong brand, marketing is generally ineffective and selling is like beating your head against a wall of sales resistance. A strong brand is the rock-solid foundation for all marketing, because every other aspect of a product's identity—its logo, how its ads are written, who its spokesperson is—is based on that brand. Branding is the reason customers consider a product in the first place.

Branding is *always* about emotions. Good branding campaigns inspire powerful feelings in their target markets: envy, confidence, humor, or the desire to be "cool," for example. Rather than sell or drive home a message, branding *influences* the decision-making centers of the mind. For business owners, Personal Branding is largely about inspiring confidence that you can do the job and that you're good to work with during the process. But nothing is more effective than a Personal Brand that says, "I'm the one to get it done for you." Only slightly less important is having a Personal Brand that fits the culture of your prospects. If you're an accountant trying to get business as an auditor for small software companies, your brand should suggest you're conservative and know high-tech.

When you have a strong Personal Brand out in the world working for you, you'll *attract* new business without even trying. Prospects will come to you after multiple exposures to your brand, and they'll come 90 percent sold on you already. All you'll need to do is close the sale. We've seen it time and time again. New business with no work. If that's not cool, nothing is.

Branding Is Everything

Everything you do affects your Personal Brand. That includes:

- The way you walk, talk and dress
- Your education, neighborhood and profession
- Your choice of spouse, car and friends
- The way you sell, negotiate and meet your obligations
- Your customer service and presentation skills
- How you follow through on your promises

The Brand Continuum

The relationship between selling, marketing and branding can be best illustrated by something we call the Brand Continuum. Imagine a continuum, a state of being that continues infinitely in both directions, using Salesman A from Company A, selling Brand Widget as an example.

Brand Widget

The category of "sales assets" can include sales pitch, personality, physical presentation, personal appearance and negotiating skills.

Brand Widget

Notice that selling is contained as part of marketing. Marketing includes many factors outside the control of Salesman A: product, price, performance, lead generation, advertising, market research, product development and customer service.

Brand Widget

Notice *both* sales and marketing are parts of branding. Branding encompasses everything contained in sales and marketing, plus any or all of the following: company ownership, company location, company facilities, position of product, company and product name, slogan and reputation.

Because of this, sales and marketing help build brands, and vice versa. In short, everything you do affects your Personal Brand, either by supporting it or contradicting it.

That means in this society, where attention spans are short and patience for marketing and sales messages is thin, branding allows people to form impressions instantly as information blurs past them. Before any professional or businessperson can successfully sell his or her services, he or she must cultivate a brand. It's like tilling the soil before planting seeds. You can plant without tilling, but you'll get a lot less yield for your work.

Personal Branding Disciplines

When we present the idea of Personal Branding to business owners and independent professionals, a significant percentage of them respond with something like, "But isn't branding for big corporations?" This bothers us, because that misperception is what keeps many individuals from branding themselves. Branding has nothing to do with market cap or budget. It's about influencing perception and communicating value. You don't have to run Super Bowl TV spots to do that.

The process of Personal Branding actually encompasses every way in which you interact with your clients. We've broken Personal Branding into five disciplines:

1. Personal Brand Development—Creation of tools that contain and communicate your Personal Brand without selling, such as brochures, Web sites and logos

2. Personal Marketing
    a. Print and broadcast advertising
    b. Direct response, mostly direct mail
    c. Networking
    d. Outdoor advertising
    e. Professional and client referrals
    f. Sales
    g. Seminars and client events
    h. Website development and marketing

3. Customer Service
   a. Customer relationship management software

4. Public Relations

5. Personal Presentation
   a. Appearance
   b. Mannerisms
   c. Speaking

Become Your Chief Branding Officer

Who is your Chief Branding Officer? If branding encompasses every aspect of your business, who can act as your company's Chief Branding Officer? That's right: You. Most corporate CEOs think branding belongs in the marketing department, but they're wrong. There is only one person in any company—from a sole proprietorship to a 100,000-employee, multinational operation—with the influence and authority to do the job: the CEO. You are the CBO—Chief Branding Officer—of You, Inc.

Getting from Handshake to Brand

Before this all gets too abstract, let's lay out the process, step-by-step, from the creation of your Personal Brand to the new prospects walking in your door:

Step 1: You craft a Personal Brand based on the attributes that create a sense of value for your target market.

Step 2: Your brand determines the design of your business card, the style of your Web site, the target markets you pursue—all your branding decisions.

Step 3: You launch your marketing, sending direct mail to your target market, posting your Web site, writing articles for carefully selected publications, and so on.

Step 4: You continue your marketing and PR efforts over a period of months, gradually letting your brand establish itself organically as prospects become aware of you.

Step 5: You see the first benefit of your Personal Branding, as longtime clients and prospects alike respond to your sales efforts more favorably.

Step 6: You see the second benefit, as prospects who "heard of you" begin to appear from nowhere, contacting you for meetings or appointments.

Step 7: As you continue your brand development (it never stops), you begin meeting with and closing new clients. You find it's easier, as they come to you looking for reasons NOT to work with you, instead of needing to be sold.

Step 8: You realize greater revenues, both from new clients and the fact that increased demand has allowed you to charge more.

Brand First

The point of all this information is simple: Before you spend a dime on a Yellow Pages ad, new business cards or a snazzy suit, create your Personal Brand. As a business owner, your Personal Brand is especially important, because there's no corporate barrier between it and your prospects.

Even if seeing the first benefits from your brand takes six months, it's worth the investment, as long as you can support yourself in the meantime. It's far better to live with no Personal Brand for a while and start with a blank slate than to create a bad brand in haste, then try to undo the damage months later.

The Difference Between Success in Business, Marketing and Branding

We're not zealots. It's possible to build a successful business without ever building a Personal Brand. All we're saying is, it's much easier, faster, more effective and more rewarding to build a business you can enjoy—one that leaves you time to relish your success—with a strong brand than without one.

In fact, business, marketing and branding success aren't necessarily connected. Business success means survival, the ability to produce a steady income and pay your personnel. It doesn't imply anything about growth, happy clients or your own happiness. Often, it's the result of long, long hours.

Marketing success means you have the ability to attract new business by direct mail, advertising and so on. It doesn't guarantee you can get those clients back, or that you're turning a profit. Marketing means you are able to offer something of value to generate new business. Marketing is expensive.

Branding success, however, implies marketing and business success. You can't build and maintain a successful Personal Brand without strong marketing, great customer service that creates loyalty and generates referrals, a sustainable business model, consistent profits that enable you to reward your people, and time to enjoy the fruits of your labor. It's the best of all worlds.

Personal Brand Case Study

David Bach
David Bach Finish Rich, Inc.

Business: Financial education books, seminars, newsletters, videos
Online: davidbach.com

David Bach was a senior vice president at Morgan Stanley, and a partner of The Bach Group, which during his tenure managed over a half billion dollars for individual investors. His financial planning business emerged from his now nationally licensed Finish Rich Seminars. His philosophy—values first, money second—started a national movement that is revolutionizing how people learn and act with their money. His insights into the need for lifestyle financial education for people of all incomes led him to become a world-renowed author and speaker. Today, he's the author of the national bestsellers *Smart Women Finish Rich*, *Smart Couples Finish Rich*, and *The Finish Rich Workbook*. An internationally recognized financial advisor, speaker and educator with books in six languages and 20 countries, Bach will relase three new titles in the next twelve months (*The Automatic Millionaire*, *Start Young, Finish Rich* and *The Finish Rich Dictionary*).

How It Started:
Bach stumbled into his niche completely by accident. He held a series of seminars on money and investing for women, and while he expected 20 – 30 women to attend the classes, he got 200. He realized there was a tremendous need for what he could offer. "I was raised by a grandmother who taught herself how to invest," he says. "I thought all women were in charge of the money, but many were not. So I started meeting with widows whose husbands had been managing the money. I taught that first class to bring our own clients up to speed."

As so often happens, the title of the seminar hooked prospect after prospect. "Smart Women Finish Rich" has an emotional impact on people, Bach says. "The title was a very important decision. When I wrote a book based on the seminar, the material I had been teaching for five years, I used the same title. I applied the knowledge of what I had been teaching for years and packaged it to reach millions. Many people think you package your knowledge to make money. The truth is you package your knowledge to help more people. The more people you successfully help, however, the more you succeed. It's a wonderful circle of life, where you live and finish rich."

Most Important Steps in Building a Personal Brand:

Bach says that even though he set out to build his company around the Finish Rich brand, people continued to be attracted to his Personal Brand, so that became the cornerstone of the company. "People are ultimately buying into my brand because of me," he says. "They like the way I teach, the way I communicate."

Biggest Success:

Television, in a word. Bach has turned his common-man approach to financial education and a tireless PR effort (he's given thousands of interviews) into appearances on every major television talk program, from *The Today Show*, *The Early Show*, *The View*, and *The O'Reilly Factor* to shows on *CNBC*, CNNfn and PBS. The PBS program about *Smart Women Finish Rich* aired for two years and was instrumental in making the book a bestseller. He's currently working on his second PBS show, *Smart Couples Finish Rich*.

On Personal Branding and Loving What You Do:

"To do this, you've really got to love what you're doing. You have to be driven with a purpose. A lot of people want to write a book and be a brand, but they don't want to do the work. Writing the book is just 10% of it. You then have to get the message out. People have to find you and that takes traveling the world, sharing your story. I've been sharing my message of financial empowerment for over a decade. I eat, sleep and breath what I teach. It hasn't been easy. In the beginning I traveled 100,000 miles a year, stayed at all the Motel 6s and went to the book signings when there were six people there. I love what I do. I would probably write these books for free, but fortunately I get to get paid for teaching and doing this. We have a 25-year plan to really make the world a better place. A purpose makes all the difference."

Advice:

Word of mouth is the key. Bach says. "I've been to almost every state. You've got to get out there and talk to people and tell your story to the world, whether there are five people or 5,000 listening."

"Eventually you get to tell story on television to millions, and then the world finds you. But it starts small, and it starts with a passion and a purpose."

Brandstorming Sales and Marketing:
8 Great Things You Can Do Right Now

1. Calculate the Return on Investment, or ROI, from your marketing. First, add up the money it costs you to get each new customer (direct mail, advertising, printing, giveaways, etc.). Then figure the amount of revenue each customer brings in over 12 months. If you're spending more than half the revenue each customer generates to get them in the door, you're doing something wrong.

2. If you're using salespeople as the first contact with new prospects, stop.

3. Junk your current sales manual (if you have one) and prepare to write a new one once you've built your Personal Brand.

4. Decide whether or not you want to sell. Once you decide, stick with it.

5. Instead of more direct mail, send your customers a survey asking them what they like most and least about your service and business.

6. Go to BuyerZone.com, one of our favorite resources for Personal Branders, to begin looking for printers and other vendors.

7. Calculate the percentage of total revenue you spend on marketing.

8. Write down the mistakes your competitors have made in their marketing. You can learn from them.

Bottom Line No. 2: How Personal Branding Equals More Business
Differentiating you from your competition

Situation: You're a chiropractor in a busy suburban area. With the many weekend athletes around, you should be busy 24/7. But one look through the Yellow Pages reveals about 40 other chiropractors in the same area, and they all seem about as qualified as you. There's nothing to separate you from them, so much of your business depends on people choosing you at random.

Solution: You create a Personal Brand as a self-aware doctor who knows how skeptical some people are about chiropractic care. In your advertising, you position yourself as "the chiropractor for skeptics." In your ads, you dare people who think chiropractors are quacks to come in for a session, and if they're skeptics when they leave, their visit is free. No one else in your market is doing this, so you instantly stand out.

Result: Calls to your office triple as three different groups respond to your message: skeptics who need pain relief but like the risk-free element, mainstream patients who feel you must be confident in your skills to offer a guarantee, and people who like your *chutzpah* and sense of humor.

Brand Surgery: Avoiding Tragic Branding Mistakes
The Patient: Your Budget

- Don't waste big bucks on advertising in large-circulation publications that appeal to a wide target market. You'll get more bang for your buck with smaller, tightly focused publications.

- Beware of buying expensive mailing lists from mailing-list companies. They're often full of dead addresses and errors.

- Unless you're in a profession where appearance doesn't count, invest in professional apparel. This usually means dressing more professionally than your clients. If they tend toward jeans, dress in Dockers. If they prefer khakis, wear a casual suit, and so on.

- Do not hire your brother's friend's cousin to design your Web site.

- Don't get talked into printing your stationery in expensive full color (also known as four-color). It's not always necessary, and the right designer can make two colors look spectacular.

- Choose a target market for your branding campaign that's big enough to provide you with enough business. You'll only convert about 2 percent of your prospects into clients in a 12-month period, so to get 20 new clients, you need to brand to at least 1,000 prospects a year.

- Resist the temptation to jump the gun and send out direct mail or run ads "just to do something." You'll waste money to little effect, and you might damage your brand. Always remember, bad branding is worse than no branding at all.

- Resist the temptation to buy marketing products or premiums based on a "deal." Just because you can get a really great rate on a quarter page of advertising in the local business journal does not mean it's the right tool to build your brand.

- Do as much PR as possible: writing articles for local publications, being interviewed as an expert source, sponsoring public events, etc. It's very effective and very cheap.

CHAPTER 3

How Personal Branding Works

By now, you should have some understanding of why Personal Branding is such a force in business and professional success. The next step: understanding how it works. Knowing the basic principles that give Personal Brands their power will help you create and manage your brand, especially as your target market and goals change, and you're forced to make strategic decisions about your brand.

Everything Begins with Instinct

No matter how rational or perceptive we are, human beings make instantaneous judgments about people and situations, even when there's little evidence. It's evolutionary baggage from 100,000 years ago, when humans lived in nomadic, pre-agrarian societies. One of our critical survival skills was the ability to form immediate, powerful impressions of our environment or other peoples we ran across. Often, these impressions preserved our lives, telling us to run away because an animal was dangerous, or not to eat a strange berry because it smelled like poison.

Today, we do the same in a more civilized setting: a cocktail party (you may argue a cocktail party is only slightly more civilized than Ice Age North America). A woman is introduced to a man and before she even shakes his hand, she's judging him by his clothing, hair or posture. If she gets to know him, she'll make more judgments about him based on his speech and personal background. For her, his Personal Brand has begun to form. We all do this; it's in our nature to label people, objects and situations based on superficial clues, and we form strong initial impressions in 3 to 5 seconds.

People develop these "instinct reactions" about you based on a vast range of elements. Some of the most common:

- What you do
- Where you live
- Your marital status
- Where you went to school
- Where you're from
- What you drive
- How you dress
- Your vocabulary

Nudging "Professional Instincts" the Right Way

Instinct reactions in your personal life probably don't have much effect on your business. But in your professional life, they can be the difference between getting and losing a client. Those 3 to 5 seconds are critical to growing your business. Why? Because while you can dazzle prospects with your knowledge once you get them at the meeting table, the instinctive reaction to your Personal Brand determines *whether or not you get the meeting at all.*

A powerful Personal Brand is the door-opener, nudging the professional instincts of your target market in the direction you want. To do this, your Personal Brand needs to affect your prospect in two ways: to convey the idea you're the person to provide something the prospect needs in the best way possible, and suggest you're someone with whom the prospect can identify or relate to in some way. Common factors prospects will judge you by include:

- The appearance of your office
- The quality of your business card
- Your awards
- Whom you know or whom you've worked with in the past
- How punctual you are
- How you dress

Answer the Questions for Them

Based on this kind of information, prospects will conduct an internal question-and-answer session about you: Is he a professional? Is she successful? Can I trust him to do a good job? Will she understand my business? Is her work high quality? They'll often answer such questions for themselves before they even ask you. If the answers aren't in your favor, kiss the business goodbye.

It isn't fair to gain or lose a client based on these superficial factors. But that's reality. Complain about it, or build a strong brand, take control of those first 3 to 5 seconds, and answer the questions before they're ever asked.

We Do Business With People We Like

Even at its highest levels, business is about people. The 2002 merger between America Online and Time Warner largely came down to a meeting of the minds between AOL founder Steve Case and then-Time Warner CEO Gerald Levin. When the Enron and Tyco debacles became the poster children for rampant corporate corruption, where did public and Congressional wrath fall? Former CEOs Ken Lay and Dennis Kozlowski took the heat. Business will always be about relationships between people.

We live in an age when 24/7 marketing makes it easy to conclude everyone is "spinning" the truth, that everything is focus-grouped to death, and that we can't trust anything companies say. What's the one thing we can trust? How we feel when we meet a person, shake his hand, look him in the eye, and hear what he has to say. Do you know when a person is being sincere or saying what he thinks you want to hear? Well, so do the people who do business with you.

For example, Ben Cohen and Jerry Greenfield became the biggest names on the gourmet ice-cream block not by buying millions in ad space, but by starting an eco-friendly, quirky ice cream company in the wilds of Vermont. By giving their flavors fun names like Cherry Garcia, donating time and profits to environmental causes, and staying true to their funky, granola roots, Ben & Jerry became the ice-cream maker everybody smiled about.

Your Personal Brand tells a prospect you might be someone he'll like or approve of before he ever meets you. That's one more step toward winning the battle in those 3 to 5 seconds.

The Made-Up Mind Is Never Wrong

Once you're in dialogue with the prospect, you're constantly doing and saying things that either reinforce those initial perceptions or contradict them. You can appreciate the damage you do by creating one impression in the first 3 to 5 seconds, then giving off a totally different vibe later. You're fighting an uphill battle.

Personal Branding takes place in the mind, and you have a limited amount of time before people make up their minds about you. It can take months of working together, or it can take a single 15-minute meeting. But once the mind is made up, *it is never wrong*. It's an axiom of Personal

Branding. The made-up mind is always right—to itself—and it can't be changed without great effort and a lot of luck. Think of celebrities about whom you have very strong opinions. Is there anything he could say or do that would change your opinion of O.J. Simpson?

Here's the kicker, which you probably know: Prospects will make up their minds about you in a negative way a lot faster than they will in a positive way. That's because people are cautious. To quote a Hollywood saying, "Nobody ever got fired for saying 'No.'" You need to give prospects strong reasons to feel good about you and what you can do, and that begins with your Personal Brand.

Pass the Gestalt and Other Psych Mumbo-Jumbo

There are complex psychological reasons why people make up their minds so irreversibly. Lucky for us, they're boring. But since you've read this far, you're probably interested in the basics of why we set certain perceptions in quick-dry concrete. So, let's discuss two basic concepts that will give you just enough information to be dangerous at parties.

The first is a German term, *Gestalt*. Gestalts are very powerful learned ideas that, because they've been reinforced again and again through repetition and evidence, have become automatic in our minds and utterly, completely compelling. When an idea takes on Gestalt status for you, you don't even question that it's true; it just is. It's easy to see how Gestalts can be critical in brand development. Some examples common in our culture:

- Honda cars run forever.

- Teenagers are difficult to live with.

- Europeans smoke.

- Engagement rings have diamonds
(DeBeers has done an amazing job with this).

These Gestalts are based as much on opinion or prejudice as on evidence, but they're so universal and powerful, they're largely taken as fact. Your prospects will probably never form Gestalts about you, but they may have them about your profession. Keep that in mind when you choose your target market and build your brand: Are you fighting your profession's image?

Attitude

Attitude is where the rubber meets the road in terms of whether or not you get the business. An attitude is a very personal interpretation, by each person you meet, of whether you are "good" or "bad."

Good or bad? All your qualifications and training come down to that? Basically, yes. A great Personal Brand stimulates strong, different emotions in each person it touches—amusement, interest, scorn, confidence, and so on. If that person interprets that feeling as "good," the brand and its source will be regarded positively. If the interpretation is "bad," there's little chance of winning the person over at any point. You can't make the person change his or her values.

Again, you see how incredibly important it is to choose the right target market for your Personal Branding. If your main selling point is extensive experience, but you're not a great conversationalist, you need to market yourself to a target market that appreciates track record and doesn't care about getting the warm and fuzzies.

Your Brand's Three Power Sources

Let's suppose you've chosen your target market well and gotten past those harrowing 3 to 5 introductory seconds. Your Personal Brand has slipped past the palace guards, and now you have a chance to make a lasting impression on the minds of your prospects. What gives your Personal Brand its power?

1. **Emotional Impact**—The decision to hire someone, buy a product, or award a project is always based on a blend of emotional reaction and rational thinking. However, getting a person considered—making him or her part of the "decision set"—is usually about emotion first. We like to think we make buying decisions based purely on logic, but it's not so. A corporate CEO may choose an ad agency based on a variety of measurable factors, but very often, his decision to give the agency a shot in the first place is based on how that agency—and its marketing—make him *feel*. To be effective, your Personal Brand must evoke strong emotions in your target market—warmth, fellowship, amusement, confidence, admiration, respect, and so on.

2. **Consistency**—Very rarely, a Personal Brand will resonate so strongly with its target market that it generates inquiries and new business immediately. But more often, people will only notice and begin to appreciate your brand after multiple exposures. That makes it critical to keep your Personal Brand consistent from month to month and year to year. Your ad headlines and press releases can change, of course. But your overall brand mes-

sage—who you are, what you do, and how you provide value for your target market—must remain the same, so over time, prospects can become familiar with you. Remember, there's a lot of marketing "noise" out there, and it takes time to rise above it.

3. **Time**—Personal Branding is about repetition. Personal Branding is about repetition. Personal Branding is about...OK, you get the point. It's not glamorous, but it's how brands get built. Not through one exposure to your brochure or your Web site or your public speaking, but through dozens. Once you build a strong Personal Brand, you've got to get your message out to your target market, over and over, consistently, without stopping. That's how you break through the clutter. Plus, repetition and consistency tell prospects you're successful and professional. After all, if you weren't, they wouldn't be seeing your name all the time, would they?

A wonderful example of this is Lucille Ball. I know as kids, we watched (and probably you did, too) "I Love Lucy" reruns several times a week, at dinner, in the morning, during holiday marathons. It was always funny, even after repeated viewings, when you knew exactly what was going to happen. Over the last 50 years of reruns, the show's emotional appeal and consistent quality have made it a timeless classic...and given Lucille Ball an immortal Personal Brand.

Let People Sell Themselves on You

We've talked about how people hate to be "sold," and how Personal Brands grow organically. Well, when you create a strong Personal Brand that appeals to the emotions, is consistent, and hits your target market regularly over time, people will sell themselves on you. They'll form strong, positive impressions of you and *actually take credit for them.* They will think their ability to see how valuable you are is a product of their own acumen and intelligence, rather than any influence you've had over their thinking. *They'll pat themselves on the back for being smart enough to discover you!*

That phenomenon is the main reason Personal Branding is so effective: it works its way into the organic decision-making process. Instead of selling, it gives people the information to sell themselves on you. Once they do, you've got it made. That's the beauty of Personal Branding.

Absolutely 100 Percent Authentic

One of the most unforgettable Personal Brands of the last century was Will Rogers. The beloved actor, humorist and author admitted in a famous quote,

"All I know is what I read in the papers." While a marketing executive of today might dismiss Rogers as a laughable yokel, he was loved by virtually all Americans. Why? He was real.

We're endlessly encouraging businesspeople to build Personal Brands that are 100 percent true to who they are, what they love, and what they want out of life. This isn't just because we're honest men who don't believe in deceiving people, though we are. It's because authentic Personal Brands are the only ones that survive.

In this age, the powerful "baloney detectors" people carry with them are on call around the clock. So when you craft a brand that's 100 percent authentic, incorporating your likes, dislikes and flaws, it resonates with people. They know you're not snowing them. You're a real person putting yourself out there for them to see. There's power in that.

Authenticity is what keeps Personal Branding from being cynical or manipulative. Of course, some folks still insist on trying to baffle with B.S., and they soon discover...

...You Can't Brand a Lie

Branding a lie is impossible, and when lies are revealed, Personal Brands can fall hard. A perfect example is Jimmy Swaggart, the television minister who waged war on evil until he publicly admitted to an unspecified "sin" that later turned out to be cavorting with prostitutes. Despite his famous, tearful "I have sinned against you" speech and his penitence, Swaggart has never rehabilitated his image because so many of his followers felt extremely and irreversibly betrayed.

So, remember, when building your Personal Brand, stick to the advice of Polonius, the court advisor in William Shakespeare's *Hamlet*: "To thine own self be true."

The Three Levels of Brand Status

One of the most common reasons people don't create Personal Brands is they think branding is only for celebrities, or people whose work exists on a national or global scale, like politicians or journalists. Not true. The principles of Personal Branding apply on any scale, from a Hollywood studio putting the right actor's name above the movie title to ensure a big Labor Day opening, to a small business owner positioning himself with the local Chamber of Commerce.

Fact is, you don't have to be a mover and shaker to be an effective Personal Brand. There are three levels of brand status, each with its own advantages:

1. **Advocate: the Personal Brand is associated with a trend or culture—** At this level, your Personal Brand does not shape a trend or culture, but taps into it and uses its popularity to increase people's awareness and acceptance of the brand. Example: an architect sees a resurgence of Spanish Revival design in L.A., and re-positions himself to be the "Spanish Revival architect."

   Trends can and do go out of style, so it's dangerous to tie your Personal Brand too closely to one. You're better off to embrace the strongest aspects of your professional culture, from creativity to attention to detail; they're more likely to last. But of course, if you can hitch your wagon to a hot trend and ride it for greater wealth, be opportunistic.

   Example: Singer Mandy Moore is a low-level pop diva who's riding the coattails of Britney Spears and others to sell a few million records. She's got some talent, but she'll never create or symbolize a musical movement.

2. **Trendsetter: the Personal Brand influences the culture—** Trend-setting Personal Brands drive or encourage the spread of new ideas within their culture, such as an interior designer being one of the first in her region to try a new style. Trendsetters possess both the ability to identify and promote new ideas within their culture, and a strong link to the principles of that culture. As trends come and go, they stay in the limelight.

   The most powerful advantage for you in becoming a trendsetter is *differentiation*. Instead of being just another service provider in your field, you're a leader, someone shaping the progress of your profession. Keep in mind this is perception; you may not be actively doing anything to change your culture. But you're seen as a leader, and that sets you apart.

   Example: Britney Spears is a superstar, and she's the leading example of the modern, bare-midriffed, media-created pop music icon. She's talented, and a trendsetter for the current music scene, but most doubt she has the artistic ability to transcend fad status. When she fades from the scene, another pretty face will take her place.

3. **Icon: the Personal Brand is etched into the culture—** Most of us will never achieve icon status, because it's as much about luck as it is about Personal Branding skill. Icons symbolize entire cultures or movements, much as Bob Dylan is synonymous with the '60s folk scene.

   Don't worry about becoming an icon. Even if you wanted to, it's out of your control. Icon status brings as many problems as advantages, like your every action being under a microscope. Being a trendsetter will get you all the success you could ever want.

But if you're looking for an example in the world of music, you can't do better than Madonna. Her merits as an artist are up for debate, but there's no argument about one fact: She's the symbol of self-reinvention, provocation, and daring cultural commentary for female musical performers.

Visibility Is More Important than Ability

What does this all mean? It means that despite your training, skills, education and experience, if you're not being seen in the right way by the right people, over and over again, you will lose business to lower-quality competitors who are more visible.

To put it simply, *visibility is more important than ability*. Write it down, hang it on your bulletin board, have a shirt made. It makes professionals angry, but it's true. When you're trying to get business, the first step is to be considered, to get into the decision set. That doesn't happen because you're wonderful at what you do; prospects have no way of knowing that. They consider the people they see repeatedly in direct mail, in the newspaper, or at speaking engagements.

When people see your name or face consistently, they assume you must be more successful—and therefore better—than the service providers they never see. Those companies will get the calls and the business. Visibility becomes a self-fulfilling prophecy.

Lack of Visibility Diminishes Your Credibility

With such a flood of marketing information available today, people assume anyone worth hearing about has already crossed their radar screen. If they haven't heard of you, you can't be very good. Also unfair, but true. Visibility affects the perception of your competence.

Your Personal Brand is your weapon in the visibility battle. It keeps you visible to the prospect through your marketing and PR, and tells prospects about the abilities that make you worth contacting. That's why it's so important to constantly promote your brand. Brands decay over time, and if you're not keeping your brand in front of your target market, they'll assume you're out of business.

Attorney Johnnie Cochran is a great example of this dynamic. For years, he was a successful lawyer working for African-American clients fighting faulty products, discrimination, and police brutality. He had built a solid reputation as a crusader and was getting close to taking his money and retiring. Then came O.J. Simpson. Now, Cochran is internationally known, in demand, and the figurehead of an international company that employs hundreds. Is Cochran a better lawyer? No. But as he might put it in rhyme, "If you've got visibility, you've got greater hireability."

Does Ability Matter?

Of course it does. Once you've got the meeting, you've got to perform. Dazzle prospects with your knowledge and experience. Use your sales skills. If you get the work, blow clients away with the quality.

Over the long term, your ability to perform and provide value again and again is what will build your Personal Brand with each customer. Visibility and emotional impact get them in the door. Quality keeps them with you for years. They're equal parts of your effective Personal Brand.

Personal Brand Case Study

Kenny Fisher
Kenny the Printer

Position: On-time printing with retail-quality service
Location: Irvine, CA
Business: Full-service commercial printing
Online: kennytheprinter.com

A quirky name? Sure. But Kenny the Printer has become *the* printer in the business-heavy region of Orange County, CA. All because Kenny Fisher, a brash, fast-talking would-be savior for the printing industry, had a fit of indignation over the disgraceful level of service offered at most print shops, and decided to save the industry from itself.

How it Started:

In 1981, Fisher was looking to start a business, and he started smart: by looking for an industry that was not serving its market well. By that standard, printing stood out like a tarantula on a wedding cake. "There are many reasons for it," he says. "Printing, from the time you order typesetting to the time it goes to the plates, then to stripping and bindery, so many hands touch it, somewhere along the line there's going to be a breakdown."

What Fisher discovered was that printing, especially small-press printing, was a customer-experience disaster. "People jumped into it who had no background in printing, especially with the franchises," he says. "The stories are bizarre. I looked at 43 print shops as a mystery shopper, from San Diego to San Jose, and found a number of things that were wrong. The places were dumps. They didn't understand that they are retailers, they should run like Nordstrom. Instead, most printers act like you should be grateful to them for waiting on you. Then you need a rabbit's foot and a horseshoe to get your job done right and on time. It's nauseating."

Initially, Fisher's solution was to launch a revolution: a training and scheduling system designed to teach printers to turn themselves into clockwork businesses. He still trains printers and speaks around the world, and has served on the board of every printing organization in the country. But the inevitable outgrowth of Fisher's mission was his own print shop that used his system for marketing, business, operations, scheduling and customer service.

Most Important Steps in Building a Personal Brand:

Most crucial is the name, without question. Concocted over a conversation with his father, the Kenny the Printer moniker immediately differentiates the business from the endless Kwik-Prints and Insta-Copy franchises out there.

Next, Fisher swears by his ability to give customers an experience like none they've ever had at a printer before. "When you walk through the door, you're greeted with a smile," he says. "We make shopping for printing easy by bringing your choices down so it's easy to know what you need. And we give you the work when it's promised. Neighbors and businesses talk, and they say, 'Go there. You'll get it on time, and it will be right.' That's why there were 10 printers in my area when we opened, and now there's only me and one other."

Biggest Success:

"I asked, 'What made you come here, why did you leave your old printer?' They would all have a horror story of one kind or another. So I picked up on things where other printers were dropping the ball. No one was dropping the ball worse than small-press printers, except maybe car dealers."

Fisher is proud to state he has no outside salespeople, as most other commercial printers do. He doesn't need them; his business has grown to dominate the local market strictly through performance and word-of-mouth, much like Lexus or Nordstrom.

On Personal Branding and His Name:

"I've had that "who's on first, what's on second" routine with customers who didn't know the name of the company was Kenny the Printer. I didn't want it to be another Sir Speedy, etc. Those names lend themselves to the idea that you're only making copies, but Kenny the Printer would lend itself to what we have today, which is 13 different capabilities."

Advice:

"The best advice is, and it sounds corny, but follow the Golden Rule to the point that it's painful. That means if you've made a mistake, stand behind it, and if you have to turn around and reimburse the customer for thousands, do it. That's painful, but do it. Employees see it and they know we stand behind what we say. And customers spread the word-of-mouth like wildfire."

Brandstorming Your Visibility:
9 Great Things You Can Do Right Now

1. If your business has a corporate-sounding name, change it and rename your business around *your* name.

2. Trash your old business cards and stationery and reprint new ones with your new name.

3. Write letters to your customers letting them know you've changed your name and why—you want to leverage the value inherent in your name.

4. Develop a spoken statement that tells listeners exactly what you do in 5 seconds or less.

5. Find out which networking groups meet in your area and put their meeting dates on your calendar.

6. Do the same for organizations related to your profession that meet in your area.

7. List the ways prospects and customers come into contact with your Personal Brand when they deal with your business. Can they come into contact with your brand more often?

8. Do a survey of people in a public place—a supermarket or park. Ask them to name three people in the area in your line of work. Talk to at least 50 people, list the responses, and see how many times you're named and at which ranking.

9. List the competitors who have greater visibility than you and the tactics they use to become visible.

Bottom Line No. 3: How Personal Branding Equals More Business
Using the media to create visibility

Situation: You're a financial advisor in a booming economy, when everyone is making money and offering financial advice. But you want more: a self-sustaining business that will keep producing new clients even when the Wall Street bubble pops. Sound familiar?

Solution: You realize some of your competitors are advertising heavily in the local newspaper and some are doing billboards as well. People see their faces around town, assume they must be good if they're everywhere, and call them instead of you. You decide to fight back: You hire a local freelance writer to ghostwrite a column for you on smart retirement planning, and you talk the editor of your local paper into running it. Now you've got a weekly presence in the local media that has much more credibility than a paid ad. Even better, you start sending reprints of your column to your prospects every week, further reinforcing your expertise.

Result: Over the months, people begin to know you as "the financial planner with the column." They see your photo in the paper, recognize you on the street, and you start working your way into their minds. Your credibility is greater than the advisors who advertise because in your column, you're not trying to sell anyone on anything. Your visibility jumps drastically, and within three months, you start seeing a noticeable increase in business.

Brand Surgery: Avoiding Tragic Branding Mistakes
The Patient: Selling and Marketing

- Don't start your quest for new business by selling. If people don't know anything about you, why would they buy from you?

- Don't spend the majority of your time on sales calls. That's chasing clients. Let the prospects come to you through your branding. It's a better use of your time.

- Teach your sales staff about Personal Branding. Each of them should have his or her own Personal Brand for the people he or she comes into contact with in business.

- Don't confuse marketing and advertising. This happens a lot. Marketing encompasses all activities that help generate new business, from direct mail to client referrals. Advertising is one of many marketing tools. It is buying advertising space in a magazine or newspaper or airtime on TV or radio.

- Hone your sales skills and have your people do the same. Personal Branding gets prospects in the door, but when they're in your office, it's time to sell and close the deal. Make sure your sales techniques and those of your staff fit your brand.

- Don't copy. If a competitor launches a branding campaign, don't emulate it. This is a major strategic mistake. You don't want to be the follower in a category; you want to lead your own category.

the brand called YOU

Part Two:

What's Your Brand?

CHAPTER 4

Building the Brand Your Business Needs

Like any science, Personal Branding has its core concepts—the things you've got to know to understand the whole picture. Develop a clear understanding of the three essentials of Personal Branding, and you'll be ahead of 99 percent of the population—and well on your way to your own winning brand.

No. 1 - Characteristics

Personal Brands aren't abstract. They're based on characteristics you possess. People look at the characteristics you build into your brand and decide whether or not they like you, and if you can provide the value they're looking for in a product or service. You're branded by some of the following characteristics:

- Personality
- Skills
- Profession
- Interests
- Lifestyle

- Accomplishments
- Appearance
- Possessions
- Friends

No. 2 - Attributes

Each of us has hundreds of characteristics, from hair color to awards we've won. The 3 to 5 characteristics that instantly signify powerful benefits to a target market are called *attributes*. They're the foundation of any Personal Brand. For example, Michael Jordan's attributes are:

- Greatest basketball champion of all time

- Incredible leaper and athlete

- Charismatic spokesman

- Physically attractive

- Fierce competitor

- Excellence

No. 3 – Leading Attribute

Take the single most powerful attribute and that's your *leading attribute*. The leading attribute is almost always the first idea that enters someone's mind when they hear or read about another person. For example, Michael Jordan's leading attribute is obviously:

The Greatest Basketball Player of All Time

Attributes are the pillars your Personal Brand is built on, and your leading attribute is your load-bearing wall. The hard part is identifying your attributes and choosing a leading attribute. Which one you choose depends on who your target market is and what they value, because that's what will compel them to choose you over your competition.

Perception Is More Powerful than Reality

You've heard the aphorism: "Perception is reality." Debate the metaphysics of that all you want, but the fact is perception is *stronger* than reality. What we believe often influences our actions much more than what is, and that's what gives branding its firepower. Personal Branding is about influencing perceptions, choosing the characteristics that will appeal to your target market, and communicating them in a manner that makes people perceive you as beneficial to them.

So in developing your brand, keep in mind how you are perceived. Before you even begin choosing the attributes that will make up your brand, ask yourself, "How do I want to be perceived by my target audience?" Consider the values your target market holds, the ways the top people in your field are perceived, and answer these questions:

- How does my target market perceive me now?

- Is that perception in line with how I want to be perceived?

- Is it beneficial to my growth?

- What perception do I want my prospects to hold that lines up with my professional strengths and my personal passions?

- How can I make my prospects perceive me as different from my competitors?

How can you know how you're currently perceived? Try asking your customers, vendors and colleagues. It can make for some uncomfortable conversations, but be persistent and you'll get the real scoop on how they see you.

Differentiation Is Everything

Like the law of gravity, differentiation is simple, direct and utterly essential: For prospects to choose you over a competitor, they *must* see you as being different from others in your field. For your Personal Brand to pay off, you absolutely must differentiate yourself from everyone else working your target market.

The trouble is, differentiation goes against our natural human tendency to blend into the crowd, to emulate what others do because it's safe. For a Personal Brand that lets you dominate a market, you must go in the other direction, telling others why you're different from the crowd. Many businesspeople make the error of copying what their most successful competitors are doing, but all that accomplishes is to make others see you as an also-ran riding on another's coattails.

The best ways to differentiate yourself:

- Create a new category within your profession. An example would be a Web site designer repositioning herself as a designer of interactive television ads. To do this, your product or service must truly be different, not just repackaged.

- Choose a leading attribute for your brand that your competitors are ignoring. For example, if no one in your market has built a brand around saving time and meeting deadlines, build your Personal Brand around that feature.

- Offer a product or service no one else does.

- Communicate with your audience in a way no one else does. For example, if your competition tends to run dry, staid ads or brochures, try writing branding pieces that take the opposite tack: humorous, personal and clever.

A perfect example of differentiation was Mary Kay Ash, the *doyenne* of American cosmetics for nearly four decades. In her trademark pink Cadillac (she awarded similar cars to her top salespeople each year) and her highly personal approach to helping women thrive in the male-dominated business world of the 1960s, Ash became something unique: a driven, flamboyant business mogul who used the Golden Rule as her guiding principle of business.

Differentiation requires that you become an expert on your competition—who they are and how they've positioned themselves. Once you know that, you can figure out how best to differentiate yourself. Start researching.

Create a Business – Appropriate Brand

Your business brand is a set of parameters your Personal Brand must fit into if it's going to have the effect you want on your prospects. Some types of people will appeal to certain types of customers. Others will not. If you build a Personal Brand while ignoring the fact that your target market expects certain things from certain professions, you might end up with a distinct brand that reflects who you are, but actually repels the people you want as customers.

For example, if you're an attorney, but deep down you're a Margaritaville-loving frat boy who just wants to have fun, you might go whole-hog and build a Personal Brand as the "wacky, Hawaiian shirt-wearing lawyer." Distinctive to be sure, but 99 percent of prospects will run from you in horror. People don't hire lawyers; they hire you to take their problems seriously. You can't build a Personal Brand in a vacuum. You must consider what your target market expects not just from you, but from your profession.

To get off on the right foot, follow these steps:

• Write down what your clients typically expect of you.

• Write down the things you have done so far that have made you successful, and the things that have cost you business.

• Think about the aspects of your personality, background and approach to your work that best fit your client and prospect expectations.

• Which characteristics can you work into your Personal Brand that will suggest the factors that have made you successful? If working long hours has won you more clients than anything else, how can you build a brand that tells your target market about your work ethic?

- Which things should definitely NOT go into your brand?

It's the Relationship, Stupid

Think about the service providers you frequent: your accountant, your mechanic, your real estate agent. No matter how skilled they are, you wouldn't work with them if they made you angry or insulted you. The relationship matters as much as the performance—maybe even more. Have you ever maintained a relationship with someone who fouled up? You probably have, and the reason you did is because the relationships are often more important than performance.

The importance of relationships in business is a main reason Personal Branding works. When you craft a compelling brand, you do more than communicate key reasons to work with you. You allow each prospect to get to know you from a distance, to start a relationship with you. That's why we recommend your brand be built around your personal characteristics and passions. No person can form an emotional connection to a list of your degrees and awards, but when you tell a unique personal story, you'll make meaningful contact with many potential clients.

Which kinds of relationships do the people in your target market value? Creative and interactive? Rule-bound and rigidly professional? Fast-paced and chaotic? Personal and emotional? If you don't know, learn.

Good Advice Builds Trust

Everyone in your field offers basically the same products or services, right? What makes you different is your level of expertise, the knowledge of your specialty you share with customers. In short, your advice is your most important and valuable service, whether you're selling hardware or legal services.

When prospects come to you initially, you're an empty sheet of paper in their minds. How you perform for them and live up to expectations— the quality of the advice you give—determines the picture that goes on that paper. Provide reliable advice repeatedly, and you gain a customer's trust, the most valuable payment you can receive. Good advice builds trust, and trust turns customers into loyalists, referral sources, and business assets.

Personal Brand Case Study

Louis Barajas
Louis Barajas & Associates

Position: Financial services for the under-served Latino market
Location: East Los Angeles, CA
Business: Financial planning
Online: btfacts.com

Louis Barajas did something unthinkable in the world of financial services, where "assets under management" is the only accepted measure of success: He left a cushy Newport Beach firm to return to his roots in East Los Angeles. Why? He wanted to focus his energies on providing badly needed financial advice and planning to his fellow Latinos, who normally did not have access to such services.

The payoff was substantial: Barajas was chosen as one of the Top 100 Advisors in the country for 2002 by *Mutual Funds* magazine.

How It Started:

As Barajas admits, becoming a sort of prodigal son—the Hispanic kid who made good and came back—"made me one in a million. It was a great PR opportunity." He knew the niche existed, especially with a slow but steady-growing market of prosperous Latinos. Barajas knew he would stand out as someone who came back to the community, or as he puts it, "I created my own legend."

Today, Barajas works with a steady stream of more affluent Latinos, while continuing to educate lower income investors through speaking appearances and a book he has written on financial planning, *The Latino Journey to Financial Greatness* (HarperCollins).

Most Important Steps In Building a Personal Brand:

Barajas and his staff have become obsessive accumulators of print media coverage—documenting it, keeping it, adding to it, creating press kits bursting with relevant articles about his work and knowledge of Latino economic affairs.

"I've never had a PR person," he says. "We send articles out to the media, tell them, 'If you would like an opinion about finance related to the Hispanic community, call me.' We send them out quarterly, and every time we do it, I get four or five new interviews."

Biggest Success:

"We focus more on credibility marketing," Barajas says. "They say the most powerful affirmation is a third-party endorsement, and that's what I focus on: being endorsed by an objective third party. The media hasn't really created a lot of business for me, but it creates credibility when my clients go out and refer me. When a nice piece comes out, we'll get reprints and send them to clients."

On Personal Branding and Idealism:

"I used to be the Mexican Ralph Nader," Barajas says. "A pragmatic idealist. I had these big ideals of transforming the community, but I had more ideas about consumer activism. But now, people who have read my book and gotten to know me say I'm the Hispanic Dr. Phil and Suze Orman. I'm in your face, honest, my favorite saying is 'I've never seen a U-Haul behind a hearse.'

"I don't have a lot of hidden agendas. Most people who come in to this community have a lot of political ambitions. I have no political ambitions. I won't edit what I say. I'll talk about the problems with the community. People realize they're going to get honest, objective advice."

Advice:

"Be authentic. People let out certain hormones, and people know whether you're B.S.ing them or not. It's about going out and working in a niche that you love, that you're passionate about. I love helping people in the community. I'm really blessed. Whatever you feel is in your heart, do it. Find that niche you really have a passion for, your 'occu-passion.'"

Brandstorming Business Relationships:
8 Great Things You Can Do Right Now

1. List your clients in three categories: "Close Relationship," "Superficial Relationship," and "No Relationship." Why do you have close relationships with some? Can that factor be "exported" to the other groups?

2. List the customers who offer the best chance of giving you the most lucrative referrals.

3. Crunch the numbers and determine which clients provide the most per-client revenue. Your goals: to form close relationships with the high-revenue and high-referral clients, and to attract more of those clients with whom you have much in common.

4. Get a cell phone and number that you designate as a "Premium Customer Line." Give your best customers a business card that tells them the number is exclusively for them to contact you with questions or comments, and give them extended hours when you'll answer that phone.

5. Send your best clients a personal, handwritten note telling them about your Personal Branding efforts, thanking them for their business, and inviting their comments and ideas.

6. List ideas for new ways you can get each key client alone for 10 to 15 minutes of uninterrupted conversation.

7. Put "bring the family or friend to work" days on the calendar. On these days, you'll bring your spouse, child or a close friend to work in your office or shop, introducing him or her as such. For customers, this strengthens the idea that they really know you.

8. Hold an open house.

Bottom Line No. 4: How Personal Branding Equals More Business
Anticipating prospect expectations to stand out from the crowd

Situation: You're a CPA trying to land more medium-sized corporate clients needing financial audits. But you've got major competition and you're treading water, spending money on direct mail and Yellow Pages ads to little effect.

Solution: You realize the mid-level companies you're after aren't just looking for accounting services; they're looking for strategies that will help them grow into big companies. So you reposition yourself in your branding materials, talking about your talents in locating sources of capital, from equity investors to Initial Public Offerings. You package yourself as the "source of financial solutions that turn medium-size companies into major players," and send out a series of direct-mail pieces with this message.

Result: Jackpot. Suddenly, you've gone from being just another generic service provider to a solution creator, a specialist in capital development. You're getting calls from the kind of ambitious, forward-thinking companies you're dying to land as clients, and you get so much business you need to hire a junior CPA to handle your old clients.

Brand Surgery: Avoiding Tragic Branding Mistakes
The Patient: Your Relationships

- Always under-promise and over-deliver. Say you'll have something done in two weeks and do it in one. Managing expectations will have clients eating out of your hand.

- If you say you're going to do something, do it. No excuses, even if it's something small. Clients will base your trustworthiness on the smallest of factors.

- Spell out what you do and don't do in your branding materials, and again when you meet with prospects. Make it clear if something's outside your area of expertise, your clients will have to find another vendor. Then have a list of possible vendors.

- Be bold about your personality with prospects. Your quirks will drive away some, but attract others. They'll be the people with whom you can form long-term alliances.

- Never believe the "If you do this for us at a lower price, there'll be a lot more work coming down the line" gambit. It's as old as the hills, and it's really just a ploy to save money. A quality prospect will pay you what you're worth, instead of trying to get you to discount by holding out the carrot of more work.

CHAPTER 5

Putting the "Personal" in Your Personal Brand

Building an effective brand may start with identifying your attributes, but stopping there is like building a house and leaving it unfurnished. The basics are there, but there's nothing to draw people inside.

Once the foundation of your Personal Brand is laid, weaving your personal side into it makes you more than a collection of skills and benefits. While it's possible to be successful while keeping your clients at a distance, it's tough. Generally, people want to work with someone to whom they relate, someone with whom they can enjoy the time spent.

Perhaps the best reason to work personal information into your Personal Brand is this: There's only one you. No matter where you come from or what you've done, you're unique. When you thread your personality, passions and history into your brand, you're making yourself stand out from any other brand in the market—even if others have exactly the same skills and training as you.

Size Does Matter: Why We Trust Personal Brands More than Corporate Brands

Most small companies spend years and lots of dollars trying to give themselves the spit, polish and businesslike demeanor of large corporations, in the misguided belief that's what customers want. Well, in this post-Enron era, when corporations have become the symbols for greed, fraud and corruption, are you sure you want to emulate a corporation?

Most consumers are looking for exactly the opposite. They're looking for a personal, intimate experience with someone who will tailor service to them, who will go the extra mile, who's not trying to be perfect but is willing to admit and fix mistakes. A real person. A Personal Brand.

Why Personal Branding Is Stronger than Corporate Branding

- **We trust people more than corporations.** It is very hard to hide when it's your name on the door —and we know it. When we're working with a small company operated by a person, we know where the buck stops. On the other hand, how many times have you contacted the less-than-friendly customer-service department of your big phone or utility company, gotten the runaround from a service rep who didn't seem to care if you existed, and felt powerless to do anything about it? Did you ever really trust that corporation—or any corporation—again? When we deal with a person whose name we know and whose hand we've shaken, we know exactly what we're getting, and we know if there's trouble, that person will respond.

- **People have more to lose than corporations.** Despite what their marketing says, do you think your local phone company cares about losing your business? They have thousands or millions of other customers, so they're rarely, if ever, going to do more than the minimum to keep you from complaining. And the typical CEO of a publicly traded company doesn't care about the company or the customers; shareholder value is what matters. The owner of a small business or professional practice, on the other hand, needs every customer happy and telling others. He can't afford to take anyone for granted or he'll go under. Since customers often become personal friends, doing business the right way becomes personal.

- **People are more accountable than corporations.** Big corporations run you through a Rube Goldberg maze of bureaucracy to get anything done. When you're working with an individual, there are no barriers. You can talk with the decision-maker, and hold him or her responsible for making things right.

- **People care more than corporations.** Who is more likely to respond with compassion and a helping hand when there's a problem: a multinational conglomerate or the family doctor you've known for 15 years? It's nearly impossible to have a relationship with a corporation.

Bottom line, we're in an era when trust in the all-powerful corporation is in serious, perhaps fatal, decline. This is the age of the Personal Brand. Never before has there been such a "trust void" for you to fill.

Why Get Personal?

You may not be comfortable with the idea of adding a personal dimension to your professional identity. After all, aren't the two supposed to be kept separate? Maybe, in the corporate world, but as a business owner, it's critical to sell yourself as a skilled person, someone clients can talk with, someone who will listen when they have a question or a brainstorm. That leads me to the benefits of personalization:

- **Relatability.** When you work personal characteristics into your Personal Brand, you become human, flawed, and easier to understand. Prospects see you're not a company, but a human being. Suddenly, you're easier to relate to, because you operate on a one-to-one scale.

- **Common ground.** Surely you've experienced this: You meet a prospect, and when he finds out you share the same hobby, high school or car, you bond and he ends up becoming a great client. It happens all the time, and it stands a better chance of happening if you build aspects of your personal life into your brand.

- **Differentiation.** There are hundreds of dentists in your area. But how many of them skydive? Look at the Yellow Pages ads for any profession, and see how many of them say basically the same thing. Build an ad around something personal—a photo of a dentist in free fall, for example, with a clever headline—and it will immediately stand out. You can work almost any personal information into your Personal Brand and your branding, and it will set you apart from the competition.

- **Retention.** When people see the same message again and again, it loses its impact. That's a natural feature of human memory. But novelty stands out. If you're the only person in your profession who markets himself using his hobby or his style of dress, how well do you think you'll be remembered?

- **Breaking down sales resistance.** People are bombarded with marketing messages. If they see you as a salesperson peddling yourself, it's easy to shut you out. If they see you as a unique individual with personality who just happens to be providing a service they might need, it's easier to get your foot in the door.

- **Increased sales.** Given the choice between giving their money to a faceless behemoth with questionable accounting practices or a local, hard-working individual they can call anytime, an increasing number of people are choosing the individual.

- **Fun.** Bottom line, marketing yourself is a blast. Thumbing your nose at corporate dehumanization is great, and your business should be fun, no matter what it is. Personal Branding lets you take pride in who you are—and take satisfaction in letting everyone else know it.

In the end, the personal can be the difference between getting the business and getting the gate. When the marketplace is overwhelmed by competitors who all appear identical, it's the one who stands out—who gives the prospect a reason to choose—who wins.

There are few better examples of the incredible power of personal connection than Rosie O'Donnell. Following in the footsteps of Oprah Winfrey, the former standup comedian has become a multimedia star with a talk show and a recently terminated magazine. How has she done it? Aside from being funny and gifted with a sharp business mind, O'Donnell has opened her personal life—coming out as a lesbian. She's made herself open, vulnerable and utterly authentic, and people love her for it.

Four Types of Personal Brand Content

How do you personalize your Personal Brand? When you sift through all the possible personal content that can be worked into your brand, you come out with four basic categories:

1. **Personality**—Your quirks, how you speak, your sense of humor, your attitude toward the world.

2. **Background**—Where you grew up, where your family comes from, where you went to school, stories from your life.

3. **Interests**—Your hobbies, passions, obsessions, and pastimes.

4. **Lifestyle**—Where you live, what you drive, what you eat, what you wear, and so on.

Personality

This a problem for some people, because we're taught that business is, well, serious business. That approach couldn't be more wrong. The fact is, people—with senses of humor, fears, needs and emotions—run even the largest corporations.

Personality can mean a wide range of things: your sharp sense of humor, the attitude in your slogan, your style of leadership, odd habits or tastes you choose to let prospects know about, your political or religious views. Just about any aspect of your behavior can be woven into your brand.

However, before you start working personality into your Personal Brand, *make sure your personality is appropriate for your target market.*

Nothing will turn off a potential customer faster than inappropriate behavior. Know your target market and the people in it and you'll know how much personality to add to your brand, and at what intensity. Some tips:

- Be safe when working personality into printed materials. You can dial down your behavior with a client that's not quite in tune with you, but you can't dial down a brochure.

- Go into a prospect with the more subtle aspects of your personality on display, and as you get to know the people, turn up the volume.

- Once you're established, be bold about the personality in your brand and your branding.

Background

Your personal history is a powerful weapon in building your Personal Brand, as long as you know which parts to publicize and which to leave out.

Background information can be where you grew up, what country your family came from originally, what kind of traveling you've done in the past, even your ethnicity. It can also be interesting stories from your life—adventures, tragedies, funny tales or improbable coincidences. People love to learn about the things that shaped you, because it helps them understand you and your actions.

Providing a sense of where you came from can help others develop an affinity for you. Perhaps you and a prospect both have Native American heritage, or you and the CFO of a corporation both spent time living in Ireland. Promoting your life story gives them the chance to make those connections. Some tips:

- Research your target market to discover where the trends lie. Are a majority of your best prospects of the same religion? Did they graduate from the Ivy League? Do they tend to come from musical families? Discovering the backgrounds of the people whose business you're after will help you decide which parts of your background to make public.

- Beware of maudlin stories. You don't want people feeling sorry for you or feeling that you're trying to manipulate their emotions.

- Tell stories about your life in detail. People love to learn about other people.

Interests

If you're a sailor, build a Personal Brand that has boating as an integral component. Once it's established in the local sailing community, you'll have an immediate bond with anyone in that community.

Interests can be hobbies, sports you play, things you collect, passions for theatre or politics, cooking or wine, or just about anything else you do when you're not working. Interests are a powerful way to differentiate yourself, because they're easy to grasp and to file away in people's memory banks. Some tips:

- Make sure your target market will be receptive to information about your hobbies or activities. Some businesses such as law are very serious, and talk about your bowling league may not go over well.

- If possible, promote an interest of yours that complements an interest common in your target market. For example, if you're a physical therapist or personal trainer, promoting your love of outdoor sports might be a good move.

- Be cautious about over-promoting your interests as part of your Personal Brand. You don't want people to think you're more into your hobby than your work.

Lifestyle

Lifestyle offers a chance to connect with people who may not live like you do, but want to. They can get a vicarious taste of that life by working with you.

For example, you live at the beach and surf almost every morning. No matter what profession you're in, you could design a logo and business card that depicts you in a beach setting or on a surfboard. Voila! You've tied yourself to beach culture.

Lifestyle information can be about where you live, the hours you keep, the car you drive, the clothes you wear, or even the places you hang out. Communicating this part of your Personal Brand is usually less about marketing and more about living the brand—dressing the part, taking clients to a restaurant or other meeting place that fits your lifestyle, and so on. For example, if part of your Personal Brand positions you as a lover of fine culture, show up for a dinner meeting with a rare bottle of fine wine. Some tips:

- Lifestyle can be the most volatile aspect of your Personal Brand. There are people who may refuse to work with you because they don't like your politics, your hair or your sexual orientation. Decide whether or not that matters and brand accordingly.

- If you're going to claim a lifestyle, be able to back it up. Don't build an image as a surfer dude and always look paler than 1 percent milk.

- Political affiliation, religious faith and the place you live are all part of your lifestyle, and you can connect with others through those characteristics as powerfully as something that's "edgy."

Stirring the Personal Touch into Your Brand

Here are four strategies for communicating your personal side to your target market:

1. **Your environment**

2. **Your behavior**

3. **Your branding materials**

4. **Your level of interaction with your target market**

1. Environment

Turn your office, studio or mobile workspace into a reflection of your personal side. If you're a nut about European travel, fill your office with maps and souvenirs from all over the continent. If you're an edgy, irreverent creative type, paper your studio with strange posters and bizarre photos.

Of course, this strategy only works if you have an office and actually bring clients to it. If not, create a mobile environment in your car or on the screen saver of your notebook computer. Either way, use your surroundings to communicate something about your character. Bonus: this also makes your workspace more comfortable for you, more personal and inviting.

2. Behavior

This is the most natural way to work personal info into your brand. If your personal side is best communicated by how you act, work to let more of it come across when you deal with your target market. Some organic ways to add behavior to your Personal Brand:

- If you've been subduing your normal personality when working with clients, let a little more of it loose.

- When it's appropriate, share information about yourself—your personal life, plans for the weekend, etc.

- Ask clients or prospects about themselves more.

- Be more opinionated about your work and your clients' decisions, as long as you don't cross the line into rude.

3. Branding Materials

Including personal information and personal style in your branding materials is the easiest way to get more personal with your Personal Brand. Plenty of professionals who aren't comfortable talking about their hobbies are fine with writing a story about their college years.

In fact, your branding materials should always have at least some personal information, even if it's just a slogan that captures your sense of humor. That way, something personal about you is constantly touching your target market, enhancing your Personal Brand. Some examples:

- A Personal Brochure that tells a story from your past, illustrating how you developed the skills you use today

- A slogan that reflects your feelings about what you do

- A bold, colorful business card that captures your sense of style in what you wear and what you drive

- An animated, evocative Web site that appeals to the emotions and tells more of your personal story

- A series of direct-mail pieces you use to share ongoing tidbits from your life with your prospects and clients

4. Level of Interaction

How personal do you get with your clients and prospects? Is it strictly business? Do you exchange Christmas gifts? Do you go out for drinks, or to basketball games with some of your best customers? Your interaction with your target market is a very important and natural method of promoting your Personal Brand, and if you're not thinking about it in a strategic way, start.

It's rare that a Personal Brand is well-served by becoming less intimate with clients. Normally, being close and friendly with clients in a non-business way will only help your business. But don't assume anything. Look closely at the brand you want to build. Be sure your level of client interaction suits your Personal Brand. If not, you need to gradually adjust your interaction, either by carefully increasing your involvement with key clients or by slowly scaling it back.

When Not to Get Personal

Of course, getting personal may not be right for you. Either you're not comfortable being anything other than purely business, or your profession doesn't consider sharing any hint of your non-business persona appropriate.

That's 100 percent fine. We're not saying you MUST work personality, stories from your childhood or the fact you're obsessed with baseball stats into your Personal Brand. In most cases it helps considerably, but that may not be true in your case. Great. Remember, the Golden Rule of Personal Branding is "to thine own self be true." Your brand must be who you are, and if that means it's all business, that's what it should be.

Our advice? Write down all the aspects of your personal side that might work well with your Personal Brand, from your outdoor activities to tales from your college years. You might be surprised to discover what makes your brand truly three-dimensional.

Personal Brand Case Study

Jonice Padilha
J. Sisters Salon

Position: Brazilian beauty treatments in a family atmosphere
Location: New York, NY
Business: Beauty services
Online: jsisters.com

Seven Brazilian-born sisters came to the United States in 1987, intent on introducing American women to their culture's beauty secrets. Working tirelessly and creating a place with a Cheers-like sense of welcome and family, the J. Sisters have turned their West 57th Street salon into a New York institution and a mandatory stop for celebrities ranging from Gwyneth Paltrow to Vanessa Williams. The J. Sisters boast a rarity: a group Personal Brand.

How It Started:
After working in their family's salon in Brazil since they were teenagers, the sisters saw a demand for Brazilian-style beauty techniques in the U.S. With little money beyond the operating costs for their location, they relied on publicity generated by anyone and everyone who would pass around positive word-of-mouth. Today, J. Sisters International also has eight of the sisters' nieces working at the salon.

Most Important Steps in Building a Personal Brand:

The big break for the J. Sisters came when *Elle* magazine wrote a flattering piece about the salon in 1991. "They fell in love with us, so they started recommending us to all these other magazines," Padilha says. The increased business enabled them to hire a PR firm, and the salon was on its way to becoming a piece of New York culture, and doing about $3.5 million a year in business to boot.

Biggest Success:

"Success has come through relationships," she says. "People have to experience what we do for themselves. You come in and you see we've got kind of a family relationship with clients. All these 15 years, there are people I know who lose everything, and when they come to me I say 'Come and spend a day with me.' We create a bond with people. Thanks to our relationships, we have the status where we 'have to come' to parties and events."

On Personal Branding and Staying Involved:

"I still come in, in the morning, and make coffee. Lots of little things make a difference."

Advice:

"People think they can open a business and it runs itself. Wrong. Follow your heart. If you really love what you do, follow your heart and help comes from all directions. Sometimes I feel sickness, when I come into a place and don't feel a good atmosphere. People come in and talk to me, say 'Do me a favor,' and I do. It benefits my business. When I'm sick, everyone calls me, 'do you need anything?' That's the kind of friendship I create with my clients."

Brandstorming Your Personal Story:
7 Great Things You Can Do Right Now

1. Write your personal story in rough form, focusing on interesting stories from your past.

2. Talk to family, friends, or teachers about things from your past you may have forgotten about.

3. Collect photos and mementos for later use in marketing materials.

4. Look at your target market. Which aspect of your past, such as a university or military service, do your clients and prospects relate to the most?

5. Polish your personal story, have it read by a few friends and colleagues, and edit accordingly.

6. Start looking for unique items associated with the dominant story from your past that you can use in your branding. For example, if you've been a big world traveler, travel articles and exotic maps are a possibility.

7. Look at your main competitors and determine how personal or impersonal their Personal Brands are. This will help you differentiate yourself by being more personal than your least personal rivals, and less personal than those who go over the top.

Bottom Line No. 5: How Personal Branding Equals More Business
Making a personal connection with your prospects

Situation: You're a general contractor with a business problem—nobody knows who you are. Worse, in your market there are lots of new home developments, with few buyers who want to do immediate renovation. You need to find a cost-effective way to appeal to the owners of older homes and income property owners who want to renovate. But how?

Solution: Something else that's big in your area is baseball—college ball, Little League, and so on. You played minor league baseball for a few years, and you coach Little League. In fact, you're a certified baseball nut. So you decide to work this into your brand, figuring people—especially men—who share your love of the game will respond. You create a new business card designed so it looks as if a baseball's seams are running through it, order baseball tickets and baseballs with your logo and name on them to give out as promotions, become a sponsor of the local college team, wear a Cubs jersey with your name on the back to every job, and start sending the people on your e-mail list a "Construction Tip of the Day" along with a "Baseball Fact of the Day."

Result: Within a few months, you're known as the "baseball contractor." It's been effortless and fun, and you've connected with men from all over the county who love baseball and wish they'd played, and gotten dozens of new referrals. Most important, you stand out from all the other contractors in your area.

Brand Surgery: Avoiding Tragic Branding Mistakes
The Patient: Getting Personal

- Don't share too much information. Some people hold the outdated but persuasive idea that business should be all about business.

- Avoid the controversial stuff, unless your target market thrives on it.

- Don't make up a lifestyle just to get into a lucrative market. Your lies will quickly catch up with you and crush you.

- If you have a sick, twisted sense of humor, best to keep it under wraps until you know the people you're dealing with very well.

- In building an environment to reflect your personality, creative is good. Clutter or tastelessness is not.

- Don't embarrass or anger your family or friends in telling personal stories. You don't want to lose loved ones while you gain business.

- Don't take out ads that tell people how hip you are, or how much you're into coin collecting. Show, don't tell.

- Make sure your personal information doesn't leave people scratching their head about what you do.

the brand called YOU

Part Three:
Branding Strategies

CHAPTER 6

Specialize or Sink

When you started your business, strategy probably wasn't on your mind. You were focused on pure survival: start your office, save money, get customers, pay your bills, and avoid having to work for someone else. Strategic thinking was a luxury.

But if you've been in business for a couple of years or more, you're probably less worried about day-to-day survival and more about how to grow your business into what you had in mind when you first hung up your shingle. That's when building a powerful Personal Brand becomes important, and in building that brand, thinking strategically is paramount. In the next three chapters, we'll look at the four critical strategies you must employ in building a successful Personal Brand. The first of those is specialization.

Do Less, Be More

Specialization means when you brand yourself, you narrow down the scope of who you are or what you do, packaging yourself as a specialist in a smaller, more precise range of services. Specialization is powerful because most professionals cover themselves by telling prospects they do everything. As a result, they all look the same. Even more important, these generalists lose the opportunity to highlight their expertise in any one area. Specialization lets you pick a few lucrative, in-demand areas of your business and build your brand around them.

Specialization can be extremely powerful. For example, Bob Vila can be summed up in one phrase: "home restoration." The home-restoration sensation that made Vila a symbol began with *This Old House*, the PBS program he hosted beginning in 1979. During the restoration of homes throughout New England, Vila's bearded, genial face became associated with a "you can do it" philosophy that infected much of the U.S. with do-it-yourself disease. As identified with home renovation as Martha Stewart is with home decorating, Vila polishes his Personal Brand on his show *Bob Vila's Home Again.*

Bottom line, you must specialize. Otherwise, you'll be just another anonymous service provider, with no reason for prospects to choose you over anyone else. It really should be "specialize or die."

Brands Should Both Attract and Repel

It's natural to want your Personal Brand to attract the most people possible. But it's a huge mistake, and if you succumb to the temptation to try to be all things to all people, you'll end up being nothing to anyone.

One of the hardest and most valuable lessons to learn in Personal Branding is that a brand that drives away the prospects you don't want is as valuable as a brand that attracts the ones you *do* want. Why? First off, some prospects will waste your time or cost you money. But more important, if your Personal Brand is strong, clear and persuasive enough to prevent some people from contacting you, it's going to be powerful enough to exert tremendous influence over your ideal prospects. It's a great litmus test of your Personal Brand: If everyone likes it, rethink it.

One of the best corporate examples of the perils of the "be everything to everyone" branding approach is K-Mart. K-Mart went Chapter 11 because it had no well-defined brand identity. You shopped at Wal-Mart if you wanted really low prices, and at Target if you wanted hip style and value. But why did you shop at K-Mart? The company never gave consumers a compelling reason why it was different from its competitors, so they didn't know why they should shop there. As a result, consumers defined K-Mart's brand as, "cheap stuff." It's a sad example of how weak, ineffective branding can sink a company. We've even come to call such vanilla, middle-of-the-road branding "K-Marketing" around the office.

The Benefits of Specialization

- **Differentiation**—Instead of being a generalist who tries to be all things to all people, you set yourself apart from your competition by doing a few things very, very well.

- **Presumed expertise**—When you tell people you're a specialist in something, they naturally presume you're especially skilled in that area.

- **Perceived value**—Experts can demand more money. Brand yourself as a specialist in a desirable area and you'll be able to charge more than a generalist offering the same service.

- **Easier to understand**—Human perception processes simpler ideas better than complex ones, so your Personal Brand becomes more memorable when it's built around a couple of very clear benefits. People are more apt to see your value when they can easily understand what you do.

- **Focus on your strengths**—If you specialize in the things you do best or enjoy most, you'll probably do better work, enjoy yourself more, and make more money.

Targeting: Don't Specialize Without It

We've talked about target marketing throughout this book, but what is it? Very simply, it's choosing a specific audience for your Personal Branding campaign based on their culture, lack of entrenched competitors, growth potential, and ability to generate the income you desire. Choosing the right target market—and learning *everything* you can about how it works and how its people think—will make or break your Personal Branding campaign.

By targeting, you reject the idea that the best way to build a business is to hit every living person with your Personal Brand and marketing and hope some of them show interest. That's a primitive, ineffective way of getting clientele. Targeting lets you focus in on the specific markets that are most desirable, either because of their wealth, their size, their need for your service, or some combination of all three. It lets you reject the "desperation marketing" that's the equivalent of door-to-door sales.

The benefits of targeting:

- **Higher-quality clients.** Instead of chasing every bottom-feeder who comes along, you can go after exactly the people you want, people who understand the value in what you do, and who will provide you with a more robust income.

- **More effective spending.** Logically, if you're not spending money to chase after everyone in your market area, your return on marketing investment will be improved.

- **More focused messages.** You can tailor your Personal Branding messages to your target markets, allowing you to be more focused on their needs— their "pain," as marketing professionals call it—and to produce stronger responses.

- **Less time marketing.** When you're no longer trying to get everyone's business, you'll spend less time pursuing clients and more time working with them.

- **Greater profitability.** Less marketing time + greater marketing ROI + better paying clients = a more profitable business.

- **Stronger referral base.** Once you penetrate a group and educate them on why you create value, you'll create a referral base that feeds on itself. Within your market, two clients tell four people, they tell eight, and so on.

- **Focused efforts.** The greatest part of being in business for yourself is you can do anything you want. The most challenging part of being in business for yourself is you can do anything you want. When you target market, you focus your energies and build momentum much quicker and with greater force. Would you rather cut wood with a laser or with a baseball bat?

Choosing Your Target Market

Let me reiterate: Choosing the right target market and learning all you can about it will be one of the most important steps you take in building a successful Personal Brand. Approach it with deliberation, patience, and dedication to getting all the facts before you decide on a market.

In specializing, choose one target market initially. It will become the focus of your Personal Branding. If, up to now, you've been trying to get the attention of everyone in your market area, stop. Stand firm and resist the temptation to chase every possible customer on the remote possibility you *might* be losing business. You are, but you'll be gaining much more than you lose. Let your competition chase everyone on the street and waste their money.

How do you define a target market? Start with these criteria:

- Income

- Where they live (example: targeting a single planned community)

- Profession

- Age group

- Religion

- Political affiliation

- Recreational interest (example: golfers)

- Industry (for companies)

- Size (for companies)

- Professional or fraternal organizations

- Lifestyle (examples: gay, environmentalist, etc.)

To select your target market, start by looking more closely at groups of people or companies in your region, and categorizing them by the above criteria. Let's say you're a financial planner. You might end up with a list that looks like this:

- Market 1—Six professional groups for legal professionals

- Market 2—Members of bank and investment company Boards of Directors, all wealthy executives with incomes approx. $200,000+

- Market 3—Boating community at local marina, lots of bankers and executives

Look at every distinct group that may lead you to the final goal: paying customers who are ideally suited to want what you offer. Examine every possible target market and ask the same questions:

1. Do I enjoy working with this group?

2. Does it have the potential to increase my income?

3. Do its members need what I can provide?

4. Based on their culture, values and background, will they perceive the value in my Personal Brand?

Take the time to do your research: Read trade journals, attend professional meetings or trade shows, and talk to the people in the markets.

Now pick one market and focus on it exclusively. Why just one? Because you'll be learning about the principles and tactics needed to build and maintain your brand, and that's challenging enough with one market.

How Big Should Your Target Market Be?

That depends on your income goals, what kind of staff and resources you have on hand, and above all, how you want to balance your work time with personal time. For some people, a target market of 1,000 individuals or companies is perfectly reasonable. For others, 100 homes are all they need. Here's a basic guide to figuring out how big your target market should be:

1. **Income Goal**—How much income do you want to make in the next year?

2. **Per-Client Revenue**—What is your current average revenue per client?

3. **Client Volume**—Armed with the knowledge of how much an average client generates for you, how many clients will you need to meet your income goal?

4. **Prospect Count**—Find out how many prospects who fit your ideal target market profile are in the geographic area you plan to service. You can do this by hitting the Yellow Pages, paying a research firm, or contacting a seller of direct-mail lists to find out about people of certain income levels living in your area.

5. **Market Penetration**—Divide your number of current clients by the number of prospects in your service area to get the percentage of potential clients who are actual clients.

6. **Market Analysis**—Based on your market penetration, calculate how many prospects you'll need to target to bring in enough clients to meet your goals. For example, if you currently have 50 clients and need 100, and your 50 clients represent 1 percent of your ideal prospects, you'll need to reach another 5,000 prospects to ensure another 50, or 1 percent of them, become your clients.

Once you've done the numbers, ask the following questions:

- Can you realistically target the number of prospects you need?

- Can you realistically service that many clients?

- Do you need to market to a different demographic instead?

- Is any of your competition stepping up to grab market share, or is the market wide open?

- Are your goals reasonable?

The Three Steps to Specialization

Once you've done the heavy lifting of choosing a target market, you can decide on a specialization. You can't do it before. For example, if you're an insurance professional working with the elderly, it doesn't do a lot of good to tell them you specialize in helping people save for college.

Follow these three steps in developing the specialization for your Personal Brand:

Step One: Choose Your Target Market

Follow the steps above.

Step Two: Tailor Your Products or Services to Your Market

Personal Branding is about finding an unmet need and offering a product or service that fills it. So look at your possible target market and ask, what's it looking for? It could be anything from faster service to a supplier of specific electronics. Once you determine this, look at ways you can customize your product or service to meet that need. For example:

- Offering new products or services

- Changing the name of your product or service

- Emphasizing a different aspect of your product or service in your branding materials

- Raising or lowering your price point

- Emphasizing certain qualifications in your personal background

Step Three: Develop Your Business Model

Now you must gear your business to attract the desired prospects. Design your business around your prospects—who they are, what they want, what they can afford, and so on. Some examples:

- **Office location**—One of the easiest ways to capture market share with a target market is to be where they are. Move your office to a place that's convenient for a large portion of your prospects, or that has a high visibility factor.

- **Office style**—Design your office environment to appeal to your target audience.

- **Web presence**—If your target market is Web-savvy, invest in a Web site that will give them more than they expect. Online order-tracking and appointment-setting features, downloadable articles and fact sheets, animation—all ways to give prospects a beneficial Web experience.

- **Prospecting**—How do your prospects feel about direct mail? Cold calling? Face-to-face meetings? Learn how they respond to the Personal Branding tactics in your weapons locker and only use the ones they embrace enthusiastically.

- **Billing and pricing**—If you know your target market, you know their incomes. Set your prices accordingly. Make sure to set up a billing system that suits how your clients live: electronic, monthly retainer, and so on.

• **Service programs**—Most important, develop a service program with automatic "triggers" that keeps your business in touch with your clients as often as possible. If your clients like to eat out, reward referrals with local restaurant gift certificates. Set up a phone calling system that monitors client satisfaction before, during and after business is conducted. Create a mailing that asks for written "How can we do better?" information.

The better you know your target market and the more you specialize to meet its needs, the more market share you'll own.

Common Mistake No. 1: Diversification

Sometimes, business owners can't pull the trigger. No matter how badly they want to specialize, it's too scary. So they make a huge error: They try to be all things to all people. It's impossible. Don't do it.

Diversification muddies the waters, creates confusion, and weakens your brand's strengths. Worst of all, diversification plants seeds of doubt in the minds of prospects. It's natural to read an ad or brochure for a service provider, see a laundry list of services as long as your arm, and think to yourself, "If he does so many different things, he can't be very good at any of them. "

Common Mistake No. 2: Dilution

Dilution takes a successful, specialized Personal Brand and ruins it by trying to branch out too widely, to be a specialist in too many areas. Like an army that suffers when it stretches its supply line too thin, the farther you get from your core specialty, the more you risk diluting your Personal Brand and losing the perception of you as a specialist.

A good example of the damage dilution can do is Calvin Klein. For decades, his brand of clean-lined, stylish attire set the standard for the industry. Then he made a critical tactical error: He decided if he was a specialist in mainstream retail, he could make even bigger profits in discount stores. Hence the appearance of Calvin Klein clothes at chains like Costco. Sure, he sells more of his low-end product. But in the long run, he's done heavy damage to his Personal Brand by robbing it of any sense of exclusivity.

Resist the temptation. Leave a Personal Brand alone once it's established and working. It's critical to retain the tight, stubborn focus that made the brand a success. Change that formula and 99 percent of the time you'll drain the unique energy that makes the brand compelling.

Tips for Better Specialization

1. **Be aware of emotional needs**—Sometimes, a target market doesn't need a service to fill an unmet need. They need a vendor with a sense of humor, or someone who's renowned for always meeting deadlines. You can specialize in such areas. One example is author Robert Bly, who saw an unfilled need in 1980s men seeking a path back to traditional masculine values after a decade of "sensitivity." His book, *Iron John*, filled this void and turned Bly into a guru.

2. **Create something new**—Far-fetched? Tell that to the people who created new Internet industries. If there's no void to fill, develop a Personal Brand that offers a novel product, service or benefit. This can be risky if there's no demand for what you create. But if it works, you'll have *first-mover advantage*. If you're stumped for something new, look at what the competition is doing and do exactly the opposite.

3. **Focus and get smaller**—Hone your Personal Brand like a knife. Instead of constantly doing more, do less. Direct your promotional energies and performance to the single specialization the brand is built around, ignoring opportunities to diversify. Become the only person specializing in one service that's in hot demand, and you'll get rich.

Personal Brand Case Study

Dr. Barry Friedberg
Cosmetic Surgery Anesthesia

Position: Nausea-free cosmetic surgery anesthesia
Location: Corona Del Mar, CA
Business: Cosmetic Surgery Anesthesiologist
Online: doctorfriedberg.com, pkaffiliates.com

In 1986, Dr. Barry Friedberg was an unhappy physician in a group practice on the verge of being co-opted into California's new managed care system. "I said to my people, 'It's an American thing to work more and make more, but it's a decidedly un-American thing to buy into a system that makes you work more and make less.'" Following a bitter break from his practice, Friedberg launched his career outside the hospital setting. After a year spent wondering what to do next, he found the mission that has made his Personal Brand: cosmetic surgery anesthesiology that dramatically reduced nausea and vomiting.

How It Started:

"I wanted to differentiate myself from the nurse anesthetist," Friedberg says. "I went to a symposium about surgery and anesthesia, and the doctor spoke about using Ketamine during cosmetic surgery." Pointing out that many surgeons use narcotic anesthesia that often causes nausea and vomiting, he continues. "There was an office in trouble for a death because of using narcotics in an inappropriate fashion. That was the beginning—there was nothing in the literature about Propofol blocking Ketamine hallucinations. It was a fabulous technique: everybody got happy from the Propofol, and as a side benefit, no one was throwing up."

Friedberg had hit the Personal Branding jackpot—he had found the unmet need. "Anesthesiologists think pain is the major patient concern," he says, "but the No. 1 patient concern is nausea and vomiting. I've spent the last 10 years waving my arms and saying this. Now I'm the hero: All my patients love me, doctors love me, and the nurses love me, because they don't have to clean up after a patient has thrown up."

Most Important Steps in Building Personal Brand:

Friedberg has morphed into as much of a problem-solver as an anesthesiologist, flying all over the world explaining to disbelieving physicians that it is possible to anesthetize patients in a different, more patient-friendly way.

He also taps multiple channels for getting the word out to a community that resists change: pens with his name on them that he gives out at speaking engagements, ads in trade publications, articles on the topic in key trade journals, and more. Today, he's probably one of a handful of anesthesiologists in the nation with two publicists, one for the trade and one for national press.

Also, in a bold move, Friedberg founded his own professional organization: SOFA, the Society for Office Anesthesiologists, which merged with SOBA, the Society for Office Based Anesthesia, in 1998.

Biggest Success:

Since he can't be everywhere at once, Friedberg made a smart move: He retained a publicist and, with her guidance, established a Web site and the basics of his branding. Doctorfriedberg.com regularly gets 2,500 unique visitors every month. It has become *the* online clearinghouse for information about cosmetic surgery without PONV (post-operative nausea and vomiting).

On Personal Branding and Convincing Doubters:

"If I wasn't getting this patient feedback, I wouldn't do this. The Web site was designed to educate the public. That's the only way to force change—educate and create demand. There has to be a force to make physicians change. The mindset of anesthesiologists is almost impossible to change.

"The force for that change is patient demand. That's what keeps me running. I get e-mails from surgeons all over the country. I get this feedback all the time: 'It's simple, it works.' In 10 years, I've had 13 patients succeed in throwing up. We don't need a double blind study, because everybody who's picked it up says, 'It works.'

"Cognitive dissonance hits the people who come and see: what they see is at too great a variance with what they believe. But the people who believe it and try it tell me how great it is. Those enthusiastic responses keep me going."

Advice:

Friedberg suggests if you're offering something new, get an angle. "I had to get an angle, so people would think I had a self-interest approach to this, rather than for simply improving patient outcomes for the sake of it," he says. "Now I'm morphing from Don Quixote to Don Corleone. I found a new angle: coming to your office and consulting with you. It makes me seem more like a money-grubbing SOB, which makes people more comfortable."

Brandstorming Specialization:
7 Great Things You Can Do Right Now

1. Purchase a copy of the *Lifestyle Market Analyst*, the best book ever for analyzing consumer demographics (published by SRDS and Equifax).

2. Write down all your possible target markets: geographic areas, religious groups, industries, ethnic groups or nationalities, etc.

3. Analyze your business. Are there 1 to 2 areas that provide more them 50 percent of your revenue?

4. Take a close look at your competitors to determine if they specialize and if so, how.

5. Break down your business model and flag dysfunctional aspects like training or billing. You'll need to correct these as you revise your model for your specialization.

6. Talk to 20 or 30 of your current clients and top prospects and ask them what needs they have that aren't being met.

7. Resist the pull to generalize by compiling a referral list of colleagues who specialize in areas that are related to but not the same as your specialty. Then when the off-target business comes, be ready with the referral.

Bottom Line No. 6: How Personal Branding Equals More Business
Capturing a unique market niche

Situation: You're a business efficiency consultant in San Diego, working with companies to help them streamline their operations and run more cost-effectively. You're good at what you do, but you face a two-headed problem: The term "consultant" doesn't really tell anyone what you do, and you've got at least 20 competitors in the metro area, all offering the same services as you. A few can outspend you on marketing from here to next week. So you're stagnant.

Solution: You take a closer look at your business trends over the last three years and see that 60 percent of your income has come from working with companies that do business 24 hours, such as convenience-store chains and all-night restaurant chains. Spotting a potential specialty, you investigate and find no one staking out this territory. Quickly, you establish a new Personal Brand by simply changing your name to "24/7 Business Consulting" and adopting the slogan "Efficient Thinking for Companies that Never Close." You begin marketing yourself to such companies, not just in San Diego, but all over California, figuring your specialization gives you an edge.

Result: You figure right. Corporate parents of convenience stores, supermarkets and gas stations burn up your phone lines when they see that you specialize in their business, exclusively. You no longer need to outspend your competitors. You've out-thought them.

Brand Surgery: Avoiding Tragic Branding Mistakes
The Patient: Specialization

• Be flexible. If someone offers you lucrative business outside your specialization, take it. You just don't have to make it part of your branding campaign.

• Beware of a specialization that's too narrow to give you a viable target market.

- Beware of specializing in your own obsession. You may find Civil War Re-enactment fascinating, but if only a tiny percentage of your total market shares that view, making it the cornerstone of your branding is a mistake.

- Ignore those who tell you you've got to do it all to earn enough clients to stay in business.

- Keep your ear to the ground. After you launch your specialization, if you find customers are going elsewhere to find services you used to offer, you may have misread your market.

- Avoid jargon and clichés to describe what you do. In your speech about your work, be as precise as possible.

#

CHAPTER 7

Driving a Stake in the Ground

Positioning means staking out a place for yourself in the minds of your target market, so they identify you with a single powerful idea. Look at it this way: When we process the products and people that enter our minds daily, we file them away in mental file folders, labeled everything from "Discount Prices" to "Reliable Plumber."

When you actively position yourself, you control what goes on the label of your folder. You're telling your target market how to categorize your Personal Brand and how to think about you.

People sometimes confuse specialization and positioning, so we're going to point out the clear differences:

• You specialize independent of your competition, thinking only of what your target market needs. You position yourself in relation to your competitors, trying to occupy a space they don't.

• Specialization is about the service or value you offer. Positioning is all about the idea your Personal Brand evokes in people's minds.

• Specialization is about focusing and making yourself different from competitors. Positioning is about "owning" a segment of the market by having your target market identify you with a certain product or service before anyone else.

For example, you're an independent architect. You decide to market yourself as an expert in home renovation using recycled materials. That's your specialty. But when you create a position to market that Personal Brand, you want people to file you away in their minds as "the eco-friendly architect." That's your position. One is about specific value; the other is about how people think about you and the way you make them feel.

Famous People and Their Positions

Confused? Don't worry. Positioning is one of the hardest Personal Branding concepts to grasp at first. It helps to think of your mind—everyone's mind—as a gold field. Everyone's trying to stake their claim, to capture a little bit of space—to "own" a piece of your mind for their product or service. Positioning is staking out that claim. Here are some great examples of personal and corporate positions:

• Mary Kay: *The flamboyant first lady of direct-to-consumer cosmetics*

• Charles Schwab: *The alternative to Wall Street investing for every man*

• Walt Disney: *Family entertainment visionary*

• Martha Stewart: *The patron saint of beautiful homemaking*

• Calvin Klein: *Classic fashion that never goes out of style*

• Jimmy Buffett: *Margaritaville, music and the good life*

Strong positions stake out an area that's different from anyone else's. Their goal is to stick their label on your mental file folder, so when you think of "expensive performance car," you think of BMW first. There might be no difference between the performance of the BMW and the Mercedes, but they're positioned differently.

Orville Redenbacher would never be anyone's idea of the ideal commercial pitchman, but with his nerdy appearance, homespun delivery and astonishing name, he was memorable. However, his genius was in positioning his product as the first "Gourmet Popcorn." Was there anything different between Redenbacher's popcorn and any other? Not likely. But that doesn't matter. Positioning exists in the mind, and in the minds of consumers, Orville Redenbacher *was* gourmet popcorn.

Benefits of Positioning

If a Personal Brand's job is to influence how your target market perceives you, your position tells them where you fit into the competitive landscape. Picking the right position becomes crucial, because positions are hard to change once they're ingrained in your market; if you choose the wrong one, you'll lose business to people who are positioned in a way that's more appealing or relevant.

The benefits of positioning:

• **"Top-of-mind" status**—You're the person prospects think of first when they need a certain product or service. If you're positioned as "the sales trainer who does standup comedy," when companies are looking for an entertaining way to train their staff, you'll be the first one they think of for the job.

- **Filtering**—Prospects will call you more often about the services you want to provide, and you'll waste less time dealing with people who want things you don't do or which aren't profitable.

- **Emotional appeal**—A strong position can slip past sales resistance to stimulate the emotional need that makes people call you.

- **Clarity of value**—The more clearly prospects understand what you do, the more value they'll see in your work. Clear positioning adds perceived value.

Boiling You Down to the Basics

The purpose of your Personal Brand is to tell prospects how they should feel about you. To do that effectively, the message can't be complicated or confusing. Remember, you're not trying to tell your entire story in 10 seconds; you can get in-depth after you hook your target market. To keep your brand simple, clear and concise, build it on the three core elements of your positioning:

1. Who You Are

2. What You Do

3. What Makes You Different or How You Create Value for Your Target Market

Tell your target prospects these three things in a compelling, emotionally engaging way and you'll stand an excellent chance of turning them into clients.

Part No. 1: Who You Are

Telling people who you are is so basic that many companies forget all about it. It's similar to the misguided notion that because you find what you do fascinating, everyone else will. Thousands of businesses fail because of this fallacy.

Fact: People don't know who you are—and don't care—unless you tell them why they should. One of the three goals of a Personal Brand is to tell people who you are, to make them understand, in a few well-chosen words, some of the following:

- Your profession

- How long you've been doing it

- Your educational background

- Where you're from

- Your accolades

- What your passions are

The description of your Personal Brand should communicate the most important one or two ideas about who you are in statements like these:

"A Stanford-educated engineer…"

"A Chicago native…"

"An award-winning graphic artist…"

"The fourth-generation child of Greek musicians…"

Think Differentiation

Which is more intriguing?

"A Russian-speaking, military brat journalist…"

"A magazine editor…"

Both are accurate descriptions for a man we know, a flamboyant journalist who grew up all over Europe due to his father's military career. But of the two, which would make you want to know more about this person? The first description, of course. It jumps off the page and makes the subject seem unique. That's precisely what your "who you are" statement must do: differentiate you.

So in crafting a statement of who you are, think about what makes you unique. Chances are, you have something in your background or lifestyle that's very interesting to others, from the college you attended to an extreme hobby to your family's ethnic background. Don't be discouraged if you're not sure; you're too close to be an impartial judge. After all, you're you every day. Ask a friend or family member what about you stands out. Ask several and you'll end up with a list of characteristics.

The idea here is to turn you from a service provider into a person, to label you in the target market's mind so they think, "Oh yeah, that's the lawyer who was an All-American football player." The more unique you can make yourself, the stronger your Personal Brand will be.

One caveat: Keep in mind the type of person your target market wants to work with professionally. Don't paint yourself as an ex-hippie if your target market is investment bankers.

Part No. 2: What You Do

We're stunned at how many companies fail to tell people what they do. This comes down to that old disease, which we'll call Self-Evident Disorder. Businesses with this malady think somehow, through telepathy, people know what they do without being told.

Here's the key: It's not enough to say you're an accountant. How many accountants, or real estate agents, or whatever you do, are in your area? One hundred? Two hundred? Do you want to be lumped in with them? If being chosen by no more than a random finger point at the Yellow Pages is your goal, great. If not, you've got to get past the general description of your profession and tell people what you *really* do.

What you do is all about the specific services you're really good at, or that are in high demand. Take a look at your entire range of services and ask yourself:

- Which aspects of my work are most sought after?

- Which ones make me the most money?

- At which am I best?

- Which do I enjoy the most?

Find the aspect of your service that fits all these descriptions and you have your "what you do" descriptor. For example, if you're a real estate agent and you look closely at your business, you realize 65 percent of your clients come from selling fixer-uppers to buyers looking for income properties. In that case, your descriptor becomes:

> "…matching buyers seeking spec homes with high-value, classic properties…"

With a little marketing spin, you've become a specialist in a unique, lucrative aspect of your profession. This sort of packaging is possible for any profession, once you put your business under a microscope and discover where you truly get your clients.

Avoiding Generalizations = Creating Value

Marketing as a specialist is nerve-wracking for some businesspeople. They don't want to specialize so narrowly that they chase away valuable business. There's some validity to that; if you can't identify a niche that has the potential to give you a growing income, don't manufacture one. You can't specialize if no one wants your specialty.

But if it comes down to a choice between general and specialized, *always* choose specialized. That's what professional marketers do: identify a market that's potentially lucrative and under-served, position themselves as specialists, and seize control of it. Begin by being as specific as possible in describing what you do. Break out the profitable elements of your service as cleanly as possible, so instead of "professional auto detailer," you get "specialist in restoring pollution-damaged automotive leather, wood and chrome."

When crafting your statement of what you do, always imply a sense of value to the target market. You'll state the value outright later, but there should be a sense of it in this descriptor. Our real estate agent implies she knows the right fixer-uppers in her farm area, while the auto detailer specifically talks about restoring premium surfaces. Remember, you're selling yourself as a provider of value your target market simply can't go another day without.

Part No. 3: How You're Different or Create Value, or Your UVP

That segues us right into value. This is where the rubber meets the Personal Branding road. This is when you'll tell your prospect how you differ from your competitors or how you create unique value for him or her.

If you're in marketing, you may have heard the phrase "Unique Selling Proposition," or USP. That's a single, powerful idea that gives a prospect a reason to buy from you. In positioning yourself, you're creating a UVP, or Unique Value Proposition: one idea that tells prospects how you can benefit them, or why you're different from everyone else in your market.

Know the Unmet Need

In crafting this descriptor, you're looking for a need your target market has which is not being met. This is absolutely critical—if you can identify a need your market is dying for, and fill that need, you'll get rich. Of course, if it was that easy 80 percent of small businesses wouldn't fail within five years, but that just cuts down your competition, doesn't it?

In determining your benefit, you're really looking for a *critical unmet need* you can meet with your skills and abilities. The thing is, it doesn't have to be a specific service or product. An unmet need can be a quality, some way in which you're different from the competition, or a better price—anything your market hungers for but isn't getting. Examples:

- The ability to meet deadlines

- Technical knowledge

- A sense of humor

- Extra personal attention

- Hourly pricing

As long as your target market needs it, and you can fill the need, you've got your benefit. Tell your target market you're the professional to provide that thing of value they can't get anywhere else. To use our imaginary real estate agent again, here's her benefit statement:

> "...and managing all tax aspects of income property sales to the benefit of buyers and sellers."

If there's no other real estate agent in the area claiming to be an expert in the tax consequences of income properties, this lady's going to clean up.

Writing Your Personal Brand Statement (PBS)

Take the three core aspects of your position, line them up as a single sentence, and you've got your Personal Brand Statement, or PBS. This is the essence of your Personal Brand. If we once again use our fixer-upper-obsessed Realtor®, her PBS would probably read something like this:

> "A San Francisco native matching buyers seeking spec homes with high-value, classic properties and managing tax aspects to the benefit of all parties."

A little editing produces a tight, clear statement. Nowhere does it say "real estate agent," because it doesn't need to state that. Her profession is clear from the description of what she does. In two words, she's told prospective clients everything they need to know to decide if she's someone to consider when buying or selling a fixer-upper residence.

Once you write your three positioning elements, practice writing your PBS. Not all the parts will fit together smoothly at first, and that's normal. Edit, change words, and streamline until you get a concise statement that neatly summarizes you.

How Do You Use a PBS?

No one will ever see your PBS. Yes, that's right. Once you've tortured yourself over each syllable, no one in your target market will ever see it word for word. That's exactly as it should be.

Your PBS is designed for your eyes only, to be a compass for your Personal Branding and the marketing driven by your brand. You write the PBS not for your prospects but for yourself, as a way of setting in stone the identity you want to communicate to your target market. Once it's written, you've got a constant reminder of the professional niche you've chosen and how you offer value to your market.

Your PBS will be a constant presence as you build your Personal Brand, determining the direction and focus of your messages and overall marketing. Does a certain direct-mail piece work? Check it against the PBS. Does your slogan reflect your niche? Again, stand it up against your PBS and see if they mesh. If not, change your slogan. Print out your PBS and tack it to your office wall as a reminder of your brand, to keep you focused and moving in the right direction.

Interview: Al Ries and Laura Ries

Is the word "branding" constantly on your lips today? Thank Al Ries. Together with onetime partner Jack Trout, Ries brought the esoteric concepts of marketing and branding into the public eye with their seminal books, *Positioning* and *The 22 Immutable Laws of Marketing*. Since then, Ries and Trout—and later Ries and his daughter and current partner, Laura—have opened the eyes of the business world with niche-defining books on positioning, branding and more. Their latest book, *The Fall of Advertising and the Rise of PR*, is a perceptive, insightful dissection of why advertising is becoming irrelevant for a new brands.

We spoke to Al and Laura Ries from their offices in Roswell, GA, about the evolution of positioning and Personal Branding.

Q: How has the concept of positioning evolved since the first book?

A: Years ago, there was a kind of myth that said if you work hard, you get ahead, the people who work the hardest get ahead the fastest, and so on. Yet our personal experience says that's not necessarily true. The people who get ahead are the ones who get noticed, inside and outside the company. One of the stories in (the book) *Horse Sense* is about a time at Citibank when the CEO had the names of 75 people who were identified as people with potential talent. If you weren't on that list of 75, you were never going to get a big job at Citibank. How do you get on that list? Visibility.

Most people still just believe in the "hard work and keep your nose clean" theory. I think people believe life is fair, and that God will decide that I should be promoted. It's the Calvinist work ethic, the idea that you get what you deserve. But it's not true.

Q: Where is the greatest value in a Personal Brand in this age?

A: Nothing works in America like celebrity. Look at Suzanne Somers; she's famous for being famous. You get famous in the larger world through publicity, through mentions in the media. It's helpful if you can focus on a single idea you want to communicate. Sometimes it's hard to verbalize, but just visualize Martha Stewart, Donald Trump. They are successful for being successful.

Getting publicity is achieved through doing something, but also being first at what you do, being unique and different. You have to think about where people are going to file your name in their mind, what attributes people are going to associate with you. In my mind, a safe car is a Volvo, a driving machine is a BMW. Stand for something and then communicate what you stand for, and do it in such a way that you get it inside people's minds.

Q: Your book Horse Sense *talks about attaching yourself to a great idea and riding it. How does that apply to Personal Branding?*

A: The book was initially called *Positioning Yourself*. We determined the best way to position yourself is to get outside yourself and hook onto some product or service. The problem with most people is they want to do it themselves, by proving to the world they're terrific.

Take an entrepreneur. He needs to find an idea, product or service. Here's the trick: Most entrepreneurs who get wealthy did not invent anything; they found better ways to promote it. Howard Schultz didn't found Starbucks. He bought it.

In a nation of 281 million people, I might have one or two ideas inside myself that can make me wealthy, but look at the choices I have: I can look around at the other 281 million people and find an idea none of them have thought of, or I can promote something better than anyone else.

It's rare for someone all by himself or herself to come up with an idea or concept that becomes an enormously successful something or other. By looking around, you get free market research. People are doing something and you say, "That looks interesting. I can start a business focused on that." Sometimes, you do something based on negative input. The guy who started Holiday Inn stopped at a motel, and they charged him for each kid. So he started his own motel chain.

Q: What principles of positioning are evergreen?

A: You build any brand by getting into the mind. You build brands in the mind, not in the marketplace. That's true with your career. Unless people think you're important, successful and smart, you're not.

PR is crucial. That's what our latest book is all about. One of the biggest mistakes business owners make is blowing their money on advertising. People won't even pay attention to it. We only suggest it as a maintenance tool. You only pay attention to an ad if you already know and like the company.

The biggest single point is you have to stand for something. People have to associate you with something. Henry Ford stands for the automobile. It's not enough to be a name people know; you have to be known for something.

Also, you're better off with a single concise idea. As an entrepreneur, you have to be out front promoting the idea. We've talked to entrepreneurs who don't want to be out there, they want to stay in their offices. Sorry, it doesn't work that way. Behind every successful brand is an entrepreneur who is willing to get out and promote it.

Strategies for a Stronger Position

- **Be consistent!** Once you choose it, stick with your position and keep your messages consistent. It will take time for your positioning to become widely known in your target market. Give it that time.

- **If you can, choose something new.** Not always possible, but if there's a position you can fill that no one in your market has ever tried before, give it a shot. You never know when something unlikely will be a huge success.

- **Work your position into your slogan.** You will do a slogan. When you do, write a slogan that captures the essence of your positioning statement.

- **Speak your position.** Prepare a phrase so when people ask you what you do, you can tell them in a way that reflects your position. People often forget this, and sabotage their positioning in conversation.

- **Emphasize your position with extras.** Find ways to drive home your position with clients and prospects—special direct mailers, premiums, thank-you gifts like sports tickets, whatever. Try to locate creative ideas that will remind people of the niche you occupy—for example, a chiropractor sending good clients a free back massager.

- **Protect your position against interlopers.** Competitors will try to copy your position if you're successful. Prepare for this, first by making sure your target market knows you were the first in your market to occupy your position, and second by reinforcing it all the more strongly after you see a competitor's message. Remember, in Personal Branding, he who moves first laughs last.

Personal Brand Case Study

Todd Eckelman
Todd Eckelman Photography

Position: The people photographer
Location: Portland, OR
Business: Commercial Photography
Online: eckelman.com

Todd Eckelman wasn't terribly different from any freelance creative professional trying to establish himself—he would take any job of any kind to pay the bills and build his portfolio. "I used to be nothing but a product photographer," he says. The key to his current success (shooting star athletes for Nike, among others) was making a simple yet brave decision: the decision to specialize and position himself as a photographer of people. The result has been more national work and many more opportunities.

How It Started:
Eckelman repositioned himself in his mind, then went out after the kind of work he wanted, switching what he showed from his portfolio. He also stayed versatile, becoming known as the guy who could shoot one company's athletes, and another company's executives. Plus, he doesn't turn away every product project; he just bases his branding on his position as the "people photographer."

Most Important Steps in Building a Personal Brand:
"I do direct-mail pieces, and I have the Web site. The direct mail gets people to the Web site. Plus, if you go to any search engine, I think you'd find me. I've done print ads in a magazine called *Archive*. I never really did get a lot from other resource books; I get more response from direct mail."

Biggest Success:

"I've built my brand on being easy to work with, on being fast. I'm the guy who gets it done, and is conscious of the budget. I'll try to come in under budget most of the time if I can."

On Personal Branding and Putting the Eggs in One Basket:

"When I first started, I had one big client called Codaphone, I made the mistake of basing a lot of stuff off the income I was getting from them, and then I lost my biggest client all of a sudden. It was a big lesson to learn: you can't just have one giant client and count on them always being there. I realized I needed to have a broad base of clients. I wasn't working enough to get new clients."

Advice:

"Never stop marketing, something I need to force myself to do more. You need to be doing some sort of marketing all the time. Every other quarter I'm doing something. My things are pretty distinctive. You need to do something all the time, but it needs to set you apart. Do something that makes you different from the others. Direct mail is a hit-and-miss proposition. I've done some cool T-shirts and didn't get one response from that. Go figure.

"When people call, they're talking directly to me. A rep would be one way I could be constantly marketing, because he or she would be selling for me. A rep is valuable as someone to get you in the door, someone who's known."

Brandstorming Positioning:
7 Great Things You Can Do Right Now

1. Get to know how your competitors are positioned. Make a wall chart listing each of their names and their positioning, if any.

2. Write out Who You Are

3. Write out What You Do

4. Write out How You Create Value

5. Stake out your position immediately with your current clients by sending a personal letter explaining your branding efforts and your position.

6. Train your employees by sharing your Personal Brand Statement with them.

7. Prepare to defend your position should a competitor try to take it from you by listing strategies for fending off such interlopers.

Bottom Line No. 7: How Personal Branding Equals More Business
Creating an effective position

Situation: You're a freelance Web developer in Los Angeles, where every geek with six weeks in a Learning Annex Web design class is after your prospects. You're scrambling for consistent business and dying for a way to separate yourself from the inexperienced masses who are giving your profession a black eye.

Solution: You write your Personal Brand Statement with an eye on highlighting your experience while subtly bashing your Johnny-come-lately competitors. Your PBS: "A UCLA-trained Web architect with 10 years of programming language fluency, for corporations seeking an online presence that's more than an interactive brochure." You translate that statement into a new Web site that focuses on case histories of your best work, as well as a semi-humorous primer: "How to tell an experienced Web developer from a novice who just wants your money." You drive traffic to the site with a direct e-mail campaign.

Result: Prospects love the candor of your site, and from your case histories they learn that you know your business and have made good things happen online for some major companies. Within a few weeks, you've got meetings and proposal requests for half a dozen new prospective clients...and you're no longer one of the crowd.

Brand Surgery: Avoiding Tragic Branding Mistakes
The Patient: Your Positioning

- Don't grab a position that's too esoteric just because it's available. There may be a reason for that.

- Make sure your skills can back up your position. Remember, performance is everything.

- Avoid positioning yourself with trends. They have a nasty habit of disappearing, along with your business.

- Try not to copy others' positioning, unless you feel they're extremely weak in terms of marketing and customer satisfaction. Copycats almost always lose...expensively.

- Enjoy your position. You're packaging yourself as "The one who can do X," so you'd better enjoy X.

- Don't get into claims of quality in your position. That can start mudslinging with competitors. Just state the facts about what unique space you occupy. Then perform like nobody's business.

- Don't try to be too sophisticated with your position. Simpler is better. If you have a ready market as "the elegant caterer," sticking your nose in the air as "the French gourmet caterer" will probably just cost you business.

CHAPTER 8

Branding Channels

Many Ways to Get Your Message to Your Target Market

Advertisements in your local newspaper. Letters sent to a desirable group of prospects. Referrals from loyal customers to a group of friends or colleagues. Monthly e-mails sent to people who've hit your Web site. These are all *branding channels*: the routes by which information about your Personal Brand gets from you to your target market. Understanding what branding channels are and how to use them is the third vital Personal Branding strategy.

What Are Branding Channels?

Irrigation channels carry water. Branding channels carry information about you—your values, abilities, specialization, position, you name it. Once you've created your Personal Brand—and the specialty and positioning that go with it—that brand reaches your prospects and clients via branding channels

But they aren't just branding channels. They're also marketing channels, used to generate new business or clients. Back in Chapter 2, we made the case that all marketing is a part of branding. Channels communicate the essence of your Personal Brand—what you can do, how you create value, the abilities and philosophies you're known for—to influential people through marketing.

The Eight Branding Channels and Their Tools

There's almost no limit, given enough time and money, to the ways you can get your message to your target audience. For clarity, we've broken down the most cost-effective, useful branding channels into eight distinct categories, representing 95 percent of the branding work you'll ever do. As you develop your Personal Brand and gain experience in promoting it, you'll naturally gravitate toward the channels that fit your style and your business, but it's important to have an awareness of them all:

1. Client Referrals
   a. Referral Request
   b. Personal Brochure
   c. Premium Offer

2. Professional Referrals
   a. Referral Request
   b. Reward or Incentive Program
   c. Endorsement Letter or E-mail

3. Direct Mail
   a. Sales Letter
   b. Catalog
   c. Personal Postcard
   d. Mailing Calendar

4. Networking
   a. Business Card
   b. Personal Brochure

5. Seminars
   a. Personal Brochure
   b. Seminar Manuals
   c. PowerPoint Presentation

6. Public Relations
   a. Media Kit
   b. Press Releases
   c. Editor Relationship Program
   d. Sponsorships

7. Warm Calling
   a. Phone Script
   b. Product and Service Information

8. Web Site
   a. E-Newsletter
   b. Product and Service Offers

Secondary Channels and Tools

These remaining channels will only work for about 5 percent of the companies that use them. That's because they all require large budgets and long exposures to create brand awareness. Most likely, your money is better spent elsewhere.

We suggest avoiding these second-tier channels until you've gotten all you can from the primary channels. These tools, in general, are wonderful for gaining greater visibility and credibility, but are very poor at making the phone ring. People in town will know who you are, but will not pick up the phone to call you based on a billboard or TV ad. These tools simply make the first tier of branding channels more effective, but they're worthless for actually launching a Personal Brand.

1. Print Advertising
   a. Display Advertising
   b. Classified Advertising
   c. Yellow Page Advertising

2. Outdoor Advertising
   a. Billboards
   b. Bus Benches
   c. Airport Signage

3. Radio Advertising
   a. Host-Paid Radio Show
   b. Commercials
   c. Infomercials

4. Television Advertising
   a. Host-Paid TV Show
   b. Pay-for-Guest TV Show
   c. Commercials
   d. Infomercials

5. Tradeshows and Special Events
   a. Booth
   b. Premiums
   c. Product and Service Literature
   d. Banners

Have Five Ways to Reach Your Target Market

Building your Personal Brand takes consistency and repetition. But repeating your branding message over and over, using the same methods, becomes ineffective, then annoying. That's why experienced brand builders use multiple channels, coordinated to work together, to drive their branding message home. It's like attacking the same target from many directions; your chances of hitting go up.

To maximize your effectiveness, obey the Rule of Five: Employ at least 5 channels to reach each target market. If deployed so they complement each other, channels work beautifully, and build each other's power.

Does this work? Think about how you make a decision to buy a product, for instance, a new computer. Do you make your decision based on one exposure to one message? No. You see an ad, then a few days later hear about the computer from a friend, then see an article in a magazine the following week. Together, these channels convince you to make a buying decision.

Think Synergy

Inexperienced marketers think in terms of one tool, one goal. You place an ad to generate phone calls. You send out a press release to get a blurb in the paper, and so on. But to get the most from the money you spend, you've got to think like a Personal Brander. You've got to get your channels feeding off each other. You've got to generate *synergy*.

That means the whole is more than the sum of its parts. When you design a branding campaign that uses multiple channels in a synergistic way, you get two results: Each individual channel drives home your message on its own, and each channel increases the effectiveness of one or more others. For example:

You hold a public seminar to promote your legal services (Channel 1). At the seminar, you hand out copies of your Personal Brochure and explain the contents (Channel 2). The brochure leads people to your Web site for more information, and you gather e-mail addresses of attendees for your e-mail newsletter (Channel 3). After the seminar, you send reminder e-mails to attendees, and direct-mail pieces to those who didn't attend with the highlight content (Channel 4). Finally, you tape the seminar and send audiotapes to your local radio station with a brochure and an invitation to attend your next seminar and run a story (Channel 5). That's multiple channels, working together, giving your target market multiple chances to respond. That's ROI.

As you learn about channels and put together your own marketing to build your brand, always think, "How can I integrate my channels? How can each make others better?" Jenny Craig is a terrific example of synergy. A former housewife who beat her own weight problem, Craig masterfully promoted her Personal Brand into 652 weight-loss centers around the world. But the visibility of the centers was supported through advertising,

PR and personal appearances by Craig herself, a hero to millions of women struggling with their weight.

There Are No Bad Channels, Only Bad Branders

Branding channels are like high-performance cars: they're only as good as the person at the wheel. All branding channels work; the question is, is a channel right for the business that's using it?

Take the example of a branding client of ours, a financial planner who's been using seminars to target widows over age 65. Because widows would generally rather find a financial advisor they like and trust instead of trying to understand a lot of Byzantine financial data, the seminars flopped. So our client switched to another tactic: sponsoring monthly bingo at the local community center, even going so far as to personally announce the bingo numbers. The bingo cards even featured his logo and phone number! His business has soared because of his creative use of a channel, and his hard-earned knowledge of his specialty market.

Inclusive and Exclusive Channels

There are two categories of branding channels: *inclusive* and *exclusive.*

- **Inclusive Channels**—You don't have much control over who sees the message, so you'll probably attract a larger response but lower-quality prospects. This works for building seminar attendance and a mailing list.

- **Exclusive Channels**—You can control who sees your message, but you reach fewer people. This is ideal for target marketing and times when you need to winnow down larger groups into hot prospects.

A strong branding channel strategy uses some of both.

Inclusive Channels

1. **Seminars**

Seminars take time, planning and the ability to speak comfortably in front of groups of people. Consequently, they're not for everyone. Also, your profession may not lend itself to seminar-style presentations. However, 80 percent of the business owners we've talked with are in businesses where seminars would benefit them, so chances are when you're ready, a seminar will help you grow.

In a seminar, you get a captive target market, usually without charging them admission, and give them a sales pitch disguised as education. The idea is to deliver your Personal Brand message in person to a large group, then get as many of them as possible to meet with you later individually, to close them. Seminars are also a perfect venue for distributing materials and information.

There are two types of seminars:

1. Public, which you advertise in the community and anyone can attend. Public seminar target markets are usually lower-quality prospects who demand little.

2. Private, which you promote to a company, Chamber of Commerce or other group, and get a smaller, more desirable target market (which will probably also be more demanding).

- **What it's good for:** Making face-to-face contact with your Personal Brand to a large number of people. Getting a chance to sell prospects on your skills, experience and unique services. Distributing literature, capturing contact information, and making appointments that will lead to sales.

- **What it's bad for:** Saving money (advertising, materials and hall space are expensive), identifying qualified prospects, conserving time (the planning, execution and follow-up involved in a seminar are all very time-costly).

- **How it can work with other channels:**

  - Hand out information packets to all attendees, including such things as your Personal Brochure, articles about you, and testimonials

  - Tell people about other events you're holding

  - Get attendee addresses or e-mail addresses for your direct-mail list

  - Use the seminar as an excuse for a press release to generate media coverage

  - Make the initial acquaintances that turn telemarketing into "warm calling"

- **Using seminars more effectively:**

  - Know what kind of target market you want: large, public and varied in quality, or small, private and demanding.

  - Practice your public speaking again and again.

  - Provide quality handouts.

  - Keep it in the 60 to 90 minute range, no more.

- At one seminar, promote upcoming seminars.

- Make sure every person leaves with some printed material.

2. **Public Relations**

   PR involves working with the media to generate coverage of you, your business, and your outside activities, such as charity work and sponsorships. There's more media than you might think: local newspapers and magazines, local radio stations, cable TV stations, local network affiliates, online media, and even non-local trade publications that cover only your profession.

   PR also involves sponsorships of causes like local Little League teams and area charity events. Sponsorships attach a freight of goodwill to your name while getting your name in front of a large number of people in your community.

   For the most part, working with PR means using press releases and follow-up to generate coverage about your business. Your goal is to get news briefs, calendar listings or even features printed or broadcast about you. But good PR also means cultivating positive relationships with journalists based on mutual benefit. Get to know the print and broadcast editors and reporters in your area, and at the trade publications that cover your profession.

- **What it's good for:** PR might be the most powerful Personal Branding tool around. It's free, has great credibility, and in the right medium, wide coverage. It increases public visibility and awareness of who you are and what you do and enhances your credibility as a professional. Readers and listeners assume if you're featured in an unbiased medium like the press, you must be good. PR is great for creating awareness of events like seminars, charity sports tournaments, and so on.

- **What it's bad for:** Producing consistent, regular exposure. You have no control over editors, so you can't guarantee you'll get coverage from month to month.

- **How it can work with other channels:**

  - Create higher awareness of you, making both networking and referrals more effective

  - Drive target markets to seminars

  - Promote specific projects such as a Web site or magazine column

  - Turn you into a local "celebrity," making telemarketing more effective

- **Using public relations more effectively:**

  - Cultivate relationships with editors. Get to know them and their needs rather than simply bombarding them with press releases.

  - Send a Rolodex card and a cover letter to editors presenting yourself as an "expert source" in your field, and offering to be interviewed at any time.

  - Write your own column for a local publication, or have one ghostwritten for you. This is the one way to guarantee a regular press presence.

  - Learn and follow standard press-release format.

  - Send a press release whenever you have news, even if it's just a new hire. Multiple exposures make editors remember you.

3. **World Wide Web**

   Having an easy-to-use site with lots of useful information and features gives you a 24-hour information and branding center your clients and prospects can access anytime. That's powerful stuff. You can control their user experience, capture contact data, distribute information, and drive home your Personal Brand with graphics and copy. Done right, your Web site is a powerful tool for building your brand with prospects, the media, and influencers in your profession.

- **What it's good for:** Serving as an all-hours information center for anyone who wants to find out about you. What do you want to give clients and prospects? Case studies? A way to e-mail their friends about you and receive a free gift as a reward? A no-pressure way to check out your services? Financial calculators to figure out their retirement needs or mortgage payment? Helpful articles to download? A way to purchase your merchandise any time? You can do it all with your site, if you make the investment and know your goals.

- **What it's bad for:** Filtering prospects. You'll get plenty of hits from people who you don't want as your customers. It's also not useful for technophobic clients or people with slow connections who won't use the Web very often.

- **How it can work with other channels:**

  - Allow people to download digital versions of your brochure

  - Promote your seminars, sponsorships, and other events

  - Give editors a quick, easy way to learn about you for a story

- Get visitors to sign up for a promotion or newsletter and increase your direct-mail database

- Give referred prospects a place to go to check you out

- Allow you to do online polls of seminar attendees to find out how you can make your seminars better

- **Using the Web more effectively:**

  - Hire a professional Web designer and programmer. Do not have your cousin do it.

  - Promote your site in all your marketing, from ads to your brochure and business card.

  - Refer new contacts to your site to find out about you.

  - Refresh articles and other information on your site monthly, so users have reason to come back.

  - Make sure your privacy policy is posted, so users feel more comfortable about giving you their contact information.

  - Make your site less about design bells and whistles and more about clear, obvious user benefits.

4. **Advertising**
   When you run a Yellow Pages ad, buy space on a billboard, run a spot on a local radio station or run a Web banner, you're advertising. We recommend avoiding advertising until you have made the most of other branding channels. Advertising is expensive and requires months of exposures to generate any results.

   Once your Personal Brand is established, however, good advertising is a great way to spread awareness and solidify your hold on your target market. There's an intimidation factor to advertising that can make your competitors think twice about taking you on in your market.

- **What it's good for:** Reaching a large group of people without any effort from you. You just place the ad, pay the fee and wait. You can be seen by 100,000 people in hours with advertising. It's great for letting people know your name, your face and what you do.

- **What it's bad for:** Reaching a targeted target market and controlling the quality of your leads. Once you place an ad, it's fair game, and even if you place it in a highly targeted trade publication, you'll still attract people who aren't good prospects. Also, it's not easy to create ads that "pull." For really strong ads, you usually need an agency. Yellow Page advertisements tend to attract one-time customers who are very price sensitive. We don't recommend Yellow Page ads for most high-end professional service providers.

- **How it can work with other channels:**

  - Direct people to your Web site by publicizing your Web address

  - Promote an upcoming seminar

  - Make people aware of your name, so they're more receptive when you call them

  - Complement sponsorships

  - Add credibility to client referrals by making you more visible

- **Using advertising more effectively:**

  - Ask people to respond to your ad in some way, such as providing a number and asking them to call for your brochure.

  - Include your Web address, logo and slogan in all ads.

  - Refresh your ads periodically, no less than once every three months for ads that run continually, such as Yellow Pages ads. New layouts and headlines attract attention.

  - Make ads benefit-oriented—about the customer, not about you and how wonderful you are.

  - Offer readers a discount on your product or service when they mention the ad.

5. **Tradeshows and Special Events**

   You shouldn't even consider doing tradeshows or other big professional events until you've been an active Personal Brander for at least a year. That's because your branding and marketing message will still be in the refining stages, not ready for the chaos and short attention spans of a big tradeshow. With the costs of exhibit booths, shipping, accommodations, giveaway items and more, it's also *very* expensive.

   Once you are ready, a tradeshow, professional conference or other vertical event can be a wonderful opportunity to set up an exhibit and get your story out face-to-face.

- **What it's good for:** Networking, networking, networking. People at tradeshows and conferences are there as much to make contacts, as they are to make buying decisions. Maybe more. Your collection of business cards following a big event will be worth its weight in platinum. A tradeshow is also a powerful way to step out of a regional niche and get wider exposure. Tradeshows are also boffo for making splashy demos of new products or services, and if you can worm your way onto a panel discussion team, you can further increase your visibility and reputation.

- **What it's bad for:** Establishing any sort of meaningful dialogue between you and your prospects. There's just too much going on at a show. The vast majority of people who come into contact with you will take your brochure, accept your free gift, then dump them at day's end and never think about you again. Considering the cost, tradeshows and conferences don't generally show great ROI.

- **How it can work with other channels:**

  - Provide the press with a media event to cover

  - Give you a busy channel for distributing your Personal Brochure

  - Serve as a platform for speaking engagements and follow-up networking

  - Build your contact database for direct mailing

  - Allow you to display your Web site to a large audience

- **Using tradeshows and events more effectively:**

  - Try to use recycled exhibit booths and other show facilities. There are companies that specialize in this.

  - Attend only those events that focus on your target market exclusively.

  - Attend smaller events. The large shows may have the glitz, but you'll be lost in the crowds.

  - Have a memorable giveaway item at your exhibit.

  - Have a video or DVD demo of some product or service, if appropriate, to capture people's attention.

  - Be certain to have a way to either get a business card or scan an attendee badge so you can build a contact database from your show. It's the only way you'll get ROI.

The Details: Exclusive Channels

1. Professional Referrals

Referrals, how do we love thee, let me count the ways. Nothing is better for generating business than a referral. It's free, it's personal and it has all the credibility of the person behind it. If you never do anything else to promote your Personal Brand, cultivate a referral channel and you will succeed.

Professional referrals occur when a colleague or someone in a field related to yours recommends you to their client or customer. For example, if you're a real estate agent, sources of professional referrals are not just other Realtors®, but "associated professionals" such as mortgage brokers, appraisers, contractors, real estate attorneys and escrow companies.

These people already have a high degree of credibility with their clients, so when they recommend you, you're almost certain to get a phone call. Just do the math: since each of your associated professionals can have dozens or hundreds of clients, a few good professional referral sources can be your gateway to all the new business you can handle.

The reason more business owners and professionals don't leverage this channel? They think referrals happen spontaneously. Wrong. You must cultivate a referral base, ask for the referral, make it easy for the referring party to tell someone about you, and then reward the person providing the referral.

- **What it's good for:** Generating lots of new business from a few sources, without spending a lot of money. Cultivating your referral base is more about choosing the right people, building mutually beneficial relationships, and making it easy for them to send you referral clients.

- **What it's bad for:** There's almost nothing bad about professional referrals, provided you take good care of the clients sent to you. The only risk with any kind of referrals is you can't control what's said about you.

- **How it can work with other channels:**

  - Set the stage for a phone call or direct mailing

  - Prepare someone to receive your Personal Brochure

  - Direct someone to your Web site

  - Make a prospect more receptive to articles or other PR

- **Using referrals more effectively:**

  - Identify your associated professionals and talk to them about setting up an informal arrangement where you refer clients to each other.

  - Make sure the first target of your Personal Branding is your pool of associated professionals. If they don't know what your brand's all about, they can't refer you.

  - Make sure your referral pool has copies of your Personal Brochure or other materials to hand out.

  - Ask for the referral. Put your referral pool on a regular direct-mail plan (every other month at most) to remind them of you and the value you can offer their clients.

  - Practice *quid pro quo*. Be sure to refer clients to your associated professionals.

  - Set up an incentive or reward program for people who send you clients. This is illegal in some professions, so do your homework before proceeding.

  - Above all, treat referral clients like royalty. Take better care of them than you do your other clients, because that's the only way you'll continue to get referrals.

2. **Personal Referrals**

   No ad or brochure can get you in the door with a new client faster than a referral. The thumbs-up from someone who's used you and experienced your good work is all the endorsement you need to get business. If you have a group of happy clients, it's time to leverage them and turn them into a referral resource.

- **What it's good for:** Spreading the word about your abilities and value in a very personal, effective way. Nothing builds your Personal Brand better than a great story from someone who likes you, trusts you and wants to help someone else get to know you. Some professionals get all their new business through referrals. That's how powerful this channel is. You turn your happy customers into an army of unpaid marketers.

- **What it's bad for:** Predictability. You can't control what people say about you, and you can't make them say anything. Until you have a constant buzz going with a large group of referring customers, it's dangerous to rely too much on referrals.

- **How it can work with other channels:**

  - Prepare people for your telemarketing call

  - Send prospects to your Web site for information

  - Get them calling for information about your seminar, or to request a Personal Brochure

  - Set the stage for a networking opportunity

- **Using referrals more effectively:**

  - Ask for the referral! So few people actually ask for it, it's a wonder they ever get them. If your customers like you, they'll be happy to help you grow your business.

  - Give customers materials, such as brochures, to hand to friends or colleagues whom they refer.

  - Create reward programs for clients who refer friends or relatives to you.

  - Establish customer-service programs to ensure referred clients are treated like gold.

3. **Direct Mail**

   Direct mail is the most strategically important channel for developing your brand, because it lets you customize your message, reach prospects directly, and add offers or benefits that encourage recipients to contact you. Direct mail can be a wide range of pieces: letters, postcards, boxes and other "dimensional mailers," newsletters, and so on. We recommend color Personal Postcards because they're cost-effective, more likely to be read than letters, and they can beautifully communicate your Personal Brand.

- **What it's good for:** Communicating with prospects regularly for months or years. A strong, consistent direct-mail campaign is one of the best ways to generate a consistent flow of new business. It's also great for creating a relationship with clients, sending news and holiday greetings, promoting new services, and inviting clients and prospects to participate in promotions and open houses. Direct mail is a customized precision tool.

- **What it's bad for:** Low budgets and prickly prospects. Direct mail only works if you mail high-quality pieces consistently, and that takes money. If you're not willing to or can't make the investment, don't do direct mail now. As for the prickly prospects, some people loathe all direct mail.

- **How it can work with other channels:**

  - Promote seminars and other events

  - Inform people of articles or columns running soon

  - Ask for referrals

  - Inform recipients about new material on your Web site

- **Using direct mail more effectively:**

  - Mail consistently. For example, once a month to all your clients and prospects, forever.

  - When possible, offer your prospects a benefit, such as a free service or a premium, for contacting you. You can also offer a direct discount, such as "Get 20% your purchase when you present this postcard."

  - Make sure your phone and Web information is prominent on your mailers.

  - Know your target market and design messages to suit them. If they're older, talk retirement or travel. If many of them are engineers, talk up your Web site and keep things linear and direct.

  - Spend the money to make your mailers beautiful. High-quality paper, rich color and good printing make as much of an impression as your message.

4. **Networking**
   Networking involves making contacts with colleagues and influencers in your profession, most often at public gatherings and at professional get-togethers such as Chamber of Commerce meetings. The goal: to get people familiar with you, to lay the groundwork for productive relationships, and to hand out materials people will keep, usually your Personal Brochure.

- **What it's good for:** Letting players in your profession and your target market know you're out there, learn your name and what you do, and come to like and trust you. As we know, people do business with people they like, so networking can be a bonanza. It's about building relationships that will slowly turn into business generators. Networking is a powerful tool for long-term growth because it's exclusive, letting you create relationships with only the people who you feel will help you succeed.

- **What it's bad for:** Producing immediate business. Networking for the purpose of generating quick sales is almost always a dismal failure. People don't want to be treated as resources for your business. The best networking, and therefore the best business relationships, involve mutual benefit and the building of trust.

- **How it can work with other channels:**

  - Generate referrals

  - Allow you to hand out your Personal Brochure, which drives people to your Web site

  - Gives you the chance to tell people about your seminars, newspaper column, etc.

- **Using networking more effectively:**

  - Join professional organizations where you'll meet people who work in your field or with your target market.

  - Focus on creating relationships with professionals whose clients might have a need for your services; they're incredible sources of referral business.

  - Always have Personal Brochures to hand out.

  - Avoid selling. Treat social occasions as what they are: chances to make friends and start dialogues. Everyone knows the subtext is business; there's no need to drive it into the ground.

  - Have a follow-up plan for contacting people you meet who would be good prospects or referral sources.

5. **Warm Calling**
   Cold calling is a terrible waste of time. We're talking about so-called "warm calling," in which you call after having already made contact with the prospect at a seminar, through an inquiry, or by referral. This kind of telemarketing allows you to further a budding relationship by offering information or benefits.

- **What it's good for:** Taking a relationship to the next stage and setting up the meeting, where you hope to get the business. Talking, answering questions and letting the prospect get to know you and develop a level of comfort.

- **What it's bad for:** Busy schedules. Telemarketing is the opposite of advertising, in that it's very time-intensive. You need to set aside chunks of time from your busy life to make calls; we don't recommend you have others make them for you.

- **How it can work with other channels:**

  - Capitalize on referrals

  - Lets you invite people to seminars or events

  - Ask to send a Personal Brochure or add people to your mailing list

- **Using warm-calling telemarketing more effectively:**

  - Only call people who've come into contact with you in some way.

  - Always have a benefit to offer people who listen to your pitch.

  - Converse, don't sell. You're trying to establish trust and get the meeting, not close a sale.

  - If prospects say they're not interested, ask if they know anyone who could use your services. You have nothing to lose.

  - If people ask to be removed from your calling list, do so immediately.

  - After a successful conversation, send a thank-you card or gift prior to your scheduled appointment with the prospect.

Making the Most of All Your Channels

- Always cross-promote. Put your Web address in your press releases, refer to your advertising in your direct mail, and hand out seminar invitations at networking events. Always be thinking of ways to let one channel enhance another.

- Make sure your baseline information—name, logo, slogan—are consistent and visible in everything you do.

- Don't over-commit. Five channels are optimal, but you may not be ready for five. Maybe networking, direct mail and the Web are all you have time and money for right now. Even better, maybe they're bringing you all the business you can handle. Great. Stick with them, and when you want to grow your company, add channels.

- Always be building your database. In all contact with the public, try to get contact information—for consumers, corporate executives, editors, etc.—whenever you can.

Donna Maria Coles Johnson

Create the Life You Love

Position: Advocate of women's empowerment and life change
Location: Bowie, MD
Business: Attorney, consultant on life transformation, advocate for
        makers of natural handmade cosmetics
Online: donnamaria.com

Attorney and creator of a program called "Create the Life You Love"
Donna Maria's story is unusual, but in a sense she's a textbook example
of someone leveraging the full power of Personal Branding: the power to
remake yourself from the ground up and to create the professional life
you've always imagined.

How It Started:

In 1992, Donna Maria was an attorney and not liking it very much. Then
she discovered a subculture—people who made handmade soaps—and
found that many of the ingredients for making the soaps were right in her
kitchen. Sensing a paradigm shift, she stunned her father by quitting her
law practice, opening a shop, and staying up all night making soap.
Unfortunately, it didn't last. She didn't like retail, and got tired of shoplift-
ing losses. So she headed back to her 9-5 law practice feeling like she at
least had a story to tell.

Turns out she had more. "When you have a passion, you can't just turn
it off," she says. Donna Maria was making good money as general coun-
sel for MCI (later to become the ill-fated WorldCom), but she couldn't get
her cosmetics experience out of her mind. She didn't want to make products for sale, but she loved making them, knew the business side of
things, and wanted to turn her experience and her passion into something
greater—a business that would help women entrepreneurs realize their
dreams and transform their lives, while making everyone a good living.

So Donna Maria hired a Web designer, wrote a book (published in 2000)
and formed Donna Maria's Handmade Beauty Network, an organization
focused on meeting the needs of the small individual manufacturers of
handmade cosmetics. HBN now has over 350 member companies, and provides legal and business consulting. More important from a Personal
Branding standpoint, Donna Maria branded her own name and formed don-

namaria.com to promote her "Create the Life You Love" lectures, workshops, books and articles.

Most Important Steps in Building a Personal Brand:

Without question, Donna Maria's Personal Brand came about because she listened. "I started to hear people refer to me as my first name, people started to know me by that name alone," she says. Inspired, she turned Donna Maria into its own Personal Brand, launched a Web site for that brand, and launched her "Create the Life You Love" program. She now gives seminars and speaks all over the U.S., helping women learn how to achieve their goals through small-business ownership.

The savvy to see that her own Personal Brand was organically changing into something she had not anticipated has positioned Donna Maria as much more than a legal and business advocate for soap makers—it's made her a crusader for women's empowerment.

Biggest Success:

Donna Maria has become a master at leveraging multiple channels to reach her very receptive audience. First and foremost are her Web sites, especially handmadebeauty.com, which serves as an information and communications center for her members, vendors and everyone in her industry. She publishes an online newsletter, writes articles for major fashion and beauty magazines, and cultivates press coverage for HBN members by developing relationships with editors. With her database-enabled Web site, Donna Maria says she can run her entire enterprise from her laptop.

But her biggest success? "It would be serving the people that I already have as clients really well," she says. "That means a couple of things to me: being very responsive, and being available to them 24/7. It's serving the needs of the people who've decided I'm worth the membership dues and legal fees."

Donna Maria works tirelessly to cultivate referrals. "I create informative memoranda and hand them off to friends in this industry. And I follow up. I also promote my member businesses in my online newsletter. I can give my members coverage of their new business, new product line, even press coverage in *American Spa Magazine*, for $100 a year.

"The great thing is I can provide services to so many people with a single action, and make it available on the Web site. I can do the same for 10 members or 300. The Web design is created, the forms are there, the designer just changes the date, and it's done."

On Personal Branding and Online Research:

"I'll find online businesses, order their products, then if their service is good, recommend them to a magazine," Donna Maria says. "I also contact the trade magazines and let them know about this growing niche of people. The established cosmetics community wants to know about this growing group of entrepreneurs, and they will often run a few features on them."

Advice:

"What is so exciting about what I've done is anybody can do it. I just tossed my talent out to the universe and said 'Here I am.' When I self-published my book, the publisher called me and I didn't have an agent. I didn't have any money, so when an order came in, I'd run by Kinko's and copy it, then run by the post office and mail it.

The first step is to try something small and see what happens. I think anyone can do that: Take your passions and interests and any education you've had in life and do it. When you take what you love, and do something you can enjoy, and make a life out of it, you can do it."

Brandstorming Channels:
10 Great Things You Can Do Right Now

1. Itemize your branding and marketing budget.

2. List the channels you can afford and the ones you're comfortable using.

3. Examine your target market and determine which channels are most likely to reach them, based on their consumption habits, lifestyle and interests.

4. Research online for organizations related to your profession and explore them for networking opportunities.

5. Update your database software.

6. Start with direct response: Begin compiling a database for "warm calling" and direct mailings.

7. Begin the process of choosing a commercial printer, photographer, writer and/or designer.

8. Contact publications that are ideal for future advertising and request rate cards.

9. Look at your target market and begin shopping around for possible referral incentives. Web sites like incentives.com and giveanything.com are excellent places to start.

10. Assign or hire a branding manager who will manage the day-to-day activity of your channels.

Bottom Line No. 8: How Personal Branding Equals More Business
Leveraging the right channels to reach your target market

Situation: You're a wedding planner in a big city, with plenty of competition. Your problem isn't lack of inquiries, but lack of qualified prospects. You want to restrict your work to affluent families looking to spend at least $30,000 on a wedding, and you're tired of wasting your time meeting with couples who have $5,000 and a prayer.

Solution: You need to reach more affluent people with your Personal Brand, so you start some integrated channel marketing: private seminars for 10 to 20 women held in bridal stores; a high-end brochure with beautiful glossy photos you hand out at all events; a coordinated Web site that positions you as a wedding planner for those who want an elegant, complex event; direct mail to former clients that asks them for referrals in exchange for gift certificates to baby stores; and telemarketing to seminar attendees. Everything is top-quality; this approach is expensive, but you're making an investment in your business. At the same time, you pull your Yellow Pages ads and any other directory ads to cut off the flow of bad prospects.

Result: Over a few months, the flow of low-ticket prospects slows to a halt; when they do come in, you've got other planners to refer them to for consultations. Instead, your seminars reap a bonanza of business. You get 2 or 3 clients each month from the seminars, and because these clients are encouraged to spend at the bridal shop where the seminars take place, the shop owner gives you even more referrals. Within six months, you're as busy as you can be and making more money from wealthier clients.

Brand Surgery: Avoiding Tragic Branding Mistakes
The Patient: Your Channels

- Expensive channels aren't always the best ones. Don't be seduced by the dollars.

- Don't starve your channel. Once you open it, keep branding and marketing information flowing through it consistently.

- Stick with a channel for at least six months. Some take time to establish and show results. Abandoning a channel too quickly can waste your investment.

- Don't adopt a channel out of envy. If you see a competitor's splashy TV ad, don't rush out and spend thousands on your own. Stick with the targeted channels that have worked for you.

- Forget about what it costs, as long as it's getting results. If a channel costs $20,000 per year but brings in $100,000 in revenue, it's worth it.

- If there's trouble in one channel—such as a speaking engagement that flops—isolate that channel from the others until the trouble is fixed. Don't cite the speech in an article or press release.

CHAPTER 9

Customer Service

Back Up Your Brand with Great Performance

Ask nearly any business owner or professional why his or her business has beaten the odds and thrived, and you'll hear variations on the same theme: "Because I provide great customer service." It's true; though everyone claims to take great care of customers, few actually do it. It just sounds good in a brochure.

But customer service is more than just making people happy. In the cable TV industry, the connection from the outside main cable to the homeowner's TV is called the "last mile." Customer service is the "last mile" for your Personal Brand. The experience you provide your customers will either support or contradict the promises you make with your branding campaign. Once your branding and marketing get a prospect in the door, performance turns your Personal Brand from hype to flesh—or failure to perform alienates your prospect forever.

Your goal as a Personal Brander is simple: to complete the picture of your brand by creating satisfying—and from time to time, extraordinary—experiences for all your customers. When you perform as advertised repeatedly over time, you'll create the most valuable of all business currencies: trust.

Have a System

As important as customer service is, smart business owners and professionals don't leave it to chance. The best businesspeople develop a proactive customer-service program that operates on a pre-set schedule, without the boss' involvement, to continually reach out to customers and make them feel cared for, communicated with, and listened to at all times. It may sound like a lot of work, but the benefits are tremendous:

- Happy clients who are easy to deal with during your relationship

- An unpaid sales force giving you spontaneous, gold-plated referrals

- Customer loyalty, leading to more consistent income

- Greater tolerance for change such as price increases

Knowing What Your Customers Want

You probably know the best referrals are unsolicited, and when customers love your service enough to refer others to you without being asked, they're going to send tons of business your way. The question is: How do you provide that winning service and those incredible customer experiences?

You do it by learning what your customers want, or creating "client awareness." Then you wonder how to accomplish that. Here's how:

Customer Research Methods:

- **Formal Market Research**—Locating or purchasing demographic data from sources like USA Data and The *Sourcebook of Zip Code Demographics* can give you the refined, pure information about the people in your geographic target market: what they earn, what their political leanings are, how educated they are, how many of them own a home, etc. With such data, you can get a general picture of who your customers are, what they value, and how they live.

- **Informal Market Research**—This type of research involves sitting down with your clients in a relaxed situation (offering to take a few of them to lunch, for example), and taking down their responses to carefully chosen questions about your business. Some questions we find useful:

  a. What keeps you coming back to do business with me?

  b. What could I do to make it easier for you to work with me?

  c. Where have I fallen short in the past?

  d. What services or conveniences would you like to see me offer?

- **Keeping in Touch**—The most basic option of all, simply keeping in regular touch with your clients—without any list of questions in mind—is perhaps the best way to constantly keep a finger on the pulse of your business. The most important aspect of this: let your customers know candidly that you'll be keeping in regular touch with them, and invite them to reciprocate when they have questions or ideas. Two excellent ways to establish a 24/7 communication channel:

a. Client Surveys—Send your customers a survey twice a year asking what you're doing well, what could improve, and what they recommend for improving your service.

b. Response Lines—Let clients know there are always-open channels they can use at any time to share their thoughts or concerns. We suggest:

   1. Phone—Set up a dedicated voice-mail line called your "Customer Feedback Line" or something similar, and let customers know they can leave a message anytime with their ideas. Always respond to these messages within 24 hours.

   2. E-mail—Create a special e-mail address (feedback@you.com, for example) customers can use, and establish an auto-response that sends a message like, "Thank you for your e-mail message. I will review your thoughts and respond within 24 hours." Then follow up as promised.

When you've put your client-awareness systems in place, log all the data you gather for analysis. What you learn should tell you everything from how customers like your office wallpaper to their plans for retirement. This in turn can help you tailor your service to create the best possible experience.

The Right Customer Service Attitudes

Customer service is also an attitude. Creating memorable customer experiences must become part of your business model, not just a policy. Remember, customers are in the process of creating a new experience each time they interact with you. Will that experience enhance your Personal Brand or damage it? Some attitudes you should be adopting personally and building into the training of your staff:

1. **Love your clients**. You can't fake it and nothing can replace it. Everyone in your company must treat your clients with care and respect. If you don't love your clients, you'd better get another client base or another business.

2. **Develop a client-centered culture.** Your culture determines how you and your staff interact with your clients. Develop a company culture that naturally places the focus on meeting the clients' needs.

3. **The overriding theme of everyone's work should be, "A customer's satisfaction is my responsibility and most important mission."** It should not be, "You can't please all the people all the time." It's everyone's job to do everything they can to make the time and money the customer is spending worthwhile in the customer's eyes.

4. **The customer is always right—in his own mind.** This ancient adage has been debated and torn apart for decades, but like a spicy meal, refuses to go away. That's because it's true; perception is reality, and when you're dealing with a customer, you must remember his version of what's going on is the only one that matters. If you approach customer service from that perspective, you'll rarely go wrong.

5. **Under-promise and over-deliver.** Every customer or prospect who comes to you will have a set of expectations; some reasonable, others not. How you live up to those expectations will have a great deal to do with the customer's satisfaction. So you must *manage customer expectations*, and one of the best ways to do that is to tell the customer something will take two weeks, and then do it in one. Or promise a certain amount of work for the price, and then do 50 percent more for the same money. Of course, you'll know you were able to do the work faster or deliver more all along, but your customer won't. He'll be expecting less, but getting more—and he'll be thrilled. Disney's theme parks are a wonderful example of under-promise, over-deliver. When you get in line for a ride, they have a sign that tells you the wait will be 45 minutes. But when you board the ride and check your watch, it's always 30 minutes or so, and you're pleased. They've just made you happy to stand in line for half an hour! Brilliant.

6. **Customer service is everybody's job.** Every one of your employees must understand and live by this credo, even if they don't have direct contact with the customer. So many businesses throw around empty slogans about "The customer is the most important person in our business…blah, blah, blah" that they lose their meaning, so take another tack with your people. Sit them down and openly talk about what good customer service means for the business (strategy, referrals, growth) and how it affects them (positive feedback, more pleasant work, better pay, promotion). When you're done, print your customer-service reasons and give a copy to every employee to post at individual workspaces.

7. **People make mistakes.** It's not the mistake that kills; it's the cover-up. Nixon learned it, so should you and your people. Your customers don't expect you to be perfect, and you won't be. So when you do make an error, don't tap dance, deny or "spin." That's the worst thing you can do. If your business is legitimately at fault, admit the mistake and go above and beyond the call to fix it…at your cost. If the blame is shared, talk to the customer about the circumstances and about sharing the costs. In our experience, at least as many long-lasting business relationships have been created over the correction of a problem as over impeccable customer serv-

ice. Why? Because when you pull out all the stops to make something right, you prove you're as good as your Personal Brand.

8. **Anticipate.** Think of the times you've been delighted by a company or service provider giving you just what you wanted *before* you asked for it. That's not ESP, but anticipatory thinking. When you really get to know your clients—their families, their milestones, their tastes, their professions-you'll be able to start anticipating what they need before they ask, whether it's a free massage in your reception area or tickets to a sold-out ballgame. When you start anticipating and filling your clients' needs, you'll score *huge* points.

Improve and Never Stop

The real challenge of customer service is it never ends. You don't just institute a policy and leave it there. You must always be learning, listening and adapting to continue giving customers experiences they can brag about to others (and turn into lucrative referrals).

To make this happen, create a Customer Service Manual listing the procedures you and your people will use to give customers rewarding experiences. The basic content we recommend:

Your Customer Service Manual

- **Basic Customer Service Policies**—When to give refunds, shipping options, key contact people, etc.

- **Customer Complaint Procedures**—Processes to follow in handling a customer problem, from scripted questions to ask to complaint forms to have the customer fill out.

- **Things to Observe**—Cues to look for when a customer is unhappy, which you can use to head off complaints before they occur.

- **Customer Surveys**—Survey forms your employees can give out at the end of a visit or project to learn how you can improve.

- **Key Customer Notes and Preferences**—Write down anything important about how your best customers like to do business, from how tolerant they are of waiting to their reaction to a free gift in the mail.

Most important, sit down every six months with your staff to go over any and all customer complaints and/or praise. Look at the causes of complaints and examine ways your entire business can improve customer service.

Constant improvement is the goal; in these feedback sessions, you should strive for the following over time:

- Fewer overall customer complaints per period
- More resolved customer complaints
- More referrals per period
- More positive survey results per period

Recovering From a Customer Service Crisis

The question is not, "Will I have unhappy clients?" You will. The question is, "What do I do about it?" Courtesy of customer service trainer and "client experience" consultant Chris Tooker, here's a common sense, effective process for turning a service failure into a chance to shine:

1. **Listen and acknowledge the complaint.** Listen empathetically, and acknowledge how the customer is feeling (angry, frustrated, disappointed, insulted, etc.). Let them know you hear and feel their complaint personally. Validate their displeasure with phrases such as, "I understand how you feel," "I can understand why you are so upset," or "That certainly is not right, is it?" Often, customers are afraid of being seen as malcontents when they complain. Let them know they are right—and are, in fact, helping you—when they speak up.

2. **Apologize.** Admitting there's a problem and taking responsibility for it goes a long way. Sincerely apologize for the situation and let the customer know how disappointed you are with what's happened. Use phrases like, "If I were in your shoes I would," "I certainly wouldn't want to be treated that way..." or "You're handling this extremely well, considering the way you've been treated."

3. **Let them know you can do better.** Tell the customer that this mistake is not indicative of the work you or your company do, and that you are going to make every effort to make sure that it doesn't happen again.

4. **Ask what you can do to make things right.** Flat-out ask your customer, "What can I do to make you happy?" or "What can I do to remedy this situation?" This is scary, but critical to a successful recovery. Be genuine and assure them that you are going to do everything you can do to resolve this situation as quickly as possible.

5. **Maintain and verify communication.** Once you understand the problem and have found a solution, get in touch with the client to let them know. Say something like, "I'm working personally on a solution, and by the end

of the day tomorrow everything will be as you requested." Keep communicating with the client until the problem is solved.

6. **Thank the customer.** Once the crisis is over, send your customer a note thanking them for alerting you to the problem and providing you the opportunity to make sure it never happens again. Thank them for their business and for giving you the opportunity to keep it.

Keep your sense of humor, be pleasant and personable, and remember, you can't fix crazy, but you should at least try to help.

Getting Rich Through a Love Affair with Your Clients

Few professionals have ever managed to turn customer service into a gold mine like financial advisor Ron Carson. Based in Omaha, the L/PL Financial Services advisor was on pace to gross $6 million in 2002 at the time of this writing—all while taking three months off to travel around the U.S. with his family. Sound like a man who's sold his soul to the devil? Nope, just a guy who's developed a customer-service system to make his clients feel like the most important people in the world.

For one thing, Carson has only 350 clients—carefully chosen for their affluence and their appreciation of his personal and professional style. Carson's brilliance lies in his approach: he doesn't service a clientele, he maintains a community by surprising his clients with gifts and "random acts of kindness" that give his Personal Brand absolute 24-karat, top-of-mind status.

Carson's receptionist is also his "director of first impressions," responsible for greeting clients with baked goods and stocking their favorite beverages. He has taken clients on cruises, golf outings with Arnold Palmer, and Cornhusker tailgate parties. He ties his staff's bonuses to client satisfaction. Most important, he stays in contact, calling at random just to chat, not about business, but about anything.

The result is a level of client loyalty that's off the scale, and a lifestyle 95 percent of us would run over our mothers for. Ron Carson creates unmatched customer experiences, and that love translates into huge success.

Personal Brand Case Study

Dr. Todd Walkow

Position: Orthodontic for all ages
Location: Newport Beach, CA
Business: Orthodontia

Dr. Todd Walkow saw an opportunity in adult orthodontics, so he bought an existing practice from a Newport Beach orthodontist who had not been leveraging the full potential of his business. But rather than portray himself as a large practice, Walkow made a very smart strategic branding decision: to build his business on his Personal Brand.

How It Started:

The doctor whom Walkow bought out had an office in a superb area of the affluent Southern California city, a great clientele, and tremendous growth potential, but was leveraging almost none of his advantages. Walkow saw the potential not only in the existing business, but in a unique orthodontic niche.

"There's a big, growing sector in adult orthodontics," he says. "People are looking into better aesthetics, so there's a huge, growing market for adult orthodontia. Most people predominantly thought of orthodontia as something for kids. But adults didn't feel as intimidated."

Most Important Steps in Building a Personal Brand:

Walkow knew he would be at a disadvantage if he tried to position his practice as a big company. Fortunately, he knew his greatest strength was his patients' comfort level with him, the person.

"Since I'm one doctor, not a multi-practitioner practice, I needed to sell myself," he says. "People are coming to see me, not an entity. The best way to use that was to name the business after myself, not a catchy name. When people are at the supermarket or the soccer field, they're not saying some entity; they're using my name. If I was going to sell myself, I needed to sell my name."

Biggest Success:

"When patients come here, we do internal and external marketing. Internally, I try to make the experience the best I can, from having a really well-trained staff to patient care, making sure the patients are always getting the best care and attention possible. Contests, special promotions,— we always have things out for the kids, toys with my name on them. We have awards for people who take great care of their braces, Patient of the Day awards, the patient's name on a sign when they come in. It's all about making them feel like part of our dental family when they come in. We do all the little, special things we can to make it a better experience.

Externally, we give patients things that have our name and the brand on them—T-shirts that kids wear to the beach, moms wear to the gym. We keep the community informed that we're here. We also do outreach to dentists in the area, bringing in other dental practices to our office for 'lunch and learn' sessions. We want people to think of us when they think of orthodontics in Newport Beach."

On Personal Branding and the Patient Experience:

"I tell my staff, we can do all these great things for patients, but if we do one negative thing, they're going to go out and talk about that."

Advice:

"The best way to build your business is to establish your name as your brand. It takes time, and it takes a lot of outreach to the community and existing clientele. My philosophy is, the more you can do to get people to see and use your name more, and to associate something positive with your name, the better."

Brandstorming Customer Service:
13 Great Things You Can Do Right Now

1. Every time you greet clients, act as if they are the most important client in the world...*and mean it!*

2. Thank-You Notes—Personal Postcards with handwritten notes thanking the recipient for anything

3. Birthday and Anniversary Cards
   a. Send client a reminder a week in advance of upcoming anniversary.
   b. Send client a reminder a week in advance of spouse's birthday.

4. Receptionist
   a. Hire a live receptionist and train him or her in customer service and phone etiquette
   b. Install an easy-to-use, voice-mail system

5. Reach out with a dozen "touches" per year—Communicate with clients at least once a month via mail, e-mail, the phone or in person

6. Holiday Greetings and Gifts—Send gender/faith neutral tokens (wine, gift certificates, movie passes, theatre tickets) when appropriate, with a personal note

7. Client-Friendly Reception Area
   a. Provide quality food and beverages
   b. Have appealing, timely décor with quality, comfortable furniture, and current magazines and books
   c. Ensure that everyone who walks by asks, "Hello, have you been helped?"

8. Begin a client newsletter—Print if your clients are not online, electronic if most of them are

9. Hold "Client Appreciation Nights" at a local restaurant

10. Hold Client Appreciation Seminars where you sit down with all your customers, educate them about your business, and invite their questions and feedback

11. Commit "Random Acts of Kindness": spontaneous gifts, surprise car detailing at customers' offices, and so on

12. Referral Services—Develop a network of businesses and service professionals you think your clients will need, and when they ask you "Do you know anyone who...?" come to the rescue with a referral.

13. Condolence Cards and Flowers—Show your concern at difficult times

Bottom Line No. 9: How Personal Branding Equals More Business
Differentiating yourself from the competition

Situation: You run a florist shop in a suburban area where businesses are swallowed in a sea of subdivisions and vast shopping centers. Getting noticed is tough, and because it's a bedroom community with lots of families, lots of people need flowers. So there's lots of competition. You're doing OK, but you and your three-person staff want an advantage over the other six florists in town.

Solution: You need to differentiate yourself, and since flowers are a commodity, the best way to do that is by offering fantastic, thoughtful customer service that anticipates the needs of your customers. You and your employees develop a Customer Service Manual with three areas: Before, During and After the Sale. You start doing things like offering each customer a complimentary corsage that matches her outfit, whether she buys anything or not. You launch a "While You're Away" service that offers to care for customers' flowers and houseplants while they're on vacation. You even start offering free flower-arranging classes on Saturday mornings, and place a PC in your store with a feedback form that sends customer comments and requests straight to your database.

Result: Now that you're getting to know your customers, you find out that 50 percent of them work in the other stores in your huge shopping center. So you start sending those stores flowers every week. Referrals go through the roof, and people start coming to you for flower-arranging tips for events like weddings and school reunions. You've repositioned yourself as a flower expert and built a great local referral base that's not going anywhere.

Brand Surgery: Avoiding Tragic Branding Mistakes
The Patient: Your Customer Service

- Never over-promise. You'll create expectations you may not be able to meet. Be realistic in what you say you can do.

- When you do promise, always deliver. If you don't, your customer will immediately assume your Personal Brand is hot air and you'll never see him again—except as someone poisoning your prospect pool.

- Hire carefully. Watch out for people who treat the customer-business relationship as an arm-wrestling match. Look for people with strong communication or problem-resolution skills.

- Don't over-communicate with your customers. Once a month is fine, unless there's something special going on they should know about. You want them to feel each communication is fresh, not that you're bugging them.

- Meet deadlines and be on time. Surveys show nothing makes consumers angrier than having their time wasted.

- Never take customer dissatisfaction personally.

the
brand
called *you*

Part Four

Power Tools for Your Personal Brand

Personal Brochures

The One Tool You Can't Live Without

You know the strategies. You know the theories. Now comes the bread and butter: the tools you'll use to take your Personal Brand from an abstraction to a powerful market force, redefining you and influencing how you're seen by your target market.

Making the Business Card an Endangered Species

We're not really proposing you kill off your business card, of course. Business cards have a place, and we've got some ideas for changing those as well. But when you're trying to make an impact in the market and really drive your Personal Brand home with a new contact or a prospect in your office, nothing works as well as a colorful, emotionally appealing, high-quality brochure. Many people give them out *instead* of their business card.

You probably have a mental image of a small business brochure: three panels, fits in a No. 10 envelope, black ink, probably printed on a laser printer on some cheap Kinko's brochure template, filled with sales copy that bores the reader to tears. Get that picture out of your head. The Personal Brochure we're talking about is a professional-quality, full-color marketing gem that's created in an unusual size (like square), uses beautiful color photography, and tells your personal story in a way that captures the reader's imagination.

A Prospecting Tool, Not a Sales Tool

Handing out a Personal Brochure will not get you business by itself. It's vital that you understand that, or you'll misuse your brochure and waste your investment. A Personal Brochure is a tool for building rapport. It's a vehicle for your personal story and your position, telling readers who you are, where you come from, what's important to you, and so on. It's not a sale closer.

A good Personal Brochure has two jobs. One is to make prospects *know* you. By that, we mean come to understand something about you. We're dead set against filling a brochure with bragging points about your education, training, etc. That's sales information, and no brochure is going to close a sale for you. That's your job. Your Personal Brochure's job is to help the prospect feel a sense of connection to you, to break down natural sales resistance by *not* trying to sell him. Great brochures talk about life lessons, memorable anecdotes from your younger years, exciting achievements—everything *but* the sale.

The Personal Brochure's second job is to make prospects *trust* you. That's less about the contents of the brochure and more about the look and feel. Think about how you've felt in the past when a service provider has handed you a cheap, flimsy brochure that looked like it came off a Xerox machine. You probably couldn't get to the door fast enough.

Now think about how impressed you are when someone hands you a glossy, beautifully printed piece on expensive paper. They could be selling porcupines and you'd be well down the road to buying one. Quality tells prospects you're successful, you're doing something right, and they can put themselves in your hands.

What's your own marketing brochure like? Are you embarrassed to hand it out? If you're smiling to yourself in chagrin, you know exactly what we mean. Having a great brochure gives you an advantage over competitors who might have twice your experience, but don't know how to package themselves.

Six Steps to a Great Personal Brochure

For most people, unless you're a writer, designer or photographer, creating a Personal Brochure is probably an intimidating and frightening prospect. But not to worry. These steps apply whether or not you're going to create your own brochure or hire a freelancer or ad agency to do it for you. Follow them and you'll find yourself with a strong, effective Personal Branding tool.

Step One: Pick a Single Attribute

You can't be all things to all people, and you don't want to try. Your objective in developing a Personal Brochure is to convey your Personal Brand in a way that's not only emotionally affecting, but also clear. You can't do that if you're talking about your experience in one paragraph and your Internet smarts in the next.

Before you make any decisions about the design or content of your brochure, pick the single most compelling way in which you provide value, and make that the focus of your brochure. Remember, the point of the brochure isn't to sell the prospect, but to break down sales resistance and get you closer to the business.

Step Two: Map Out Your Personal Story

You are your best product, and the Personal Brochure is about selling you, not what you offer. The heart and soul of your brochure is a biography that tells your story and makes the reader come away as if he or she knows you.

There's common sense to this. Ask yourself how you feel when someone is obviously trying to sell you, on a car lot, for example. You have a negative reaction. So in your brochure, it's important that you reveal yourself as a human being rather than talking about your accomplishments. If you can make an emotional connection with the reader, you'll begin to build the trust that's the key to sales.

Your personal story should comprise from 75 percent to 90 percent of your Personal Brochure. This is a soft sell, in which the person is more important than the product. Your prospects aren't stupid. They'll quickly figure out this is a brochure from a contractor, agent or interior designer, and any selling your brochure does will have about zero credibility. A look inside you, however, at what shaped you as a person, is wonderfully unexpected and quite believable.

Consider some of the following when working on your story:

- How you grew up

- Family stories

- Your education

- Major life experiences that shaped you—travel, military service, etc.

- First jobs

- Life lessons or mentors

Does this really work? Think back on television coverage of the Olympics. Between events, the airwaves are bursting with personal stories, "Triumph Over Tragedy" tales and all sorts of inspirational tales about the athletes. Love them or hate them, we watch them because they're about overcoming obstacles to reach goals, something that touches almost every one of us.

Step Three: Write Your Story

Whether you or a professional writer does the job, follow these guidelines for more effective Personal Brochure copy:

- Use the third-person, objective point of view. Readers associate third-person writing with objectivity, and it makes your piece seem more journalistic.

- If you use the first person, only talk about your personal experience, not the results you have achieved. Otherwise, you'll appear to be bragging.

- Keep the text positive. Don't mention sad stories or negative possibilities.

- Present your text in paragraphs, not bullets. People like to read a good story, and research shows without doubt that narrative outperforms short, bullet text every time. Use bullets sparingly.

- Be candid. Consumers have a strong internal lie detector, and they'll see right through equivocation or empty, overblown promises.

- Avoid clichés like the plague (just kidding). But do avoid clichés.

- Use subheads to break up the text. Short headlines between major sections of copy break up the text and make your brochure much easier to read. Make the subheads powerful and interesting.

- Start the brochure with a strong headline that has emotional value.

- Finally, keep the text brief: 250 to 400 words on the interior of your brochure will be enough for most formats. You want to leave people wanting more, not tire them out.

Step Four: Knockout Cover, Appealing Layout, Great Photos

Your Personal Brochure needs a compelling cover. The most beautifully written and designed piece is worthless if no one wants to open your brochure when they see it, or if they don't even pick it up.

Your cover must stimulate your reader's curiosity, screaming, "Pick me up!" It should feature an image with "stopping power," that is, the power to catch someone's eye and make the prospect pick it up to see what's behind the intriguing image. Equally important, it needs a powerful headline that conveys a strong message about your Personal Brand.

Do not put anything on the cover that relates directly to your business, products or services. If readers so much as smell a sales pitch, they'll pitch your piece in the round file. Rather than sell, your cover should create unbearable curiosity. Always put your company name and logo on the back of the brochure.

Once readers open your Personal Brochure, your interior layout should be clean and attractive, leading the reader into the text. Use plenty of "white space," empty space where there's nothing: no text, no graphics. Amateur designers think you must fill every inch of space, but pros know that dense copy and excessive graphics look ugly and unprofessional. Proper spacing and clean lines invite readers in to enjoy your story.

When it comes to photos, go with a professional. Don't use your Olan Mills studio shots, and don't hire a friend to take them. Hire a pro to take candid shots in your office, on the job, at home, or engaged in a hobby. As with most things, quality photos say a lot about you. To find a photographer, ask friends for a referral or visit www.photographers.com. Plan on investing between $500 and $1,500 for quality photographs.

We usually recommend two sets of photos to our clients; one set in a work or professional setting and the second set in a personal setting. The first set shows you working with clients or staff, and the second set expresses the more personal nature of your life with friends, family, pets or a hobby.

And, for the love of peace, avoid the creatively bankrupt headshot, or "mug-shot." They were fine for your high-school yearbook, but they have no place in your Personal Branding.

Step Five: Choose an Unusual Brochure Format or Size

Brochures in the usual 8 1/2" x 11" format that fold to fit into a No. 10 envelope are a waste of your money, because it's very easy to throw away a No. 10 envelope without ever opening it. Large formats attract more attention and offer dramatically increased readership rates, especially when they arrive in the mail.

In our experience, the best shape for Personal Brochures is usually a square, because square materials remind us of invitations and tend to be looked at more. Consider brochures at 6 x 6, 7 x 7 and 8 x 8 sizes, and talk to a pro designer about other alternatives. The most common brochure formats to consider:

Description	Most Common Configurations (in inches)		

Single Fold

Four page brochure with one parallel fold.

Folded	*Flat*
6 x 6	12 x 6
7 x 7	14 x 7
8 x 8	16 x 8

Bi-fold

Six page brochure with two parallel folds.

Folded	*Flat*
6 x 6	18 x 6
7 x 7	21 x 7
8 x 8	24 x 8

Less Common Sizes		

Gatefold

Eight page brochure with three parallel folds.

Folded	*Flat*
6 x 6 (intermediate fold is 12 x 6)	24 x 6
7 x 7 (intermediate fold is 14 x 7)	28 x 7
8 x 8 (intermediate fold is 16 x 8)	32 x 8

Accordion

Six or eight pages, two or three folds.

Six pages		Eight pages	
Folded	*Flat*	*Folded*	*Flat*
6 x 6	18 x 6	6 x 6	24 x 6
7 x 7	21 x 7	7 x 7	28 x 7
8 x 8	24 x 8	8 x 8	32 x 8

Book

Saddle stitched book. Common page counts would be 4, 8, 12, 16, etc.

Folded	*Flat*
6 x 6	12 x 6
7 x 7	14 x 7
8 x 8	16 x 8

Folders

Folder with pocket(s) and insert(s). (left)

The folder may also include a saddle stitched book bound into the folder. (right)

Folded	*Flat*
9 x 12	18 x 12

A Standard folder comes with one or two 4" pockets, glued on the outside edge, and usually the left pocket has slits for your business card. Inserts would be 8 1/2 x 11.

Custom Brochure or Folder

Any one of the above brochures or folders can be customized in terms of size, shape, complexity, or finish.

Step Six: Invest in High-Quality Printing

Crisp, quality printing on rich, glossy paper says as much about you as the contents of your brochure. Always print your piece in four-color (full color).

Choose an experienced printer who can handle typesetting for you, and don't choose the printer who gives you the lowest price quote. You're not looking for a few pennies here; you're looking for someone to produce your most valuable Personal Branding piece. Make sure your printer uses a four-color press at 175-line screen or greater, and make sure you pay for proofs, also called "pre-flights" or "match prints." This is a necessary step as this will be your last chance to proofread the brochure before it is actually printed. Print your brochure on heavy, high-quality paper, at least 100-pound gloss cover stock. As for quantities, we recommend you print at least 2,500. If that seems like a lot, you'll use them. Plus, per-unit cost drops as quantities rise.

Don't make the mistake of some proud brochure owners: hoarding your brochures and not handing them out because they are "too nice to give away." You're supposed to hand the brochures out; they can't get you business unless they're in the hands of your prospects. You can always print more when you run out.

The emergence of digital printing has offered small companies new alternatives for producing brochures. Digital presses allow you to run smaller quantities at manageable costs, and jobs can often be run in 24 hours. The resolution isn't as high and you can't do complex folds, but if you need a few brochures fast, digital is a great option.

Add it all up and 5,000 brochures will typically cost you about $7,500, or about $1.50 each, when you factor in writing, design, photography and printing.

Ten Ideal Uses for Your Personal Brochure

Once your brochure comes back from the printer, and you've stopped admiring it, it's time to put it into action. An important point: Personal Brochures are not cold direct-mail pieces. They're too expensive. Ideally, your brochures should be sent to people you already know or given to people by you in person.

The first thing you should do is give a copy of your Personal Brochure to everyone remotely associated with your business: colleagues, media contacts, friends. After that, choose any or all of these uses for your brochure:

1. Mail two copies to all your current clients, one for them to keep and one to pass along to someone who might need your services.

2. Mail a copy to each prospect in your database with whom you've had contact, along with a cover letter.

3. Give at least 12 copies to any professionals who are good referral sources and encourage them to pass the brochure along to their clients.

4. Use it as part of your "12 Month Branding Campaign," as described on page 189.

5. Use it as part of your "Six Week Marketing Blitz" program, as detailed on page 189.

6. Use it as a substitute for your business card in networking situations. Hand the brochure out at public events and speaking engagements. If it's too big to carry, get contacts' business cards and mail them brochures as soon as you get back to the office.

7. Hand it out at seminars as part of your information package.

8. Include it in press kits and information packages you send to the media.

9. Take plenty of copies to tradeshows and special events. Every visitor to your exhibit booth should receive a copy.

10. Place it in appropriate locations, from Chambers of Commerce to hotel front desks.

Personal Brand Case Study

Kyle Boschen
Attorney at Law

Position: Triathlon-running estate attorney
Location: Denver, CO
Business: Probate law and estate planning

Kyle Boschen knew he was just another estate attorney in the eyes of potential clients. Fortunately for him, he had the savvy to see that to build a practice that would grow consistently, he had to differentiate himself from the thousands of other attorneys in his field. So he hung his Personal Branding hat on something he loves to do: run, swim and cycle distances that would make 95 percent of us sick to our stomachs.

How It Started:

Boschen decided even before he entered law school that he wanted to get into estate planning. He liked the tax element of it, as well as helping families plan their futures. "It's a positive law practice, where you're helping people out," he says. "I'm not into adversarial relationships."

Boschen knew his penchant for competing in triathlons would set him apart from his competitors, so he decided to build his Personal Brand around his sport.

Most Important Steps in Building a Personal Brand:

In 2002, Boschen decided to invest in a Personal Brochure based on his triathlon theme and began distributing it in "race packets" he would take to triathlons. The brochure told the story of his passion for racing as well as educating prospects on his abilities as an estate attorney.

"The feedback has been very positive," he says. "People have liked the piece. You're always worried about something so different, but I like to have my personality involved in the business."

Biggest Success:

"The network I've built has been my greatest success," Boschen says. "Usually the attorney is the end of the line when it comes to financial planning, and clients end up at the attorney for estate planning, after they've seen the CPA and the financial advisor. What I wanted to accomplish was not to be the last guy, but to be the first guy—to be the one referring other people. Doing that lets me help out the guys who have helped me out."

On Personal Branding and Relationships:

"It's amazing to me to have people out there who have a genuine interest in helping me succeed. They're really giving, the people who refer to me, and they really care about what they're doing. They really have people's interests in mind. That's been our focal point all along—to give people different service from what they're getting. We've built some great relationships."

Advice:

"Be yourself. Really show how much you like what you do. Show interest in what people are telling you. What I do best is really listen to what people are telling me, and take action on what they say. The thing I always hear is 'You really made me understand this.' There's a real teaching aspect to the practice. If you can be a lawyer but also be a person, you can enjoy what you do and whom you work with."

Brandstorming Personal Brochures:
10 Great Things You Can Do Right Now

1. Become a brochure collector. Get copies of the best brochures you've seen no matter what business they represent.

2. Decide how you'll carry your brochure to networking events. Will it fit in your coat pocket, or do you need a new briefcase to carry it?

3. Once you decide on a size for your brochure, purchase and print envelopes to fit.

4. Print mailing labels for your core customers so you can send them a copy of your brochure immediately.

5. Polish and finalize your personal story to share with your writer.

6. Determine your single greatest point of value.

7. Set a printing budget.

8. Talk to hotels, businesses, the Chamber of Commerce, etc. about placing your Personal Brochure in accessible racks.

9. Get a rack to display your Personal Brochure at your place of business.

10. Find out if your area has marketing awards. If so, get entry forms so you can enter your brochure when it's finished.

Bottom Line No. 10: How Personal Branding Equals More Business
Getting the most from your Personal Brochure

Situation: You're a mortgage broker in a down market. In your area, home sales have slowed and you're trying to bring in enough business to stay afloat until things pick up. Problem is, you're offering the same services as everyone else and there's no reason to choose you. Plus, there's a major mortgage lender in your area that does heavy consumer advertising, and they dominate the market. You need help.

Solution: You decide to do a Personal Brochure to make yourself stand out. Smartly, you decide to position yourself against the big national lender, as someone who provides one-on-one personal service and treats everyone uniquely. You craft a personal story that focuses on your own experience buying and renovating your classic home, and on what it taught you about the meaning of a new home to each buyer. You hire a designer to create your piece, a pro photographer to shoot you working on your home as well as interacting with clients, and you print a big 8 x 8 Personal Brochure that comes out gorgeous.

Result: You send 4 or 5 copies of your brochure to all your past clients with a letter asking them to pass the piece along to friends who might be in need of a mortgage broker. They do so with enthusiasm, because your brochure is exciting and compelling. Within days, you get calls from new potential clients you had never talked to before, people who read your brochure and felt you understood them. You've started a flow of regular business that's downturn-proof.

Brand Surgery: Avoiding Tragic Branding Mistakes
The Patient: Your Personal Brochure

- Don't print with a printer who uses a two-color press. Your color quality will suffer.

- Don't use photos of you at your desk or on the phone.

- Forget about funky typefaces in designing your brochure. Use serif typefaces of at least 10-point size.

- Consider designing your brochure to be a "self-mailer," with a mostly blank back where a label and bulk mail indicia can be placed. Without an envelope, your brochure is more likely to be read.

- Don't tell a personal story that will turn off your target market. Know their values and their limits.

- Ditch the thin paper. You'll get color bleeding and poor color.

- Quote out your print job to at least three printers.

CHAPTER 11

Personal Logo

Name, Slogan and Icon

What's the one piece of marketing material you already have? Come on, everybody has one. It's one of the first things you got when you went into business for yourself. Yet, you probably don't even think of it as a marketing tool, just a delivery system for your contact information.

Right, your business card. It's the one marketing piece every professional in every industry has. But almost no one makes full use of this tool. Think about it: a printed piece with your name, contact information and a description of what you do, and people actually *ask* you for it? How many people ever ask to see an ad or get a sales pitch? In getting your Personal Brand into your market, one of the first positive steps you should take is creating a business card that communicates your brand. That begins with your Personal Logo.

A great example of the muscle a logo can wield is fashion designer Donna Karan. By developing the "DKNY" logo to symbolize Donna Karan New York, she did more than create a valuable branding graphic. She aligned her fashions with New York City, the place from which all American styles come.

One Visual Image, One Powerful Meaning

Your logo is a single graphical symbol that represents your Personal Brand. An effective logo tells prospects almost everything they need to know about you: your name, what you do, your personal style, and how you create value. Your logo is used everywhere, on every piece of marketing material you create from business cards to brochures. A great Personal Logo benefits you in several ways:

• It becomes a surrogate for you, so well-known that when people see your logo they get an image of your face.

• It creates strong, widespread name recognition.

• It educates people on what you do.

• It gets you noticed.

A Personal Logo can be as simple as your name in an attractive typeface, or as sophisticated as some of the best corporate logos. But since you're trying to get every dollar's worth of leverage out of your logo, we recommend a Personal Logo that consists of these three parts:

1. Name
2. Slogan
3. Icon

1. **Name**

Nothing could be more basic than your company name, right? It's on every printed surface you use, it's how you answer the phone, and it's in your brochures. So why do so many small businesses mess it up? Two reasons: They try to get corporate, or they don't think their company name is important, so they spend all of two minutes on it. But really, what's more important than the name of your business? Nothing else has the potential to instantly identify who you are to your clients and prospects.

The most important principle in naming your business is your name must differentiate you from your competition. Look at the names of businesses or practices similar to yours, and 90 percent of them will be very similar. In some cases, such as law firms, that's because the culture of that profession demands it. Your industry, and whether you're a sole proprietor, partner or working as a larger company, will greatly influence the way you can name yourself.

Name Your Business After You

If you can, name your business after yourself. Period. In 95 percent of all cases, this is the right move. Remember, people want to do business with you, not with a company. When you name your company after yourself, you leverage any goodwill and familiarity people already have with you. You also leverage your reputation, since prospects know right away that they'll be working with you.

We know it's tempting to fall into the trap of coming up with an important sounding, corporate-esque name, but don't. Many companies do this in an attempt to capture some credibility, but is there really any credibility in a corporate name? How many times have you called a company named something like Consolidated Financial Solutions or

International Allied Realtors®, only to have your call picked up by an answering machine that sounds like it dates back to the Great Depression?

However, a company that uses a person's name isn't necessarily built around a Personal Brand. Ford was once Henry Ford, but that Personal Brand is long gone. A Personally Branded company carries the name, but also revolves around the passion, vision and principles of its founder. At the very minimum, the founder's image is still used. The late Walt Disney is a perfect example.

Charles Schwab is another. When he started his discount brokerage service aimed at the common investor, it made sense to name it after himself. But when he became a multibillion-dollar corporation, he could have easily changed the name to something that sounded more corporate. This was one of those instances when the best move is the one you don't make. Schwab knew his Personal Brand was built on a sense of connection with the little guy, and by continuing to name his company after himself, he maintained that connection.

So when you're looking for a name for your company, start with your own name. You can add other elements, of course, to suit your skills and profession. Names like these are right on the money:

- Sarah Morris Design Studio
- French Catering by Paul Lamond
- Janet Ramos Inc.
- Scott McCormick LLC

Naming Guidelines

- If you can describe what you do in a one- or two-word phrase, tack it onto your name. Examples: Creative Services, Chiropractic, Residential Renovation.

- If you're in a conservative business such as accounting or financial services, consider simply using your name with "Company" or "Inc." attached.

- If you use just your name with no descriptive add-on, make sure your slogan or other information on your business card tells people what you do.

- Use the familiar version of your name. If your full name is "William P. Jefferson III," but everyone calls you "Bill Jefferson," use that version. In other words, exclude middle initials, suffixes and designations from your company name.

- Don't add words like "& Company," "& Associates," or other professional descriptors. These words have been so overused they no longer have any meaning.

Naming Myths and Realities

Myth: "If I name my company after myself, all my clients will expect to work with me. I want to create a system that doesn't depend on me."

Reality: Whether you name your company after yourself or give it a corporate name, clients always want to work with the person in charge. Your name won't train them to want otherwise. The systems you put in place to service customers and set their expectations will.

Myth: "If I give my company a corporate name, it will create the illusion of something bigger than a one-person operation."

Reality: The quality of your branding and your service says infinitely more about your company than its name. NYSE-sounding names often mask one-man operations running out of a dingy garage office. It won't take prospects long to figure out you're small. David Letterman pokes fun at the idea that a serious corporate name means a better company with his production company name: "Worldwide Pants."

Myth: "If I change my company name, it will cause confusion among my clients."

Reality: Most of your clients don't even know the name of your company. They know *you*. Ninety-nine percent of them won't care one way or another. If you want your clients to remember the name of your company, the easiest way to do it is to name it after yourself.

Myth: "I have a strange name my clients won't remember."

Reality: We like strange names; they are difficult to remember, but once you get them you never forget them (Arnold Schwarzenegger, Monica Lewinsky). If you have a strange name, either change it or flaunt it and make them remember it.

Myth: "I'm trying to build equity into my company and eventually sell it. You can't sell a company based on a person."

Reality: There are thousands of companies worth billions of dollars built on the identities of one person: Mary Kay, Charles Schwab, Walt Disney, Dale Carnegie, to name a very few. There are three different entities at work here: you, your Personal Brand, and your company. They are all connected, but they're not all the same.

Selling a Personally Branded Company

It's time to sell your Personally Branded company. What do you do? You have two choices:

1. Don't change the name. If there's equity and value in your name, buyers will want the name on the business. Dale Carnegie died in 1955, but his brand and company live on—with his name attached. The new owners valued his Personal Brand so much they didn't dare change the name.

2. Merge and purge. Like any corporate brands that merge, part or all the existing names are used for a limited time, while the market gets used to the new brand. After a year or two, one of the names is dropped.

   Salomon Brothers merged with SmithBarney in 1997. By 2001, the company had gone back to being SmithBarney (and now is known as SmithBarney Citigroup).

Partnerships

Just because you share office space or do some marketing with someone, that does not make you Personal Branding partners. Below is a quick-glance guide to handling partner naming:

Work	Space	Naming Convention
Office partners	Share office space	Separate Names
Marketing partners	Perform some joint marketing	Separate Names
Branding partners	Clients belong equally to both partners	Shared name

If you are branding partners, use both of your last names, like a law or accounting firm. Limit the name to no more than eleven syllables. If you are office or marketing partners, use your own names, first and last for each of your firms.

Co-Branding

Perhaps you're acting as an agent for a larger company. In this situation, your Personal Brand is leveraging the equity inherent in the larger company brand. Where legally allowed, make your name as prominent as possible and minimize the company name as much as possible. The company's name does not have to be very large to be recognized.

2. **Slogan**

Your slogan is the part of your Personal Logo with which you're probably most familiar. After all, each of us can rattle off a few dozen of the most famous corporate slogans:

- The ultimate driving machine

- Think different

- Moving at the speed of business

- The best a man can get

- A diamond is forever

- Something special in the air

(For the record, these are for BMW, Apple, UPS, Gillette, DeBeers and American Airlines.)

Companies create slogans for three reasons: to tell people about their product or service, to motivate people to take action, or to convey a sense of the emotion they want customers to associate with their product, service or company.

However, you're not a major corporation. They have multimillion-dollar marketing budgets; you don't. They can afford obtuse slogans that convey pure emotion because they can also buy ads, send direct mail and open stores to tell customers what they really do. You don't have that luxury, so when you're developing a slogan for your business, it must do one of two things:

1. Tell people what you do and for whom you do it. For example:

- Massage Therapy for Professional Athletes

- Designing Eclectic Fashions for Women Over 55

- Network Consulting for the Semiconductor Industry

- Wholesale Furniture for Specialty Retailers

2. Tell people what you do and the benefit of your services. For example:

- Legal Representation that Keeps Divorce Civil

- Investment Planning for Your Family's Future

- Dance Instruction that Makes Good Parties Great

- Gentle Dental Care for the Terrified

Keep It Short and Simple

Your slogan has one purpose: to tell your prospects something useful about you and your business. But since they'll spend about 1 1/2 seconds actually reading it, it's got to be brief. Try to keep it to no more than 6 to 8 words, as tight as possible. Prospects should be able to glance at your slogan and get an instant impression of who you are and what you're offering them, whether it's a great investment or a good laugh. Other tips for writing strong slogans:

- Try to avoid the word "solutions." It's so overused that it's lost its meaning.

- Be specific. Say what you do and for whom with precision.

- Check your grammar and usage. Mistakes like using "it's" when you mean "its" can make you look foolish.

- Test your slogan on others repeatedly and if the responses aren't to your liking, keep experimenting.

- Don't Italicize or put your slogan in quotes. Many companies do this because they think it adds drama to an otherwise bad slogan. It doesn't. It only succeeds in making you look like an amateur.

3. **Icon**

   Your icon is the graphic element that goes along with your name and slogan. Not all Personal Logos have icons, but the right icon can dramatically enhance the effectiveness and retention of a logo. For example, if you're marketing your Personal Brand to the sailing community, and you work a pencil drawing of a tall ship into your logo, it tells them without a single word that you're a person with a passion for the ocean and sailboats—and that's the type of personal connection that wins business.

   Your logo icon can be anything, from an elegant-looking graphic shape (often called a "dingbat" by designers) to an illustration that's suited to your target market, your profession, or your interests. But avoid a very common mistake: cliché icons everyone in your profession uses. For example, how many real estate agents have you seen with a house icon on their business card? They probably all thought the idea originated with them. Here's a good rule of thumb: If a graphic image seems incredibly obvious for your profession—such as a chef's hat for a caterer or a quill pen for a writer—DON'T USE IT. Some other tips in choosing an icon:

- Don't use photos. They rarely reproduce well.

- Use something that can be drawn simply. Complex illustrations also don't reproduce well, especially in small sizes.

- Match your icon to the culture of your target market. For example, even if you're an avid surfer, putting a surfboard in your logo might not work well if you're trying to sell financial planning to seniors.

- Talk to a professional artist. This is the one area where do-it-yourself won't do. Unless you already know how to draw, it's worth a few hundred bucks to get something custom-done by a pro.

- Don't use your family crest. Such complex graphics rarely reproduce well in a logo format. Icons are usually small, and the finely lined detail of a family crest usually ends up a blurred mess.

Putting Together Your Logo

OK, after weeks of naming ideas, slogans, and choosing the right icon, you've got the pieces of your Personal Logo in place. Now you've got to piece them together into a single unit. Your logo should appear to be one coherent graphic, with all three elements working together.

Usually, that means your name dominates, with your slogan running underneath, and your icon off to one side or the other. Look at some of the logos of competitiors you know, or whose ads you see in the paper or phone book. This will give you some ideas. Some other guidelines:

- **Color**—There are five main colors you can use in your logo: red, orange, yellow, green and blue, and the variations on those colors like aqua, gold and violet. There are also three neutral colors: white, black and gray. You'll probably end up using some combination of main and neutral colors in your logo, and we recommend you limit colors to no more than two. Too many colors will cause your logo to look like a Dutch bed of tulips.

    Colors on the red end of the spectrum are focused slightly behind the retina of the eye and appear to move toward the viewer (try it). Colors on the blue end of the spectrum are focused slightly in front of the retina and appear to move away. That's why red is the color of energy, excitement and attention, while blue stands for peace, tranquility and relaxation. In marketing, red means volatility, blue stability. Do you think Coca-Cola's color is red and IBM's is blue by accident? Think again.

As stated in *The 22 Immutable Laws of Branding* by Al and Laura Ries, colors tend to create moods or convey feelings:

White = purity	Purple = royalty
Black = luxury	Green = nature
Yellow = caution	Red = attention
Blue = leadership	

When selecting colors for your logo, consider the mood you want to convey. This will be your principal color, used for your name and probably your icon. We recommend using black as your other color. It stands out and is cheaper to print than the other neutrals.

- **Typeface**—There are two kinds of typefaces: *serif*, the old-fashioned type you probably see in your daily newspaper, and *sans serif*, the streamlined type without all the fancy curlicues and flourishes. You'll need to choose typefaces for your name and slogan; in making this decision, your most important factor is readability. Keep things simple; stick with proven basics like Times, Goudy, Arial, Optima and Garamond.

  Serif typefaces tend to be seen as more old-fashioned, so they are used more often for traditional, conservative businesses such as financial services. Sans serif type is seen as more modern and creative, so you'll often see it used by designers, architects, and the like.

  Bottom line, pick a typestyle you like. Most companies will go with one typeface for their business name, and another for their slogan. As long as your typefaces are clean and readable, this isn't a problem. However, do avoid using all capital letters, especially in your name. It hurts readability, and comes across like shouting.

- **Size**—How big should your logo be? When you've assembled the three components, have a professional designer put them together as a single file in a program like Adobe Illustrator, so you can size your logo however you like. That's the first step.

  As for the right size, that will vary depending on the medium. Once you size your logo for your business card, you'll see why we recommend keeping your icon simple. There's just not a lot of space. Complex drawings turn to mush. But the basic guideline is, don't make your logo smaller than your most frequent prospects can read easily. In other words, if you're marketing to the over-65 crowd, and your prospects have to squint at your business card to read your slogan, you're in trouble.

A Personal Logo should be able to fit on a printed piece, be it a Personal Brochure or a direct mailer, at a size anywhere from 2 to 3 inches in one direction, and 1 to 2 in the other (most company logos are horizontal, so they would go 3 wide x 2 high). You should also be able to blow your logo up for use in outdoor advertising without it looking sloppy.

In the end, trust your good taste when sizing your logo. Make sure to test it with friends and clients before you launch it.

How to Use Your Personal Logo

Your Personal Logo goes everywhere. No exaggeration. It's your Personal Brand, so you want it on everything you do, using the same colors, the same typeface. As with all Personal Branding, consistency is everything. Some examples:

• Place it on the back panel of your Personal Brochure.

• Place it prominently on all your direct-mail postcards.

• Use in on your letterhead, mailing labels, envelopes and invoices.

• Use it at the top of each page of your Web site.

• Use it in all print or cable TV advertising.

• Print it on any outdoor advertising you do, from bus-stop benches to billboards.

• Put it on T-shirts, caps and buttons for special events you sponsor.

• Place it in PowerPoint presentations.

• Have it screened onto the window or door of your office.

• Get several polo shirts with it on the pocket, for your own use.

• Provide it to event organizers so you can get in the sponsor program.

With time and consistency, your logo and your Personal Brand can become synonymous.

Wyland

Wyland Studios

Position: The world's leading environmental artist
Location: Laguna Beach, CA
Business: Marine environmental artist, activist
Online: wyland.com

Wyland is definitely a specialist: the world's foremost marine environmental artist. Based in his spectacular Laguna Beach studio with a 90-degree view of the Pacific, this Midwestern transplant has built one of the art world's most powerful Personal Brands and franchises with his evocative, soulful paintings and sculptures of whales, sea lions, and other marine life. But the friendly, laid-back Wyland is much more than his paintings and his famous paint-signature logo: He has built a brand on goodwill and a genuine passion for environmental activism.

How It Started:

"The first thing I did when I came out here was starve," says Wyland, from his oceanfront deck, adjacent to the hotel parking lot where he painted his first whale mural. "As it turns out, I was in the right place at the right time, as Greenpeace and Jacques Cousteau were coming on. That's when I started working on my goal of being a marine-life artist."

As it turned out, Wyland exploited one of the critical principles of Personal Branding completely by accident: first-mover advantage. "The art that was done before was marine art, but what I do is marine life art, a celebration of the life in the sea, not man's conquest of it," he says. "So it was really a new art form that was evolving at the time." Pioneering a new type of marine art gave him an exclusive brand identity in his field, fueling public perception that Wyland was "the" marine artist.

Without any real intent to turn himself into a franchise, Wyland sensed that to promote his art, he needed to promote his love for the sea and its inhabitants. He proved to be a natural. "I didn't have anybody to mentor me, but by being friendly to people and using my personality, I became well-known," he says. "A lot of artists are introverted, but not me. I love people. I love the response I get to my art. I've always been hands-on and very involved, and my brand just started evolving very slowly from that."

Most Important Steps in Building a Personal Brand:

Wyland admits at one point he got tired of holding out his hand. "I didn't like the fundraising end of what I was doing," he says. "So I decided I had to be successful myself, then I wouldn't have to run around with my hand out. So I said 'Work on your art and create a very successful business so you can go out and paint these free murals and do charitable work.' So that's what I did."

Wyland and his team have built a sophisticated licensing strategy and a worldwide distribution network for his art, which is reproduced in dozens of different forms. They maintain tight control of his Personal Brand, right down to his distinctive signature and his name, which is always "Wyland." Never a first name. His Personal Brand is consistent and always tied to the same ideas: the ocean, marine life, conservation.

Biggest Success:

Despite his charisma and the appeal of his art, Wyland might have remained a successful but regional personality if not for his Whaling Walls. These enormous murals, each depicting an underwater scene of great whales and dolphins, began in 1981 with the Laguna Beach wall. They have become Wyland's signature, adorning 90 public walls and buildings around the world. His goal? Paint 100 by 2011.

Wyland says the walls, which he has always painted for free, transformed awareness of him and his work. "I went from a local artist to a national artist to an international artist in a matter of a few years because of the public art I was doing, and because of the message," he says. "I wanted to give something back."

On Personal Branding and Activism:

The trump card for Wyland has been his passionate effort to promote conservation of the ocean environment, and art and science in public schools. There's no parlor activism here; this is a man who cares deeply about the sea, its life, and about bridging the gap between art and science.

"My brand is narrowly focused and widely focused on conservation and ocean issues," he says. "The art is really the brand, the art and the message it conveys: These animals are very beautiful and intelligent, and people are captured by the art and the message on all levels."

A member of over 100 conservation groups over the years, Wyland donates money and artwork to groups that "do good work." Since 1993, he's also run the Wyland Foundation, which reaches out to millions of public school students. His big project: working with the Cousteau Society on the Wyland-Cousteau Coastal Cleanup, a five-year project that will begin by cleaning the entire Eastern Seaboard of refuse.

Wyland's clear, honest passion for the ocean and its preservation gives his Personal Brand a rare, powerful quality: a sense of higher purpose.

Advice:

"The closest thing I can compare it to is Jimmy Buffett," Wyland says. "He's a singer and songwriter, but he uses his music to inspire people and bring them together, and at the same time he has used it to get his environmental message out, which is save the manatees and save the Everglades, the things he's passionate about. That's what I think I'm doing."

Brandstorming Logos:
5 Great Things You Can Do Right Now

1. Send a personal letter to your best customers telling them why you're renaming your business.

2. Print temporary stationery with your new name that you can use to "prep" your target market while your final materials are printing.

3. Look at your competitors and identify the logos or graphic symbols that are overused.

4. To determine the best name for your logo, ask 20 colleagues, clients or friends how they introduce you to others.

5. Start using the new name of your business in conversation.

Bottom Line No. 11: How Personal Branding Equals More Business
Conveying your message with a Personal Logo

Situation: You operate a charter fishing boat in a busy resort. There are plenty of tourists, but the problem is they're not sure what service you're offering. Your business is mostly by word-of-mouth, so you don't have business cards or even a sign. You waste hours each week taking phone calls and dealing with in-person inquiries from people who want everything from a sightseeing cruise to a party boat. You need to target fishermen.

Solution: You work with a professional graphic designer to create a Personal Logo. It features your name with the phrase "Charter Sport Fishing," the slogan "Deep Sea Excitement for Expert Anglers and

Landlubbers," and an action icon of a man pulling back powerfully on a fiercely bent fishing rod. With this logo, you hope to target both experienced fishermen, but also get the people who've never done it before and want a new experience. You plaster your logo everywhere: on your new business cards, on fliers, on a sign by your dock, on the stern of your boat, and on your van—all with your phone number, of course.

Result: Your bad leads dry up to almost nothing, while your good leads triple as people spot your fliers and call you after seeing your van driving around the marina. In the space of three months, you've got fishing trips booked as far as six months out, and a newly successful business.

Brand Surgery: Avoiding Tragic Branding Mistakes
The Patient: Your Personal Logo

- Reject generic, corporate-sounding names.

- Only try to appear bigger than you are if you think no one will ask to meet your staff.

- Humor and sarcasm are great in the right context, but know your target market. "Bob's House O' Caskets" probably won't hit the mark for too many folks.

- Reject all those weird typefaces created by design students. They're all over the Internet, but they frequently print badly.

- Avoid clichés in your slogan as much as you do in your icon. Look at your competition and see how many have variations on the same theme. Then go the other way.

- Create a logo that reproduces clearly in small form. That's usually how people will see it.

- Avoid thin white type on dark backgrounds, especially if it's your slogan. In printed form, the white will sometimes fill in, leaving your slogan unreadable.

- If you're in a creative business, be creative. Your logo should reflect how you want prospects to see you.

- If you're in a serious business, like anything related to mainstream health care or money, look serious and staid.

CHAPTER 12

Personal Web Sites

"Dot Com" Your Brand

You've got to have a Web site. Today, next to a business card, it's the marketing and Personal Branding tool that more people expect you to have. At networking events, if someone is interested in finding out more about someone, this question almost always comes up: "What's your Web address?" That's because the Web is an easy, sales-free way to scope out a company and decide if you want to work with them.

Right now you're in one of two situations: you have a Web site and want to improve it, or you don't have a site and desperately want to get one. In either case, you probably have some anxiety about the complexity and the cost. Well, rest easy. The Web has come a long way since 1998's gold rush. Today, there are many low-cost options for creating your own great Web site, including Web-based turnkey services where you pay monthly and software programs that practically design your site for you.

But before you try any of those tools, you need to know why you're creating a site, what your target market wants from it, and how it can spread your Personal Brand. Whether you're changing your current site or building a new one, you need to create a Personal Web Site.

Three Reasons You Should Be Online

1. **Builds Credibility**—Your site is a public relations tool, not a sales tool. Its presence establishes you as a real company, and since even a one-person shop can have a polished, sophisticated site, your site can increase your viability in the eyes of prospects. If you have a great Web site, you must be a legitimate company. It also gives prospects a way to check you out anonymously, without sales pressure.

2. **Captures Leads**—If your site has compelling content, useful features and/or furthers your winning, interesting Personal Brand, it's the perfect tool for capturing visitor information and turning prospects into leads. The

effectiveness of the Web as a business-development tool will depend on the type of business you run.

3. **Maintains Relationships**—A Web site is a platform for you to stay in constant touch with your clients—by sending e-mail, posting information about seminars and special events, bringing them to the site for promotions, and so on. More entrepreneurs are taking advantage of the Web's expanding capabilities in this way.

How a Site Can Benefit Your Business

Having the right Personal Web Site is worth all this trouble. We've seen businesses launch a beautifully designed, well-written site that precisely targets their target market and watched it transform their business. Suddenly, they're not one or two people in a cramped office. They're a company. As far as someone surfing the Web knows, they're a big operation with multiple offices and a great track record.

The Web gives you more control over the first impression your business—and your Personal Brand—makes. It's powerful stuff. Some other things a great Personal Web Site can do for you:

1. Give new contacts a place to check you out without pressure, allowing them to surf around and learn more about you, and letting you make a strong brand impression.

2. Extend your Personal Brand into a new medium that's seen by 80 percent of the people in the U.S.

3. Provide a 24/7 information center for prospects, clients and media.

4. Give you a launch platform for e-mail communications, announcing news, and telling contacts about events and offers.

5. Help you capture visitor information and build your database.

6. Distribute literature, software or other materials worldwide.

7. Be a 24-hour store, selling your products to anyone with a credit card.

8. Increase your credibility by making you part of the "I have a Web site" crowd.

9. Increase your appeal to market segments that rely on the Web for information and research.

10. Turn you into a resource providing users with news, calculators, stock market updates, useful links to additional sites, and other value-added features.

What Do You Want Your Site to Do?

Before you develop your Personal Web Site, create a Web Plan. This is your strategy document, where you map out everything you want your site to achieve. As you know, today's Web can do a lot of incredible things, from providing online training and seminars to capturing vast amounts of personal information. But what should your site do?

Take a look at your business, your target market, their level of Web sophistication, and your company's goals. Then answer these questions:

- Do you just need an online brochure that gives information about your services?

- Do you want prospects to be able to download information and literature?

- Do you want to sell products online and accept credit cards?

- Does your target market demand rich design or features like animation?

- Do you want to capture visitor information by getting them to sign up for a newsletter or some other service?

- Will your site be an online portfolio of your work, with samples or case studies?

- Do you want customers to be able to monitor projects on your site?

- Will you provide links to other sites?

- How will your site serve your business goals?

- Is your target market comfortable with the Web? OK with it? Slightly techno-phobic?

Site-Creation Needs

Do NOT hire your cousin or a local college student to develop your Personal Web Site. People do it because it's cheap, but you do get what you pay for with Web design. Web development is a complex profession, and if you hire an amateur, you'll get amateurish results.

When you have your Web Plan and you're ready to build your site, you need three skill sets, which may come from one person, but more likely will come from two or three:

Web Design
Programming
Writing and Content

- **Web Design**—Web designers create the graphics that become your site, often including animation and other features, and in many cases can also write the basic HTML code, use the popular Web authoring tools, and even create basic database-driven sites. Web design has become so in-demand that there are a lot of Web designers out there, with a lot of different styles from staid to insane. Check out their personal sites before you hire a designer and make sure his or her style suits your target market and your industry.

- **Programming**—Programmers no longer focus on writing the underlying HTML code of a site. These days, essential tasks like coding and upload-ing site content to a Web host will usually be handled by your designer. You'll want a programmer if you're building a site with some high-pow-ered applications: complex database functions, Flash programming, or high-level security or encryption features.

- **Writing and Content**—This will usually be your lone wolf, since design-ers and writers are rarely the same person. But a writer is essential, because ultimately a pretty design is worthless if your message isn't com-pelling. Find someone who does more than write copy. Find a "content developer" who will help you map out the pages your site needs, the fea-tures you must have, and the ways to reinforce your brand. You should end up with two things: a flowchart showing all the pages of your site, and a "design document" with all your text, button names, and instruc-tions to the designer and programmer.

What Your Site Must Have

OK, you've got your plan and your team. Bravo. Now what? Well, just as no car rolls off the assembly line without tires, brakes and a steering wheel, no Personal Web Site should be without these basics:

- **A Strong, Clear Home Page.** Your home page, the first page people see when they type your site address, must reinforce your Personal Brand immediately. That means it needs to adopt the same color scheme and design style as your logo, business card and so on. Your message should be clear, strong and brief, directing users where to go depending on their needs. Your navigation should be easy to understand.

- **A Page About You.** People want to know with whom they're working, so tell your story. Talk about how you got started, how you started the business, your educational background, and so on. Anything is fair game, just as in your Personal Brochure. This section should also have biographies and photos of you and each person on your staff, if you have a staff.

- **Services.** Your site is the place to tell people what you do and for whom you do it. Talk about your services or the products you sell, pointing out features and benefits, not just facts. Tell the visitor how what you do can benefit them. If you have fixed pricing or an hourly rate, include that if you're comfortable doing so.

- **Portfolio, Case Studies or Testimonials.** Prospects invest time in cruising your Personal Web Site, so you owe them some useful information. Samples of your work, case studies of what you did for other clients, or quotes from satisfied customers are useful, and can be very convincing.

- **Contact Information.** Make this info easy to find. Have a page that at the very least has your mailing address, phone number, fax number and an e-mail link. If you want to go a step further, you can provide a mail form users fill out with their contact information and any inquiries. This can help build your database.

Other easy, common sections are lists of clients or partners, news releases, lists of useful links to other sites, and published articles that might interest your target market.

Useful and Cool Extras

There are many reasons business owners choose to add premium features to their Personal Web Sites: They need something to differentiate themselves, their target market uses the Web intensively and expects to be wowed, they want to create a big splash, they intend to use the Web as their main marketing tool, and so on. Whatever your reason, there are many cool things you can add to your site. They'll cost you more, but aren't you worth it?

- **Flash Intros.** Get into design or advertising agency sites and you'll see these a lot. Flash is a fantastic tool that lets designers create fast-loading, fluid animations with almost no limit to the types of visual landscapes you can produce. Two drawbacks: they can be expensive, and they can bore the user who just wants to get into your site. Consider carefully. If you're in a creative business, you may want one. If not, you probably don't. But talk to your designer about other, subtler ways you can use Flash in your site. There are many, including audio.

- **Downloadable PDFs.** Adobe's Portable Document Format lets you turn the layout files for brochures, ads, data sheets, and anything else printed into perfectly reproduced files that can be e-mailed and read with the free Adobe Acrobat Reader. It's a great way to deliver literature on your business. Allow site visitors to download a PDF of your brochure or report from your site.

- **E-commerce.** Create an online store where you can sell products, sign people up for seminars, and more, with just a credit card. E-commerce is easy now thanks to great turnkey software packages and online services that give you a store for a monthly fee (and will even set up your merchant account for you).

- **Search.** If you have a lot of information on your site, you can allow people to search by typing keywords into a field. Or you can let them search the whole Internet from your site, turning yourself into a portal.

- **Newsletter Sign-up.** One of the best ways to capture user contact data is by offering them the chance to sign up for your e-mail or print newsletter. The information goes directly into your database. Now all you need is a newsletter.

- **Calculators.** You've probably seen these on mortgage and insurance sites. They're applications a company places on your site while the calculating software is done on the "back end," on their servers. Calculators are outstanding if your business is related to anything financial, such as real estate, financial planning, accounting, and so on. Users can figure out their house payment, what they need to save for retirement, and a lot more. Usually, you can link these applications to your site for a monthly fee.

- **Project Sections.** Some Web sites let clients see the latest work done on a project, from home renovation to the work of a design studio. Often using Microsoft Project, project pages let users log in using a password, and can show them whatever information you choose: samples of the latest work, what's been approved and what's still being done, schedules, contact information for each person on the project, and so on.

- **Message Boards.** If you're trying to build a community among your clients, message boards are excellent. They allow users to "post" messages on your site and others to respond, creating online discussions about virtually any topic.

Content to Avoid

- **Entry Tunnels.** These are pages that appear when people type in your Web address, but all they have is a graphic or animation and a "Click to Enter" link.

- **Video.** Unless you're running a video-related company, few video applications make sense for a small business. It's very expensive.

- **Games.** You'll see sites with areas where users can go to play around, get jokes, read funny stories, and so on. They can make you seem less serious about your work.

- **Required Forms.** If you're giving away information that has value, like investment tips, you might want your site visitors to provide address, phone number, or income information before they can access the data. But in most cases, you shouldn't require information on a form beyond name and e-mail address. It's intrusive and off-putting.

- **Offsite Links.** Providing useful links is great, but make sure when users click on them, the new site appears in a new browser window (your programmer will know what this means if you don't). Otherwise, you'll be sending people away from your site, and you may never get them back.

- **Cheesy Animations.** Spinning logos, meowing cats, shoveling construction guys to signify a page under construction. Spare us all, please.

Driving Traffic

The Web is no field of dreams. If you build it, there's no guarantee they will come. You can spend thousands creating a great site and unless you drive traffic to it, nobody will ever see it and it won't help your Personal Brand. So you've got to become a traffic cop.

The first step in creating site traffic is to put your Web address on everything: business cards, brochures, ads, you name it. Anywhere your logo goes, so goes your www.mysite.com. That lets you answer the "Do you have a Web site?" question before it's even asked.

The next obvious step is to tell everyone you already work with that you have a new Personal Web Site. Send direct mail or e-mail to your client and prospect database, call your colleagues or professionals who send you business, tell your friends. Everybody likes to check out a newly launched site; it's like dropping by to scope out a buddy's new Mustang. Spread the word and if your site's strong, people will do some of the work for you.

Some Other Ways to Build Traffic:

- **URL matches company name**—If you want to find Ford online, don't you first type in www.ford.com? It's common sense. Your prospects and clients will be doing the same to find your Web site, so make it easy to find.

- **Advertise offline**—This can range from a short-term display ad run in your local newspaper to adding your Web address to your signage.

- **Search engines**—More online consumers find what they're looking for via search than any other means. But with 2.5 billion current Web pages and over seven million being added each day, searching has become a matter of wading through thousands of results. There are two ways around this. One of the best is to buy "keywords" with sites like Google. Buying search keywords ensures when people search using your terms, your site comes up near the top of the results. The other is Search Engine Optimization, or SEO, in which certain keywords are built into the computer code underlying your site, making it easier for the search engines to locate.

- **PR**—Let the print and online publications in your field know about your site. Trade periodicals often publish reviews of good sites by professionals in their field of coverage.

- **Online directories**—You can often submit your site to directories for free, or there might be a nominal fee. But it's worth it. For example, a site called www.iwantamassage.com (no kidding) lists massage therapists not just state-by-state in the U.S., but worldwide. Also, here's a somewhat stunning fact: in searches for some of the main professional services, such as legal and health care, many of the top search results are not individual businesses, but directories.

Using Your Site to Build Your Brand

Ultimately, your Personal Web Site is one more tool for building your Personal Brand. Because a Web site is so versatile and reaches so many people, many companies choose to make it their main branding tool. Whatever you do, there are many effective strategies for spreading your Personal Brand digitally.

The most important is to make your site reflect your Personal Brand the same way your Personal Brochure does. Use professionally done photos of yourself, be humorous if you're funny, make the graphics sincere and warm if you're that way, and share stories about your background.

Encourage visitors to communicate with you—ask questions, suggest ways the site could be better, and so on. This is an interactive medium, meaning two-way. Remind your visitors to interact. When they do, respond to their e-mails *as soon as possible.*

Finally, give people reasons to come back to the site by offering them something of benefit. A Personal Web Site, unlike a brochure, gives you the ability to add and update content whenever and as often as you want. That means you can offer visitors a continually updated selection of articles relevant to your local real estate market, a calendar of area events, calculators they can use in a variety of ways, the ever-shifting content of message board discussions—even things like online coupons and contests.

Be creative and think of ways to make your site a destination, not just "brochureware."

Build Your Site the Smart Way

There are Web developers on every corner, and most of them are hacks. You want a professional, and you should be prepared to pay between $50 and $100 an hour for your designer/programmer. Your Web site is a serious investment, but worth every penny when it's done right and starts bringing you new business.

Some of our insider tips for getting your Personal Web Site without getting e-screwed:

- **If you ask for any contact data, post a privacy policy.** Web users are hypersensitive about online privacy, so if you ask people to fill out a form with any personal information, have a link to a page where you promise not to share their information with any third party. Then stick to it.

- **Update your content regularly.** Nothing looks less professional than a Web site with old, outdated content, especially things like event calendars. Set up an agreement with your writer and programmer to regularly update the contents of your site, from posting new articles and calendars to adding fresh news about your services. Do it every month.

- **Test your site before launch.** Before your site goes live, sit down and go through every page and every link to make sure all links are active and all features are working. Have 10 of your friends do the same and send you "bug reports" with anything they find that doesn't work, including typographical errors.

- **Design for dialup connections.** Despite all the hype over "broadband" DSL and cable modem Internet connections, only about 20 percent of Americans have such a fast Internet connection. The rest still dial up using their telephone lines. That means unless you're marketing to a target audience in which a majority of prospects have broadband connections, make sure your designer creates your site to load quickly on a slower 56K dialup connection. This also means avoiding big graphics and fancy animations.

- **The AOL factor.** Over 24 million people in the U.S. use America Online to access the Internet. Unfortunately, AOL doesn't read many Web sites the same way as Netscape or Internet Explorer browsers do. If you're marketing to consumers, chances are good a lot of your prospects will access your site with AOL. Make sure your designer and programmer build a site that works with AOL.

- **Check vendor sites.** Sometimes you'll talk to a Web designer whose site looks awful, and he'll claim, "I've been too busy to update it." Be too busy to give him your money. Always scope the Web sites of designers, programmers and writers before you hire them. The good ones will have strong sites.

Personal Brand Case Study

Daniel Will Harris
Will-Harris Studio

Position: Wacky, irreverent designer
Location: Marin County, CA
Business: Graphic design
Online: will-harris.com

Daniel Will-Harris is a funny guy. Just ask him. Any guy who would write and publish a book called "My Wife and Times" and produce a sarcastic bimonthly e-mail newsletter called the SchmoozeLetter can't be accused of being overly serious. But that's been a huge part of Will-Harris' success in his design business: personality, and a great Web site that reflects his personality perfectly.

How It Started:
Will-Harris was an early adopter of the Web, posting one of the first 5,000 sites ever created on the Internet in 1995. He had already been doing

his own publishing and design and thought the infant medium was perfect for promoting his design work.

"Having the site got people to know I was there, see my work, and led to a job writing for CNet," Will-Harris says. "That led to working for NetObjects, which led to creating Efuse.com. You never know where things are going to end up." Efuse.com has become a very popular destination as a friendly place to learn the basics of building a Web site.

Will-Harris built his design business in a way that could only be called organic. "I moved to Point Reyes, but there wasn't any Web," he says. "I went around to local stores and restaurants and said, "You know, your menu could look a lot better." Restaurants have a very tight budget, so I would do work on spec for them, or I would work for food. The first year I lived here, I never had to pay to eat at that restaurant. There's something exciting about that.

"There are more small businesses than big ones, and they're easier to approach. For the ones I approach, I create free samples. In design, most people aren't going to know how much better their materials can look, so I design something new they can compare with their current graphics. Then they can see the difference and appreciate the value."

Most Important Steps in Building a Personal Brand:

There's no question that Will-Harris' Web site is the cornerstone of his success. It's arch, irreverent and hilariously self-deprecating, with section titles like "Esperfonto" and "MyDailyYoga." It's the gateway to his highly popular SchmoozeLetter.com e-newsletter, a ramble about life, family flotsam and occasionally the design biz.

"I think the Web is fantastic because you can do it on your own, you can display your skills globally," he says. "I've had work on almost every continent, seen by people who would not have known I existed without the Web.

"I think the reason my Web site stands out is because it's very personal. Businesses are afraid to do that; people think they need to be cold and corporate. I think the fact that you are an individual sitting in your home office is an advantage. When you are independent, you're selling your talents, skills, and personality. That stuff has to come across, and my site's always had a lot of humor and personality."

"Your Web site is your personality in pixels," he concludes. "It should really reflect how you are in person."

Biggest Success:

With over 20,000 subscribers, the Schmooze Letter has become Will-Harris' bellwether. "Schmooze Letter started when I was working for NetObjects," he says. "You have to make your own business. You have to come up with the ideas, and maybe no one's ever done it before. NetObjects knew me; I sent them a lot of e-mail, saying 'here's what you should be doing.' We had lunch, and I presented them with a lot of ideas. One of them was this online magazine.

"The idea was, there isn't really an easy site for people who want to build Web sites. NetObjects hired me and I started developing Efuse. What I figured out was that if you want people to keep coming back, you need an e-mail newsletter. If you send out an e-mail newsletter that has useful information for the people you work with, it becomes something they look forward to rather than something they resent. Because I'm a writer, I can make it funny."

On Personal Branding and Not Being Perfect:

"I learned that you can make good out of bad. Once, the software sent out 12 copies of the newsletter to everyone, and people were mad. I wrote an apology, and when you connect to people on a personal level, the introductions start to get more personal. The more personal they got, the more people subscribed. They're just personal, funny stories, and they will occasionally have something to do with Web design, but mostly they're just personal. I stay in front of these people."

Advice:

"Remind them you're there, but in a way that gives them something. People want to know what's in it for *them*. That's human nature. Give people something for free, be happy to give it to them, and they'll respond."

Brandstorming Web Sites:
10 Great Things You Can Do Right Now

1. Go to www.netsol.com and reserve your name as a URL. If it's not available, try nicknames or added words.

2. E-mail your current customers a "coming soon" notice about your upcoming new Web site.

3. Call your current clients to find out what kinds of Internet connections they have: dialup or faster connections like cable or DSL.

4. Update your office Internet connectivity to cable, DSL or T1.

5. Find and bookmark your competitors' sites for research purposes.

6. Create a training program for your employees to make sure they're all skilled in using the Web.

7. Get online and locate the Web directories that apply to your profession. Find out how much it costs to be listed.

8. Contact Web marketing companies about Search Engine Optimization services and costs.

9. Send a survey to clients and prospects asking them what they would like to see on your Web site.

10. Become a regular visitor or subscriber to www.ideabook.com, one of our favorite marketing guidance and advice sites.

Bottom Line No. 12: How Personal Branding Equals More Business
Making an impact with your Web site

Situation: You're a freelance advertising copywriter, and though you're good, you have a hard time differentiating yourself from the other copywriters in your region. Too many ad agencies think of all writers as essentially the same. You need something that will help you stand out and at the same time allow prospects to see your best work. Your answer: a great Web site.

Solution: First, you look at the Web sites of other copywriters in your geographical area. Ninety-nine percent of them are terrible: decently written, but graphically dead. You figure you can do a lot better. You decide since you've grown up by the beach in California, you'll do a beach-themed Web site that suggests your creativity, easygoing attitude and sense of humor. You hire a Web designer who can also program and launch your site, and you do the writing. In the end, you have a site that makes people think of a day at the beach. You even have your designer build in a looping audio track of seagulls calling.

Result: You e-mail your entire base of prospects, client ad agencies, colleagues and friends, inviting them to check out your site. You print your URL on your business cards and other materials, and you start advertising in the local trade publication. Within a few months, you're getting three or four e-mails a week from ad agencies, design studios and corporations looking for a writer.

Brand Surgery: Avoiding Tragic Branding Mistakes

The Patient: Your Web Site

- Don't be intimidated by the techno-jargon of Web design and back away from doing your site. As long as you hire the right development team, you don't need to know the difference between XML and HTML.

- Don't walk away from your development vendor without a "design document" that tells you the content and technology required for each site section, and a schedule.

- Don't promise anyone a firm launch date. These things have a habit of taking longer than planned.

- Once your site is up, don't simply refer anyone with a question to it. Personal interaction is always better, and will make your site more valuable.

- Know the latest technology, but don't fall into the trap of wanting to add the latest features every few months.

- Don't waste your money on banner ads. They don't work.

CHAPTER 13

Personal Postcards

Direct Mail that Actually Works

Direct mail is the most abused, misunderstood, money-wasting Personal Branding tool used by businesses. But that's not because of any inherent flaw; it's because most people haven't the slightest idea how to conduct a direct-mail campaign. When you hear your colleagues declare over a beer, "Direct mail doesn't work," it's probably because once upon a time, they sent out a single sales letter that failed to bring a flood of customers to their front door.

Direct mail *does* work. You just have to do it right. Why do you think you get dozens of postcards, letters, credit card offers and catalogs in your mailbox every week? It's not because those companies like keeping the Post Office in business. It's because direct mail pays when you know how to make it pay. The world's greatest marketers know that when used correctly, direct mail is the best tool for building a consistent, growing business. With the right tools and the correct approach, direct mail can be the growth engine of your small business—and the driving force behind the spread of your Personal Brand.

Why It Works vs. Why It Doesn't

The obvious question is, what separates the direct mailers who get results from the ones who waste their money and then badmouth the medium to everyone they know? This is typically what the unsuccessful group does:

1. **Write a sales-oriented letter on boring company letterhead.**
2. **Send the letter out to a few thousand people once.**
3. **Do no follow-up by phone or mail.**
4. **Conclude direct mail doesn't work.**

Hardly scientific. Unfortunately, most companies labor under the fallacy that sending out a piece of direct mail is a ticket to booming business. It's not. Given the massive amount of mail that comes to our attention every day, it's not shocking that people tune out about 90 percent of the mail they receive as junk.

That said, direct mail can and does work. The businesspeople who do it right—and profitably—know the four keys to successful direct mail:

1. **Quality**—Mail pieces that look and feel high quality, like they come from a successful business that knows how to market itself. Letters generally do not cut the mustard. They're so common they get round-filed before ever being opened. Consumers and corporate executives alike are proven to respond to colorful, humorous, bold direct-mail pieces with strong design and quality printing.

2. **Relevance**—Your direct mail must contain information that means something to your target market. Crucial financial data, discounts, offers of free items like special reports, news about an opportunity in the area—these are all types of information that make direct mail mean something to the recipient. Otherwise, it is junk. What about those "clever" tricks like making a piece look like it's from the IRS or marking it "time-sensitive material?" These gimmicks might get more envelopes opened, but they make people mad. You don't win clients by insulting their intelligence.

3. **Emotional connection**—Your mail can't be based on a sales message. The majority of the garbage filling mailboxes is all about "60 percent off," "Act Now and Get Your Free Widget," and so on. People are flooded with sales messages every day. If you send direct mail that goes for the hard sell, all you'll get is their resentment.

4. **Repetition**—This is the most important factor. No single direct-mail piece, no matter how brilliant, will boost your business. The most critical element to direct mail success is sending multiple pieces at regular intervals, even if you don't see short-term results. The average consumer needs 4 to 5 exposures to a mailed message to even read the text on the outside of the envelope, much less open it. Once you have a strong direct-mail format, you must mail it again and again, using a variety of messages, to wear down sales resistance and start generating responses.

Is Your Current Direct Mail Working?

If you're engaged in a direct-mail program right now, stop. Even if it's generating results, stop. Because it was started before you set out to create your Personal Brand, so it won't be consistent when you launch your brand. Besides, chances are it isn't working as well as you'd like. There are four ways to gauge the success of a direct-mail program:

- Number of responses—The people who've responded to your mailings in some way. This is especially useful for retail stores, where foot traffic is important.

- Quality of leads—The percentage of contacts that turn into paying business. Out of the people who contact you, how many are you closing? This will tell you if your messages are producing serious inquiries or just "looky loos."

- Cost Per Lead—This valuable gauge tells you what each new prospect costs you. For example, you mail 1,000 pieces per month at a total cost with printing, postage and labor of $1,500. From this, you get 40 inquiries, and spend a total of 80 hours fielding phone calls, writing proposals, and such. If your hourly rate is $50, that's $4,000 more you've spent. So whether you convert 5 or 30 of those prospects into clients, you've spent $5,500/40 or $137.50 getting each one. What's acceptable? That depends on how much you're willing to spend. If each new client generates an average of $5,000 in new business, it's money well-spent.

- Return on Investment (ROI)—This is the ultimate criterion for judging the effectiveness of a direct-mail campaign. The standard for direct-mail response is 1.5 percent to 3 percent, and if a company only receives a .5 percent response, heads usually roll. But it's really not about quantity; it's about quality. If you spend $2,000 on a mailing to 500 new prospects, and you only get three new clients, but those clients bring $20,000 in business, you've earned a great ROI.

Keep this information in mind, because even though you need to stop your current mailing, you'll use the same gauges to evaluate your new mailing with your Personal Brand in place.

What Direct Mail Can Do for You

By now, direct mail may seem like a minefield where your money goes to die. But if you do it right, you don't have to be scared of direct mail.

In fact, after your business card, Personal Brochure and Personal Web Site, direct mail is the business and Personal Branding tool you need the most. It's the one way you can develop a constant conduit of information with your clients, stay in contact with them, and be the person they think of when they need what you offer. Done right, direct mail can benefit your business in myriad ways:

• Build name and brand awareness

• Let people know your service is targeted at them

• Reinforce your Personal Brand

• Give recipients numerous, regular reminders to contact you

• Keep prospects informed of news, events and offers

• Give you a medium for notes, greetings, and congratulations

• Demonstrate through your mailers' quality that you're successful

• Constantly communicate your contact information and Web address

• Keep your current clients aware of you

• Attract a steady flow of new prospects

• Generate vastly increased referrals

Personal Postcards: The Ultimate Direct Mail

The Personal Postcard will replace every sales letter, newsletter and brochure you've ever thought about sending as a direct-mail piece. It's the most powerful mailing tool ever to hit small business. It's the quickest, most cost-effective, most customizable way to send attractive, full-color direct mail as often as you like.

A Personal Postcard is a full-color card anywhere from 6" x 9" all the way to 8 1/2" x 11" in size. Your Personal Postcard is designed to match your Personal Brochure and give your branding consistency, but their real secret is they're designed as a "shell." On one side are your logo, your photo, and some brief Personal Branding copy, along with space for a mailing label and Bulk Mail indicia. On the other side is some thematic artwork, a little marketing copy that ties into your position...and a big blank space. The blank space makes the Personal Postcard go. In this space, you can print anything from offers to news to Christmas greetings to special promotions.

Once your full batch of 1,000, 2,000 or 5,000 Personal Postcard shells is printed (and you'll be surprised how fast you go through them), you just take as many as you need for your next mailing to a local 24-hour printer, along with the text for your mailing. They run the cards through their black ink press and presto! You have gorgeous full-color cards with a message you can change each time you mail. It's the cheapest customization around, and it's what makes Personal Postcards so incredibly powerful.

Why Personal Postcards?

- Designed to coordinate with your Personal Brochure and Personal Web Site, they reinforce your Personal Brand.

- They can be easily customized, so you can send personal greetings, seasonal messages, news about the stock market, handwritten notes, anything that connects with your prospects.

- They radiate quality from the paper to the color to the photos, making you look even more professional.

- Unlike letters, they don't have to be opened, so recipients can scan the headline in .5 seconds and decide whether to read further.

- You can print 5,000 cards for $1,000 and customize 500 for another $80, making them very cost-effective.

- Mailed consistently, they're proven to work.

Designing Your Personal Postcard

Direct mail has two goals: spread and grow your Personal Brand, and generate phone calls and e-mails. To accomplish this, your Personal Postcard must be designed to do three things:

- Build name recognition

- Establish a positive emotional disposition toward working with you

- Build your credibility with quality paper, photos and printing

Design your Personal Postcard using the same graphics, colors and photos as your Personal Brochure; it should be the perfect complement to the brochure. Summarize the main copy from your Personal Brochure—your key experience, your main personal story, how you create value, and a call to action—in 50 to 60 words on the "message side," where the blank space is. Leave about 2/3 of the space on this side blank (either by using no graphics or fading them back to ghosted images) so you can legibly overprint your text.

On the mailing side, you can use your main Personal Brochure photo as large as you need it, even taking up the whole side, with your personal photo, text and contact information running over the picture. As with logos and Web sites, we recommend hiring a professional designer to help you bring your Personal Postcard to life, and to make sure you follow Post Office regulations for bulk mail.

Some other tips:

• Augment your dramatic mailing side photo with an equally dramatic headline.

• Make sure your contact information is obvious and easy to read on both sides.

• Provide a "call to action" such as "Call today for your free special report." Instruct prospects what to do next.

Writing Your Personal Postcard

Because it's based on your Personal Brochure, designing your Personal Postcard is the easy part. It's the writing that will make or break you. You've got a fully customizable shell for your messages; now you need writing that works. Here are our essential guidelines for producing postcard messages that get results:

• Always begin with a strong headline that speaks directly to the reader.

• Keep your text short, 50-60 words (75 maximum) on the message side of the card.

• Unless you're mailing to a very conservative corporate market, speak regular English, use colloquial language, and write with a relaxed, conversational style, like you're talking to a neighbor over the backyard fence.

• Get to the point. Don't waste anyone's time.

• Give each message a benefit. It might be a discount offer, a bit of relevant news, or just Happy Thanksgiving. But always send something with a reason, never just a generic sales message.

• Be frank. The readers know you're ultimately trying to sell something. Don't hide what you do or you'll insult their intelligence.

• Connect with the emotions. Tell a story, offer advice, pass on a joke, whatever. Once you appeal to the emotions, you can suggest how you offer value and ask for a call or e-mail.

• Suggest action. As long as you're not making a hard sell, it's fine to finish with an invitation to stop by your office for a cup of coffee and a chat, and so on.

- Be original. Offer to take people to dinner, run a contest on your Web site giving away baseball tickets, offer a ride in a classic car, and the like. You never know what's going to push their buttons.

Most important, *know your target market*. Know what they like, what their goals are, whether or not they have kids and what age, what their values and faith are, and so on. Know them intimately, and you'll be able to write messages that slip past their sales barriers and really touch them.

Build in Response Channels

How do you want your prospects and clients to contact you? It doesn't happen by accident. You must build "response channels" into every Personal Branding channel. Basically, give both current clients and new prospects an adequate number of options for contacting you or requesting more information, and they will choose their own. Here are the potential response channels and their pros and cons:

1. Phone Number. Pro: High-quality responses. Con: People are uncomfortable calling for fear of sales pressure, so your number of responses will be low.

2. E-mail address. Pro: Easy, no fear of sales pressure. Con: Impersonal, and people don't always check their e-mail regularly.

3. Web site address. Pro: No pressure, all your information is available without any effort from you. Con: It's hard to turn people from site browsers into prospects sending you e-mail.

4. Fax number: Pro: Easy and accessible. Con: Almost no one communicates via fax.

5. Business Reply Card (BRC). Pro: An easy way to let people contact you for more information. Con: Responses are usually low quality.

6. Mailing address: Pro: Ummmm... Con: No one writes letters anymore. The only thing that might happen is you'll end up in someone else's direct-mail database.

In all your direct mail, include at least your business phone, e-mail address and Web address. If you're out of the office a lot, also include a mobile phone number.

Six Kinds of Postcard Messages

1. Product/Service Marketing—These are product- or service-driven messages you use to promote the value you offer. Usually, they're high-impact messages that drive home how relevant what you offer is to your prospects, positioning you as a solution. Example for a financial planner:

> **When You're 70, Will You Be Living With Your Kids?**
> In 10 years or 35 years, retirement is coming. When it does, will you have enough money to maintain your lifestyle? Or will you be dependent on others? Now's the time to start planning for post-work independence. I create plans designed for many different retirement goals, from starting a business to relaxing in a tropical paradise. If you want to invest in your retirement and then forget about it, call me and let's talk.

2. News—These are bulletins of the latest news related to your field, provided by you to your customers as a service. Use the news as a jumping-off point to a call to contact you. This makes your Personal Postcard a terrific substitute for a costly (and ineffective) newsletter. Example for a chiropractor:

> **Don't even think about back surgery until you've seen me.**
> Lower back pain can make people desperate. So desperate they'll consider anything, including risky, invasive surgery, to get relief. I'm telling you there is an alternative. Chiropractic care is real medicine. In fact, recent reports show that chiropractors receive the second-most medical training in the health-care professions, after MDs. So you're in good hands...and I can probably relieve your pain without medication or surgery. Come by for a free consultation and I'll show you how.

3. Seminar Promotions—Promote your upcoming seminar to current clients and your prospect base. Example for hotel management:

> **My seminar will help you sleep as well as your guests do.**
> **Where:** [place]
> **When:** [date and time]
> **Cost:** [$$ or free]
>
> Why are hotel owners across the state signing up for my leading-edge management seminar? Because I show hotel owners how to succeed by increasing their occupancy and profit margin through tactics they've haven't tried or considered. Even if you can't attend, call me. My company's complete management system, meticulous accounting controls, and experience with all property types can help you.
>
> Please RSVP to XXX-XXXX!

4. Web Messages—These messages promote some aspect of your Web site and drive traffic to it. This is cross-promotion at its finest. Example for a physical therapist:

> **How many calories and fat grams does your workout burn? Find out at www.tomsmiththerapy.com.**
> Is your evening walk the workout you think? Or are you just fooling yourself? All exercise is great, but depending on your goals, you might need something more strenuous. Use the Calorie and Fat Calculator on my Web site to find out how much your workout is really doing for you.

5. Personal—Personal messages are wonderful ways to connect with your prospects on a personal level, beyond simply trying to sell them. This has been proven time and time again to be the most effective way to generate long-term business: get your prospects to like and trust you as a person. Personal messages can be anything: holiday greetings, personal stories, birthday greetings, and more. They don't need to have any sort of sales payoff; they exist only to let your prospects know you care about them. Example for a CPA:

> **Little League. Big Lessons.**
> My son fell in love with Little League last week, eight years after he was born and 14 years after I got my last bleacher tan in a major league ballpark. Unexpectedly, I fell in love with the game again, too—as much as he did. I was captivated by the sense of adventure, by the all-out effort given by small people whose bodies aren't really ready to do things like chasing fly balls and fielding grounders, and by the joyful astonishment my son and his teammates displayed when they did something right. Simple pleasures, simple joys...

6. Handwritten—As the name suggests, you can use your Personal Postcards to send individual notes to clients and prospects alike. Like Personal messages, Handwritten notes are a wonderful way to connect with people, whether you're congratulating someone on the birth of a child, reminding a man about his wedding anniversary, passing on a note about an investment, or almost anything else. Personal Postcards make it easy to pen a quick note and mail it.

Printing Your Personal Postcard

Print your postcard on heavy, high-quality glossy paper, just as you do your Personal Brochure. How your card feels in the hands will have as much effect on your prospects as the artwork or what it says. Maybe more.

Save money by printing large quantities. If you feel your checkbook slamming shut at the suggestion, look at it this way: If you have a mailing list of 500 prospects, and you mail to them once a month for a year, that's 6,000 postcards. That's not even counting special mailings. The fact is, big quantities lower your per-card cost considerably, so printing 5,000 cards may only cost $300 more than printing 2,500. If you're planning a monthly mailing, we recommend printing at least 10,000 pieces.

Making Sense of Mailing

First things first: You need a mailing list. In all likelihood, buying a mailing list from one of the mailing-list companies you see on the Internet or in your business mail would be a waste of your time. They're expensive, probably too big for your needs, and often poorly managed. As for compiling a list yourself from telephone directories or the like, that's a waste of your time.

The best way to get your list is to purchase it from a local newspaper or magazine that sells its subscriber lists. Assuming your target market is limited to a certain geographic area, this is a great way to get only local names without wasting money on the names of people you'll never contact.

Add the prospects already in your database and you're ready to go. If you're mailing to corporations, your needs may be smaller, maybe 100 companies. That's easy enough to compile yourself.

Once you have your cards and list, you have two choices: Have you or your staff do the mailing, or hire a mailing house. For smaller mailings such as 500 pieces, we recommend doing it yourself. You can get very good label production software from any office-supply store; in a few hours, you'll be ready to mail.

For larger mailings like 2,500 pieces, we recommend hiring a mailing-fulfillment house. For a reasonable fee, they will print your labels, stick them on, bundle your cards and get them in the mail stream while you handle other things. If you're busy, this can be a godsend. Look in the Yellow Pages for mailing-fulfillment services.

Finally, get a Bulk Mail permit. Bulk Mail lets you send batches of materials by Zip code for about half of first-class postage. Talk to your Post Office.

Three Uses for Personal Postcards

1. Twelve-Month Branding Campaign. Send a Personal Postcard each month to your current clients, friends, professional referrals, and hot prospects. The object is to keep you on their minds for that time when they're ready to do business or refer someone to you. This "drip marketing" plan features a different type of mailer each month:

Month 1: Personal Brochure with cover letter

Month 2: Product/Service Marketing postcard

Month 3: Personal postcard

Month 4: News postcard

Month 5: Personal message

Month 6: Personal Brochure with a letter asking for referrals

Month 7: Web postcard

Month 8: Product/Service Marketing postcard

Month 9: Personal postcard

Month 10: News postcard

Month 11: Web postcard

Month 12: Handwritten holiday greeting

2. Six-Week Marketing Blitz. Send one Personal Postcard per week to hot prospects for six weeks. This campaign is designed to create instant brand awareness and get the phone ringing. Use the following mailing schedule:

Week 1: Personal Brochure with cover letter

Week 2: Product/Service Marketing postcard

Week 3: Product/Service Marketing postcard

Week 4: Product/Service Marketing postcard

Week 5: Product/Service Marketing postcard

Week 6: Product/Service Marketing postcard

With the Six-Week program, mail to one target market at a time. When it's done, mail to another. This gives you the chance to gauge the effectiveness of your messages while not being overwhelmed by incoming communication.

3. Note Card. Use Personal Postcards any time you need to dash off a handwritten note or thank-you note. Personally branded note cards are unheard of, so they're a real differentiator.

Making Mailings More Effective

No matter how brilliant your Personal Postcard is, there are things you can do to improve your results. Some of the best tactics:

• **Make "Warm Calls."** Cold calling is when the person on the other end doesn't know you from Adam. With warm calling, they've gotten one or more of your direct-mail pieces, so at least they know your name. There's no substitute for personal contact. Once you've sent several mailings to your target market, start calling them to introduce yourself. Reference your past mailers, but don't sell and don't ask open-ended questions like, "Is there anything I can do for you?" Ask people about themselves. We know one financial advisor who called her direct-mail recipients and invited them to bitch about financial advisors. They loved it.

- **Follow Up.** Even if you don't call everyone, have some sort of follow-up plan for the people who respond to your direct mail. These folks should be your No. 1 priority—they represent possible new business! Have a set procedure in place, for example:

1. Receive call or e-mail from prospect.

2. If you speak directly, send a thank-you card within 24 hours.

3. If you do not speak directly, return the call (don't e-mail in response to an e-mail) within 8 hours.

4. Call within a week after your initial conversation to ask if there's anything you can do, any questions you can answer, etc.

5. Always ask for the meeting.

6. If the prospect invests time in meeting you, whether he becomes a customer or not, send a thank-you gift after the meeting. This can be something nice but inexpensive like a book or a $20 restaurant gift certificate.

- **Have a System.** Work with your staff or a fulfillment house to set up a schedule that sends your direct-mail pieces out automatically, whether you're involved or not. Lay out the tasks—printing labels, checking for deletion requests, sticking labels, bundling cards, going to the Post Office—and assign them, then post a mailing schedule on your wall so everyone knows when things go out. It's also smart to have a follow-up plan in place, where your assistant sends out thank-you cards to callers automatically, in case you're too busy to handle it.

- **Delete Names When Asked.** If people contact you to ask that they be removed from your mailing list, comply immediately.

- **Divide Up Your Prospects.** After a few months of mailing, you'll be able to divide your prospects into three groups:

  1. **Hot Properties**—These are people who have responded to your 12-month or 6-week mailing programs and seem interested in doing business with you. If you haven't already, send them a Personal

Brochure and follow it up with a phone call to discuss a meeting. Keep these people on your 12-month plan or shift them to it, and treat them like gold. Thank-you notes, personal mailers, the whole thing.

2. **Possibles**—These are people who have expressed some interest, but are not yet willing to do business. Many of them will come from your 6-week blitz mailings. Put them on your 12-month plan right away, but don't waste a lot of time on them until they make a move. Some will show further interest, while others will disappear. Those who contact you a second time should become Hot Properties.

3. **Lost Causes**—These people fall into three categories: 1) Prospects who don't respond in any way to your 6-week program, 2) Prospects who ask to be removed from your list, and 3) Prospects on your 12-month program who have not responded at all in one year, even to your requests for referrals. Stop mailing to these people and turn to new target markets. If you don't want to give up, try sending Personal Postcards to this group (except for those who have opted out) once per quarter.

Direct E-mail

Direct e-mail is a new entry into the world of direct response. With no printing, mailing costs or design fees, it's an attractive option. But it's also a different medium, and that means different rules. We could do an entire chapter on direct e-mail, but instead, some basic tips and ideas:

- **Check your prospects' comfort with e-mail.** Not everyone likes using it, and not everyone knows how. Be certain your target market has a level of tech smarts before sending them e-mail.

- **Make the subject line strong and clear.** That's what people see in their inbox, and it will often determine whether they open your mail or delete it. Put your name in the subject line so they know they're not being "spammed."

- **Provide a link to your Web site.** Always invite e-mail recipients to click and visit your site, especially if you have special promotions or offers. It's also a great idea to e-mail people links to other sites you "just thought they might find useful."

- **Give them the option to opt out.** By law, you must provide a way for people to take themselves off your e-mail list. The easiest way is to put instructions at the bottom of the e-mail: "To unsubscribe from this list, please reply to this e-mail with the word 'Remove' in the subject line."

- **Complement your direct mail.** E-mail is a great way to follow a Personal Postcard. If you're really hot after a target market, consider following up every card in your 12-month plan with e-mail, two weeks later, that touches on the subject of the last card. This lets you contact potential clients 24 times in a year.

- **Build your own list.** There are plenty of e-mail list sellers out there, and most are crooks. Instead, take the e-mail information from the postal mailing lists you buy and use an online list service like Topica, CoolList or Yahoo! Groups. This will enable you to enter e-mail addresses once and keep track of changes.

- **Say the same things you say in your postcards.** Tell stories, offer answers, highlight opportunities, and tell jokes. E-mail can be just as warm and human as anything else, and you have the potential to build a dialogue with your prospect.

Personal Brand Case Study

Wally Bock
Wally Bock Consulting

Position: Helping organizations realize the promise of the Digital Age
Location: Wilmington, NC
Business: Digital Business Consulting
Online: wallybock.com

Wally Bock specializes in tomorrow. A futurist and early Web adopter, he was one of the early subscribers to CompuServe. Today, he's a "digital-age guru" who instructs small to mid-sized businesses in how to more effectively use information technology. Bock is an example of a Personal Brand who's been able to adapt as his target market has changed over time. Today, his client list features dozens of names, including Farmer's Insurance, Bayer and Honda, as well as dozens of smaller companies.

How It Started:

Bock wrote two books that were evergreen sellers in the law-enforcement market (he's written more than 20 books to date), but his real launch came when the Internet started to appear on the general cultural radar. "People saw me and said 'He knows something about that.'"

After several more forays into publishing, Bock focused on his core business: consulting with organizations on how to get their technology to support their strategy.

Most Important Steps in Building a Personal Brand:

Bock's success has stemmed largely from a fierce determination to create widespread awareness of his Personal Brand. "I want one of two things to happen: When they hear my name, to say, 'I've heard of him,' and second, to connect my name in some way with Digital Age," he says. "If I can get the bell to go off in their heads with recognition in one-third to one-half of the places where I promote myself, I can get in the door. Once I get in the door, I can do the consultative selling stuff. If the bell goes off in an executive's head, I can talk to the executive instead of the meeting planner."

Bock also leverages multiple channels, especially mailings. "Every contact point reinforces the other stuff I do," he says. "So if they do a speech, they find out I've done a book or two. If they read the book, they find out I do speeches. If they hear me on radio or in my newsletter, they find out I have books, and so on.

"If I can hit meeting planners with series of mailings, so they see me nine months out of a year, there's a much better chance of them remembering me. I mail to my A list every month, but I mail to my B list maybe four times a year, but in a short period.

Biggest Success:

"Because I've been interviewed by major media, I can show them clips from CNBC or CNN, or clips from the *Wall Street Journal* or *Newsweek*. That's also something you work at."

On Personal Branding and Publicity:

"Understand that publicity trumps advertising most of the time. People need to see your name in print and see your slogan over and over until we're all ready to puke, because if that doesn't happen, the bell doesn't go off. And if that doesn't happen, you're not credible."

Advice:

"When you deliver value, deliver it in a narrow niche. Manufacturing guys want you to be their kind of guy. If you speak to bankers the next week, they don't care about manufacturing. But use general media to give you credibility. When I trot out the video from CNN, it gets me in the door. If Jan Nathan thinks I'm worth interviewing, I must be worth hiring."

Brandstorming Personal Postcards:
9 Great Things You Can Do Right Now

1. List all the direct mail you've done in the past year that's brought in business.

2. Talk to the clients who came to you from those mailers and find out why they responded.

3. Determine which publications in your area sell their subscriber lists for direct mailers.

4. Print your mailing labels.

5. Train your staff to label, stuff and mail your direct mailers properly.

6. Create a direct mail master calendar and post it on your wall.

7. Create a "Follow-Up Manual."

8. Make sure each employee has a supply of your Personal Postcards for hand-written notes and such.

9. Send your clients a survey asking them about their e-mail habits. Do the majority check their e-mail often enough to make direct e-mail worthwhile?

Bottom Line No. 13: How Personal Branding Equals More Business
Growing your business with consistent direct mail

Situation: You're a caterer struggling to gain market share in a saturated market. But you've noticed something: Most of your competitors specialize in food, but not service. Meanwhile, service is your specialty: you help clients pick the right menu for an event, develop themes, and even connect them with musicians and other vendors. But you need a way to highlight this major difference.

Solution: You've already done a Personal Brochure around your Personal Brand, so now you develop and print a Personal Postcard and begin a 12-month mailing to your base of about 400 homes and businesses. In your postcards, you alternate personal messages and recipes with clever, insider ideas for putting on a great party, a wonderful dinner, or a fabulous holiday event. Some revolve around food, but you send messages on everything from etiquette to decorating. Prospects start calling you to get more of the same tips, and as a result, you start building new relationships.

Result: After four months of regular mailings, your phone is ringing off the hook and you've hired an assistant. Your direct mail has positioned you as the local expert on "all things party," so you get calls from folks wanting to know what silverware to use, how to do a Cajun theme night, and a million other questions. Not only do many of these callers hire you, but they also refer you to friends. Market share is yours.

Brand Surgery: Avoiding Tragic Branding Mistakes
The Patient: Your Direct Mail

- Don't give in to your miser instincts and print your Personal Postcards digitally. It's faster and cheaper, but the quality suffers, and that will hurt you.

- Don't mail more than once a month to your longtime prospects. More than that is a nuisance.

- Keep mailing to people who become your clients. They're your best source of referrals.

- Don't fill up the blank area on your Personal Postcard with text. Less is more. Leave some white space for readability.

- Use your postcards to ask current clients for referrals once in a while.

- Don't get discouraged when you don't get any responses after your first three mailings. That's normal. It takes time for your message to percolate.

- If you're going to direct people to your Web site, make sure it's up and looks good.

- Once a quarter, purge invalid addresses from your database. You'll save money over the course of a year.

CHAPTER 14

Public Relations

or, Creating the Credibility Advertising Can't

Why would any editor want to write about you? Our answer is, why not? Where do you think newspaper and magazine editors get the material to fill up their pages, especially in small local papers where there may not be a lot of news? They cover local people—business owners, notable residents, and so on. You've got as much chance as anyone of landing a prime spot in a local—or even a national—publication. You've just got to know how to do it.

What Is Public Relations?

PR is the fine art of generating press coverage for yourself. These days, with so many corporations risking millions on stock offerings or trying to put out the fires of scandal, PR has become a major industry, with its own gurus and experts and language and procedures. But the essential fact remains: if you can develop a presence in the press, you can get big very fast. PR is fast-becoming the most powerful tool for launching any brand, replacing big-budget advertising. The right PR can *make* your career.

There are four ground rules to getting press coverage, whether you're targeting the editor of your hometown paper or of a national trade magazine:

1. Make it easy for editors and writers. Send information in the proper format and be easy to contact.

2. Don't waste their time with phone calls or empty press releases.

3. Know what they need. For a local paper, send an editor information about your sponsorship of a local soccer team.

4. Be newsworthy. Create a new type of business, new product, new category, something worth covering.

In the end, all any editor wants is a good story that can be gotten with minimal time or trouble. If you can provide such stories consistently, it doesn't matter who you are. You'll get coverage.

How PR Helps Your Business

Press coverage is the greatest, cheapest credibility builder on the planet. As you're developing your Personal Brand, it becomes crucial at some point to have corroboration, a neutral third party reminding everyone you're as good as you say you are. That's what press coverage does. More than any ad, it establishes you as an authority, someone who can be trusted. Because the media is an objective source, information printed about you in a newspaper or magazine has heft behind it.

Other Benefits of Good PR:

• **Reinforced Personal Brand**—Press coverage helps tell people more about who you are and what you do, which drives home your brand more strongly.

• **Wider awareness**—A regional newspaper with a circulation of 40,000 will tell more people about you than any direct-mail campaign you could ever mount. It's a good way to make more people aware of your name and abilities.

• **Marketing asset**—Reprints of articles can be used in promotional kits, direct mailings and even on your Web site to enhance your image.

• **Greater authority with professional contacts**—Investors, referral sources, awards committees and other professional individuals and groups will treat you with greater regard with some press attention in your portfolio. The interest of an editor validates their interest in you.

Doubt the power of PR? Two words: Tiger Woods. Name an athlete, even Michael Jordan, whose Personal Brand has benefited more from press coverage than the young golf champion. Woods isn't even particularly eloquent or charming; in fact, he's taken a beating in some publications because of his refusal to make statements about issues such as discrimination in sports. But the media can't get enough of him: He's young, ethnic, good-looking and astonishingly talented on the golf course, a sport that makes for perfect photo ops. Woods' powerful Personal Brand owes everything to the media.

Three Types of PR

Most guides to public relations focus primarily on sending out press releases and getting articles or news items published. But we're going to take you farther by also talking about other effective avenues that can produce priceless column inches for you: getting your own writing published, establishing yourself as an expert resource for editors, and sponsoring events.

1. **Press Releases and Articles**

   Sending out regular press releases on your company letterhead is the easiest way to keep yourself in front of editors and generate occasional coverage. Doing this has several goals:

   - To make editors familiar with you

   - To keep your press releases in their inbox

   - To get your release used as a short "news brief" item

   - To get a special event you're involved in listed in a calendar section

   - To eventually get the publication to write a feature-length article about you

   The idea of mailing regular press releases has a basis in editorial need: Editors need material to fill space. If they can't get it from you, they'll run house ads or filler articles from Associated Press. By providing material for short stories, you solve a problem. Then, as the editor gets to know you, you become a local or professional interest story. The more successful and prominent you become, the better story you are. It's a wonderful feedback loop.

   So to whom do you send your releases? That depends on your target market. If you're primarily trying to develop your Personal Brand to local residents, you'll want to put local papers, magazines, radio stations and TV stations on your mailing list. On the other hand, if you're targeting a certain industry, such as advertising or human resources, send releases to trade publications related to your profession, both print and Web-based. The smart way is to cover both bases: Send releases to professional publications *and* to the local media where your customers reside.

   What can your press releases be about? Anything you like, as long as it's relevant to the publication. You'll find some PR gurus telling you to send a release every month, even if it's just to report that you hired a new secretary. We don't recommend that. Send a release when you have news you think will interest the editor of each publication, even if that means sending three releases one week and not sending another for three months.

Relevance is important, not frequency. Give journalists news they can use. Some possibilities:

- You win an award

- You open a new location

- You reach a milestone, like being in business for 25 years

- You sponsor a sports team or charity event

- You launch a Web site

- You publish a book

- You open a new business

- You hire the relative of a prominent local person

- You launch an aggressive new business initiative

- You join a community group

- You run for office

- You hold a seminar

- One of your staff gets an award or special honor

How To Do It Right

- **Compile your mailing list.** Know to whom you're mailing. Get the addresses of local community newspapers, alternative weeklies, area magazines, regional editions of larger papers, and so on. You should also look to see which trade publications exist for your profession—it's astonishing how many specialized magazines there are.

- **Know press-release format.** If you send a press release in a strange format, it will never be read. Period. So know the basic professional press-release style—contact information at the top, inverted pyramid format, etc. Go to the press sections at any one of 100 corporate Web sites and you'll see professionally written releases to use as examples. NEVER deviate from this format.

- **Build a press kit.** To introduce yourself to editors, we recommend first sending them a press kit. That's a folder containing your initial press release, your personal bio, your Personal Brochure, a business card, and a black-and-white photo of you. Send with it a cover letter explaining who you are and why you've chosen to send your information to this publication.

- **Follow up with regular releases.** Once you've sent your kit, follow it with press releases as often as the news warrants. Again, spare editors the breathless report about your new secretary, but try to come up with something newsworthy at least once a month. Keep in mind, what's nothing to a national trade magazine may be Page 3 material for your local newspaper.

- **Be patient.** Don't hassle editors. Leave them alone and let your releases do their work. Most editors are time-poor and have dozens of press kits and press releases crossing their desk each day. In all likelihood, your initial efforts will either be filed with nary a glance or go straight to the recycling bin. Give it time and they will notice you, but meanwhile respect their time. Don't pester them with calls. It makes you look desperate and unprofessional.

- **Jump at the chance to get personal.** When an editor or writer finally does call, take every opportunity to start a two-way relationship. Take the writer to lunch. Send the editor a thank-you gift if a story runs. Be easy and accommodating. Make yourself available as a source for future stories in your area of expertise. It pays off.

- **Get copies.** When your article runs, whether it's a six-line news item or a feature, be sure you or your assistant get copies. Make photocopies of the coverage and keep them for future use.

2. **Publishing Your Own Column**

   Getting your own column published, either in a local periodical or a national trade paper, is a tremendous boon to your credibility. Think of the luminaries, from George Gilder to George Will, whose prestige has been enhanced tenfold by virtue of their being published on a national stage. There's no reason you can't do the same.

   A disclaimer: Many columnists who are not professional writers don't publish their own words, and you probably shouldn't either. Unless you have a background as a professional writer, you'll want to hire a ghost-writer to write your column.

   Why would a regional newspaper or a national magazine want to publish your column? Because they're always looking for new material, and because you're an expert. If you can deliver a well-written column about a subject that's of interest, you should be able to find a place to publish it.

   ### How To Do It Right
   - **Locate a good writer.** Most columns published by professionals are either produced by talented ghostwriters or they're badly written but get printed

because the person is well-known. Finding a good writer who can deliver a piece of a set length on deadline is your best strategy. Avoid the college journalism programs; you have no idea what kind of quality you'll be getting. A good way to find freelance writers these days is on the Web at sites like Guru.com. But perhaps the best way is to simply contact the writers who write for your local paper. Most reporters don't make a lot of money, and they would jump at the chance to make an extra $200 a month.

- **Peruse possible publications.** Now, where to publish? If you choose a trade publication read by people in your profession, you'll have more competition for space and you'll be subject to more scrutiny. If you're OK with that, fine. But consider a local newspaper or magazine, where your target market will be friendlier and your competition for space will be mostly amateur writers.

- **Choose your idea.** Before you choose your publication, decide what you want your column to be about. It should be something you're interested in, something you know a lot about, and something that's not being covered in the publication you're targeting. The subject will help determine where you publish. For example, if you want to write about the ups-and-downs of the local real estate market, a regional lifestyle magazine would be best. But if you'd rather talk to other massage therapists about trends in holistic medicine, try a trade magazine.

- **Get the editorial guidelines.** Every publication has them, and they'll tell you how long a column should be, which subjects are kosher, which format to submit it in, whom to send it to, and so on. Follow these to the letter.

- **Write a sample column and send it to the editor.** Once you've made your choice, hire your writer to produce a sample column. When it's done to your satisfaction, send it with a cover letter to the editor of your chosen periodical. In the letter, explain who you are, why you think your column should be accepted, and offer 3 or 4 future column ideas. Then wait and see what happens. We recommend you only send a column to one publication at a time, because if more than one accepts the same column, you're going to be in trouble.

3. **Establishing Yourself as an "Expert Source"**

This is a great way to generate press coverage, because it involves very little work or time beyond the initial effort. Here, you're establishing yourself with several editors, both local and national, as a knowledgeable, quotable source for articles in your area of expertise. Basically, you're the guy reporters call for an opinion and a quote when they're doing a piece on emerging markets stocks, athletes in the media, class-action-suit case law, or whatever your field of knowledge is.

The wonderful thing is once you're in their Rolodex, editors and reporters call you and put your name in the paper, without you lifting a finger. Beyond a twice-per-year letter or thank-you card to remind them you're still around, you don't have to do a thing.

How To Do It Right

- **Choose your field.** Even if you're a fantastic architect, we don't recommend you position yourself to an editor as the all-knowing architect. That's too broad. Choose a narrower area of specialty and present yourself as an expert source in it. For example, "architect with expertise in the county's design history and historic buildings" would be ideal.

- **Send a Rolodex card.** Have Rolodex cards printed to match your business cards, and send them to the editors at your chosen local and trade publications along with a cover letter offering yourself as an expert source, at their disposal.

- **Be accessible.** If you're going to be a source, you've got to be able to be reached. Provide editors with a mobile phone number and return calls as quickly as possible. Deadlines wait for no man.

- **Be candid and do research.** When you are called to quote on a topic, if you don't know the answer, ask to call back after you've had a chance to crack the books. Then call back within an hour. Most reporters can wait a little while for an accurate answer. When you are quoted, be direct and offer your honest, factual opinion. "Yes" and "No" answers are worthless to a busy beat reporter.

- **Repeat every three months until it works.** Every quarter, send your Rolodex card and a follow-up letter to the editors until you receive communication from them. Some will tell you to buzz off. Some will thank you and promise to get back to you. A few will express real interest.

- **Supplement your press releases.** Many smart professionals combine the sending of press releases with the sending of Rolodex cards. This dual effort gives you a better chance of getting in the paper and of being noticed; an editor who uses you as a source for a story might later remember your press kit.

Online PR

The deluge of online "e-zines" has slowed to a trickle thanks to the collapse of the dot-com bubble, but there are still plenty of specialized trade-news sites out there waiting for your press release. The great thing about the Web is you can easily access dozens of relevant e-zines without leaving your office, and e-mail information to them in an hour. The downside is they aren't read by as many people as print trade magazines.

In sending releases to trade Web sites, the same rules apply. Keep in mind if you try to sell a column to a Web site, you might be asked to produce something every week, due to the fast turnaround time and quick updating of the Web.

Finally, your Web site is part of your online PR strategy. Make sure you have a place on your site where you can post your own press releases, and in your letters to editors, direct them to your site to find more news about you, as well as useful background information that may just land you that columnist job.

Sponsorships

Sponsoring local events may not involve the press, but it does affect your relationship with the public, and there's no better definition for public relations. Let me say right off the bat that sponsorships are not right for every business. If you're strapped for cash, you're better off spending your money on direct mail and generating referrals. Also, if you're in a professional like criminal-defense law, advertising on the outfield wall of your local Little League may not be the way to go. But if you're tapped out on other tactics and are looking to become more widely known in your community, sponsorships are outstanding.

Basically, you pay to help support an event, sports team or non-profit institution, getting some free advertising in return. Some of the best things to sponsor are:

- Local baseball and soccer teams

- Museums, symphonies, and other arts organizations

- Charity events like golf tournaments and 10K runs

- Concerts

Sponsorship gets your name in front of a wide range of people, attached to something positive. It also paints you as someone who cares about your community and/or important causes. For a few thousand dollars (often much less), a sponsorship can buy you a great deal of goodwill. Some tips:

- Attend the event you sponsor and carry business cards. It doesn't hurt to subtly mention you're a sponsor.

- Leverage the sponsorship as a PR opportunity. If the event doesn't issue a press release about your sponsorship, issue your own.

- Provide your own program ad or signage. Don't let the organization create an ad for you by scanning your business card.

Personal Brand Case Study

Rainbeau Mars
Rainbeau Mars Yoga

Position: Lotus (just kidding)…Hollywood's yoga guru
Location: Los Angeles, CA
Business: Yoga instructor
Online: rainbeaumars.com

It's a no-brainer that Rainbeau Harmony Mars is a child of the early 1970s, born in a teepee under the double rainbow to a famous herbalist mother and author. But sweep aside the Summer of Love connotations of the name and you find a sincere, savvy businesswoman: part actress and model (isn't everyone in Los Angeles an actress or model?), part wildly successful yoga guru. With a Web site that features beautiful photos of this beautiful woman, and a knack for getting media coverage, Mars has become a rising star in the yoga firmament.

How It Started:

Mars began as an actress, and while working on the set of *The People vs. Larry Flynt*, actor Woody Harrelson introduced her to yoga. After learning the basics and teaching a few classes, she went to take a class from a yoga teacher she'd heard was rough on his students. "It turned out he wasn't in town, and the substitute wasn't there. At that point I had only taught 12 to 15 people. I taught the class, and the class ended up being about three hours. To this day, I still hear about that class."

Her practice began to take on a new level when celebrities came to learn, then started telling each other about their experiences. A Hollywood yoga guru was born.

Most Important Steps in Building a Personal Brand:

Mars' natural comfort level in front of the camera has led to wide exposure to the national media. Her classes started being taped for *Yoga Journal*, programs on the Oxygen network, and more. She soon began doing her own series of yoga videos, which has put her technique, warm energy, and natural on-camera poise out for thousands to see.

The PR coverage wasn't accidental. "When I did Nike or when I did a book, I had a press kit and cards listing all my upcoming coverage," she says. "People could see what press I was getting, they could see what I had to offer, and what I would add to their project."

Biggest Success:

"I try not to work personally on getting people to know who I am. I have people working with me, and there are publicity or articles that are interesting. At this point, my feeling is that when we start arriving rather than striving, that's when things move quicker. I'm not working to get people to notice; I have a team—a manager, an attorney, a publicist, a Web site—to get me noticed. All I can do is work on my craft, on my art."

On Personal Branding and Selling Yourself:

"Often, when we try to sell ourselves, we look outside ourselves, and we forget about why we do it. But when you look back inside, you see the passion and people see your passion. It's not that I consciously decided to sell myself; it's that I'm not afraid to allow myself to be sold. There are millions of people with God-given talent who are afraid.

"The key for me is to feel like I'm in the service of a higher cause. So if people are inspired by me, if my being me is of service, that's what my work is."

Advice:

"Really trust yourself. There are always so many voices, people who have been practicing a lot longer, and I say, 'I was in lotus when I was five!' It's easy to say someone else has the answers, but we need to trust our own intuition and our own inner guide."

Brandstorming PR:
10 Great Things You Can Do Right Now

1. List the print publications you want to target in your area and your industry. Do the same for appropriate TV, radio and online outlets.

2. Create a database of editors, and key writers and reporters from those publications.

3. Start gathering the contents of your press kit: a personal bio, two to three good-quality photographs of you (headshot, action shot with a client, family or personal shot) and the folders in which to send them.

4. Print Rolodex cards with your Personal Logo, contact information, and fields of expertise on them.

5. Learn standard press-release format.

6. Jot down column ideas.

7. Begin talking to local writers and journalists about ghostwriting.

8. Contact organizations or sports clubs about sponsorship.

9. Designate a press liaison in your company, someone who will interact with the media in case you're not available.

10. Read all the publications you're targeting regularly. This will help you learn what kind of material they're seeking.

Bottom Line No. 14: How Personal Branding Equals More Business
Establishing yourself as an expert with targeted PR

Situation: You're an agent representing actors, musicians and directors in New York, but you have a hard time attracting clients because you hate the hard-hitting, fast-talking style of most agents. You'd rather attract clients with your low-key manner and your genuine love for what you do, and respect for what they do. But that's a tough sale in a cynical city.

Solution: You start a PR campaign aimed at some of the smaller entertainment trade publications around the city, figuring the big trades are closed to you for now. You send releases to editors about your approach, hoping it will generate coverage. Nothing happens. Then you send a letter to an editor offering to write a column called, "The Ethical Agent: An Oxymoron for Our Times." You pitch it as a column telling actors and others how to deal with unethical representatives and how to spot good ones, and telling aspiring agents how to do the job without selling their souls. The editor bites, you hire a writer, and suddenly you're published monthly.

Result: You've repositioned yourself with this column, and created great public awareness. You get plenty of calls from the curious, and some from angry agents. But you also get interviewed by other trade papers, and best of all you get a flood of head shots, résumés and demo CDs. Slowly, you're building the business you wanted, the way you wanted.

Brand Surgery: Avoiding Tragic Branding Mistakes
The Patient: Your PR

- Don't pester editors for stories. You're one of 100 people daily who call wanting coverage, and you'll only alienate them.

- When you promise a column or release, deliver before the deadline. Time is everything to any editor or reporter, and if you waste theirs, you're dead.

- Don't send half a dozen press releases plus old articles in a press kit. That's a waste of an editor's time. Make press kits as targeted as everything else.

- Don't let an editor off the hook if she gets a fact wrong or quotes a competitor without getting a quote from you. Demand a correction or retraction or equal time.

- Your Web site can be the perfect clearinghouse for the media. Make their job easier by updating press releases on your site.

- Don't editorialize in press releases. They're supposed to be purely factual. Editors hate hype in releases; save it for the interview.

CHAPTER 15

Networking

and the Beauty of Referrals

The common image of networking is the "schmooze": a bunch of guys in loud suits standing around Chamber of Commerce mixers with vodka tonics talking about their BMWs and their golf swings. But true networking as done by smart Personal Branders is something else entirely. It's the subtle art of giving people just enough information to be intrigued, then backing off and letting them come to you.

As we've said, Personal Branding is about attracting others to you. That's never more true than when you're networking at a party, a professional society meeting, or a cultural event. In effect, you're leading with your Personal Brand; no one you meet has enough time to really get to know you, so all you can do is powerfully communicate who you are, what you do, and how you create value. Do it right and you'll make a strong impression, attracting those who want to know more.

The essence of great networking is not handing out business cards or talking about your work. That's as boring in person as it would be in a Personal Brochure. No, great networking is about communicating your Personal Brand through your speech, your attire, your conduct and your branding materials (if you get the chance to hand them out), and influencing others so they perceive you as someone with whom they want to work. The beauty of it is, even though you're carefully influencing their perception, they think it's all their own doing.

Networking Basics

Networking isn't about events. It's about seizing every opportunity to meet someone new, and laying the groundwork for a relationship with that person. Even more, it's about putting yourself in position to meet someone new. A fabulous example is Paul Viti, director of sales and marketing for the New York office of Ernst & Young. This guy is a networking madman, but he does it very simply by catching a cab. His office is in Times Square near many upscale hotels, so when Paul walks out to grab a cab for a meeting, he's got a good chance of sharing that cab with a top executive from some corporation. When Paul gets in that cab with a CEO, he's in position to get to know that person on a one-to-one basis, and he grabs that opportunity. He says he's laid the groundwork for more deals this way than all other avenues combined.

Ask yourself two questions: who are the people you want to meet, and where are your opportunities to meet them? The types of people can range widely, but here are some common categories:

- Community leaders and politicians

- Business leaders

- Colleagues in your profession

- Professionals in other fields

- Media members

- Leaders of non-profit groups

- Religious leaders

- Educators

- Prominent private citizens

Which ones should you meet? Depends on who you are. Different people in different professions will benefit from relationships with different networking contacts. That's because there are many ways your new acquaintances can benefit you:

1. Become direct clients

2. Refer clients to you

3. Become mentors and improve your skills

4. Become valuable advisors or critics

5. Provide you with needed services

6. Offer expertise in areas like business plans or raising funds

7. Provide media coverage

8. Become a bridge to influential media members, corporate leaders, politicians

9. Become friends who influence your values or lifestyle

Where to Network

As the Paul Viti story demonstrates, the question of where and how to meet the right people has almost limitless answers. But there are common environments where networking opportunities abound, and putting yourself in those environments is a matter of research, planning and initiative:

- Chamber of Commerce meetings

- Networking groups

- Professional organization meetings

- Tradeshows

- Seminars

- Sporting events

- Arts events

- Charity events

- Boards of directors

- Professional panels

- Organizational committees

- City council meetings

Do your research into every possible opportunity, from council meetings to arts events, and make a master list. Look at the types of people who frequent each environment; are they likely to benefit you? If so, put that environment on your list and give it a try. You'll know more once you make an appearance and see what happens. After 2 or 3 months, you should have a master calendar of 6 to 8 types of events or environments that will become your networking sphere. Start becoming a regular.

Networking Tips

- **Always be networking.** This sales-inspired phrase should become your guiding principle. Always be in a mindset to meet someone new, to get to know him or her, and to let the person become familiar with your Personal Brand. You never know when you'll run into a new partner, client or investor.

- **Put yourself in position to seize opportunities.** Put yourself in situations where you're more likely to meet people. Sit next to others on a plane or in a movie theater. Dine in busy, energetic restaurants. Join steering committees, non-profit boards and other groups. Be the person who listens and meets others while other people protect their personal space.

- **Just get to know them.** Don't try to extract any benefits from a person when you first meet. Remember, people want to be appreciated as people, not clients.

- **Listen.** Listen twice as much as you talk in conversation, and ask people about themselves. You'll seem like someone who really cares and a thoughtful person.

- **Always have materials.** How many times have you asked a professional for a business card and they haven't had one? What does that say about them? Don't make the same mistake. Always have your materials ready. When it's time to hand out information, go beyond the simple business card. Always have one of two things on hand: a folding, full-color business card that reflects your Personal Brand, or better yet, a Personal Brochure. Make sure your Web site address is on both.

- **Express interest.** Remember, other people are just as interested in networking as you are. So when you meet someone who may benefit you, send signals you're interested in getting to know this person better. Suggest lunch, hand over a business card, ask about a golf round, and so on.

- **Be positive.** Exude positive energy by smiling and being upbeat.

The Complementary Professional Network

One of the most effective strategies for turning your networking into business opportunities is building your Complementary Professional Network, or CPN. It's simply a group of close contacts (the "associated professionals" we talk about earlier) in professions that are not the same as yours, but which complement yours. For example, if you're a financial advisor, your complementary professionals would be other professionals who work with finance or investments: accountants, tax attorneys, mortgage brokers, bankers, real estate agents and stockbrokers. For advertising copywriters, complementary professionals would include graphic designers and commercial directors.

In building and nurturing your CPN, you're looking primarily for one thing: referrals. The idea is to create a pool of professionals with whom you can have a *quid pro quo* relationship, in which they refer clients to you and you return the favor for them. Entrenched CPNs sometimes go as far as coming up with special discount or benefit packages exclusively for members' office staffs.

Building a CPN demands some work. First, find the professionals. Then you've got to determine if you can trust them to take care of your referral clients like pure gold. Finally, you've got to formally propose a reciprocal referral relationship, with ground rules and benefits. In some states, there may be laws against rewarding professionals for referrals, so do your homework. Ask hard questions and talk to the customers of people you're considering as part of your CPN.

How formal you choose to make your CPN is up to you and its members. You can develop specific marketing tools, meetings and referral rewards, or you can make it no more complex than a promise of, "I'll have any clients who need your services call you." Either way, a rich, diverse CPN will be your greatest source of referral business.

Leveraging Your Network

Some tips and tricks for getting the most from your network of contacts:

- **Follow up right away.** The day after you meet someone potentially worthwhile, follow up with an e-mail or written note telling them how much you enjoyed your conversation and hope to do it again. Calling can make you seem desperate, so generally stick to the Internet or the USPS.

- **Keep them informed.** Even if you haven't done business with a contact yet, keep him in the loop about your activities—awards, new hires, expansion, etc. You might not want to put him on your monthly direct-mail list, but a letter or e-mail every couple of months is ideal.

- **Let them know about anything that builds your credibility.** You want your contacts to form a mental picture of you as trustworthy, professional and capable, so steer them to any information that completes that picture. That could mean telling them about a newspaper article in which you're quoted or giving them the names and numbers of a few happy clients to call.

- **Build a community.** Get your contacts together, whether it's via an online discussion board or a hosted lunch at a nice hotel. Get them talking, comparing notes and creating synergy, and you never know what can happen.

- **Be yourself.** If you're new to your business, say so. If you have an irrepressible sense of humor, tell an appropriate joke. People who appreciate who you are will be drawn to you, and will respect you for not being artificial. Sure, you won't attract everyone, but who ever said you'd get everyone as your customer in the first place?

Referrals: Your New Business Diamond Mine

Networking often leads to referrals, but referrals don't just come from networking. Referrals, as you probably know, are hands-down your best source of new business. Come on, what's better than having an existing client tell someone, "You've got to try my interior designer, she's incredible, here's her number"? Referrals have total credibility, since someone who would recommend you to a friend obviously thinks you're doing something right. A referral gives you a prospect who comes to you 95 percent sold, with no effort from you.

Why chase referrals?

1. Most people would rather find a new service provider through a referral than any other method, because of the trust.

2. Referrals are the most cost-effective way to build your business.

3. If you can mobilize your current clients to bring you referrals, you'll create a cadre of evangelists out there telling others how amazing you are.

The One Commandment of getting referrals is "Do a great job for your current clients and treat them like royalty." Send them gifts, do more than you promised, find innovative ways to save them money, remind them of anniversaries—whatever it takes to make them love you. No matter how small your budget, you can do this. Anyone can.

Be Active – Ask for the Referral!

So why don't more professionals cash in on referrals and get rich? Because they don't ask for the referral, that's why. Some businesspeople feel better about waiting for clients to refer new prospects on their own. This "passive referral" approach is never going to make you rich. Take the "active referral" approach: Ask for the referral! If you've been treating your customers right, they'll be *thrilled* to help you out.

One of the best ways to do this is to work a referral request into your Personal Postcard direct mailings (to your clients *only*) twice a year. When you mail to your clients, state candidly and politely that even if they don't have a need for your services right now, if they like what you've done for them, you would appreciate it if they would recommend you to friends and family. People like to help others, so more often than not they'll be delighted. Other methods of asking:

- Host a series of lunches or dinners for your best clients where you tell them you'd rather not be in the marketing business, so you'd love to count on them to help you grow your company. This reverse psychology will turn your guests into your personal army of marketing crusaders.

- Place a function on your Web site that allows visitors to "Tell a Friend" about you by entering e-mail addresses of people they know and sending them a pre-written message. As an incentive, you can enter site visitors in a contest for referring people.

Never be shy about asking for the referral. Often, it's the only way you'll get it.

Have a Referral System

The most successful companies have developed well-oiled machines for leveraging this valuable commodity. You've got to do the same. Our recommended components for a successful referral generation and management system:

- **Automate your direct mail.** As discussed, build at least two referral requests into your annual client direct-mail program.

- **Give clients materials to hand out.** You want to make the best possible first impression on the people whom your clients refer. To do this, make sure you give your clients a few copies of your Personal Brochure to hand out.

- **Make sure your Personal Brand is clear.** You want referring clients to be able to communicate clearly who you are and what you do. If you're not sure your brand is clear, ask your client to describe you.

- **Develop an incentive plan.** Offer your clients a program of incentives, such as restaurant gift certificates or movie tickets, for referring people to you who become paying customers.

- **Go out of your way to thank referring clients.** Clients who refer their friends or family are doing you a favor. Thank them accordingly, even if the referrals haven't turned into business yet. Send cards, gift baskets, bottles of champagne, etc.

- **Make sure old customers know how you're treating their friends.** This is so crucial, yet so few companies do it. People care about how you treat their friends or family, so update them. Send them a monthly progress report, complete with a quote from the referred client, and tell them how things are going. Even as an e-mail, it shows your older clients that you really care.

- **Have a customer-care system in place.** Most important of all, take care of referred clients like they're delicate flowers that will wilt without constant attention. Have a procedures manual that tells all your staff how to handle referral clients, from gifts to send to communications protocols. In short, do everything you can to make them love you as much as your current clients. Make sure everyone knows referral clients are their No. 1 priority, because if you handle them well, they'll refer their friends, and so on and so on and so on...

Treat People Like Trusted Friends

With networking and referrals, the bottom line is this: Treat people with respect, restraint, honest curiosity and empathy. People might ultimately decide to do business with you because of your skill, but they will only risk investing their time and effort if they like and trust you. So forget about selling. Don't "make contacts." Start relationships. Make friends. Make connections. The rest will take care of itself.

Personal Brand Case Study

Patti Glick
The Foot Nurse

Position: Friendly foot care for the workplace
Location: Cupertino, CA
Business: Foot-care consulting for businesses and organizations
Online: footnurse.com

A podiatric nurse who loved her field, Patti Glick faced a dilemma confronted by millions of working mothers: how to spend more time with her kids while continuing with her career. When a patients who worked for a company that managed health and fitness centers in corporations invited her to speak at her company about foot care, Glick made the connection. Today, she's the consultant and speaker of choice for public and private organizations whose people have jobs that stress their feet.

How It Started:

"My daughter had always called me the Foot Nurse," Glick says. "I thought, how in the world can I not continue doing this?" With her foot in the door (pardon the pun), Glick got her patient to refer her to other companies, and she got involved with local organizations in which corporations would meet and network.

When those corporations would open the floor to vendors, she would present her unique position: a foot nurse who helps people learn about their feet and how to make them feel their best. In the Silicon Valley's close-knit business community, word spread quickly.

Most Important Steps in Building a Personal Brand:

The "Foot Nurse" name (which she has service-marked) has been a huge benefit for Glick, instantly marking her as unique and different, and leveraging what she says is people's ingrained perception of nurses as kind and trustworthy. But the most important tactic Glick uses to get new business and speaking engagements is networking.

"I do a lot of networking," she says. "I attend a lot of networking meetings, though it's not an area I feel overly comfortable with. I also do a lot of cold calling. I could just call up a company and say, 'Do you have somebody in charge of a health and wellness program?'—"

Part of Glick's success also lies in her ability to capitalize on the fact that what she does is both unusual and close to the heart of anyone who has ever suffered from aching feet. Her "My aching feet—is it my feet or my shoes?" seminar is a perfect example. Her first year in business, 1996, she did about 24 talks. Now she does as many as twice that per year for such clients as America Online, Cisco Systems and Pacific Gas & Electric.

Biggest Success:

"For me, it's the cold calls," she says. "I also do foot-safety training with cities, counties, and water districts. Those people have employees on their feet all day, every day. It was a matter of calling water districts in Oakland. The safety manager flipped when he heard me. He said, 'I knew they had to be somebody out there like you!'

"People *don't* know there's anyone out there like me. When I cold call, if they have money and people with foot-intensive jobs, they're interested. Plus, you don't see a lot of nurses going into podiatry who have seen the surgical and office side."

On Personal Branding and the Web:

"One of the best things that ever happened to me was building my Web site through Big Step.com. I got very involved with the company as a user, and they ended up promoting my business as an example of what they could do for a businessperson. I had so much fun with it. And I got an article in *Inc.* Magazine! That's been the best thing I've done. I have a place to send people for information."

Advice:

"Create a memorable name. People don't remember Patty Glick the nurse, but they remember the Foot Nurse. I can go somewhere and people will say, 'You're the Foot Nurse, I've heard of you!' That blows me away."

Brandstorming Networking and Referrals:
10 Great Things You Can Do Right Now

1. List current clients who have the best potential for generating referrals.

2. Create a Complementary Professional Network database of professionals or business owners you already know.

3. Research networking groups or professional associations in your own line of work and in complementary professions.

4. Contact those organizations for information on the kinds of speakers they're seeking.

5. Create a six-month calendar of networking events.

6. Begin creating an incentive program for people who give you referrals—rewards you give, what type of referral gets which reward, etc.

7. Develop a referral customer-care program to ensure your staff treats referral customers like royalty.

8. Make a list of the businesses you've referred people to in the last year. Time for some *quid pro quo.*

9. Check your wardrobe. Is it appropriate for your networking events?

10. Rehearse your "elevator pitch."

Bottom Line No. 15: How Personal Branding Equals More Business
Networking in all the right places

Situation: You're a painter, and while your work has been well received and gets good reviews when it's exhibited, you've been unable to land that plum selling and publicity opportunity: your own show in a prominent gallery. This hurts your ability not only to further your art, but to also make a living. You're not content to be a starving artist, nor to watch less talented hacks surpass you because they have the right contacts.

Solution: You decide to get the right contacts. Never a social butterfly before, you start investigating opportunities for networking in your city and find several promising ones: a busy calendar of theater, music and museum events; several non-profit boards that work with charity causes; half a dozen new gallery shows and exhibit openings around the city each month; and regular discussion panels on fine and visual art held at your local university. You get involved in all of these, creating a master calendar to schedule your time and designing and printing funky, odd-sized business cards with your Personal Logo and a sample of your work.

Result: You throw yourself into the networking fray, and as a result you meet a wide range of philanthropists and art patrons, gallery owners, critics, business leaders, and influential people in the arts. You approach them as people and lovers of the creative arts, never as people who can advance your career, and you hone your skills so within a month you've become a charming conversationalist. You hand out business cards, people you meet discover your work on your Web site, and because they like you, they begin to contact you about exhibiting your paintings. The ball is rolling, thanks to your aggressive networking strategy.

Brand Surgery: Avoiding Tragic Branding Mistakes
The Patient: Your Networking Contacts

• Don't ask for their business five minutes after you meet them.

• Don't "just happen" to have Personal Branding materials with you. People aren't stupid. Tell them you brought Personal Brochure copies in case you met people of interest.

• Don't just focus on what they can do for you.

- Don't monopolize people. No matter how valuable they could be as contacts, tag them and let them fly away free after a few minutes. This lets you both move on to someone else.

- Don't talk about how much money you make.

- Don't ask newly referred clients for referrals before you've even done anything for them. You've got to perform before you can harvest.

- Don't panic. You may well meet, wine and dine valuable contacts, and be referred to 50 potential new clients without a single bit of new business happening for six months. It's normal. Things take time. Stay cool and don't start calling contacts or you'll seem desperate. If you know you've treated people well, in time the networking and referrals will pay off—most likely in a sudden flood of new business.

CHAPTER 16

Still More Tools

Advertising, Catalogs, CD-ROMs

We're just about finished with our tour of the major Personal Branding tools. The ones we've discussed so far are proven to work for anyone who applies them with consistency, an eye on quality, and a clear sense of what the target market wants and needs. But if you're looking for the edge that some less-common branding tactics can give you, here are a few tools to consider.

Advertising

At some level, the buying of advertising space in a publication is a costly proposition for most businesses. There are five major types:

- Newspaper and magazine
- Radio
- Television
- Outdoor
- Online

Newspaper and Magazine

This is the most common sort of advertising for small companies. Buying ad space in a regional newspaper or trade magazine lets you target a specific set of readers, whether it's area residents or professionals in a certain industry. Such advertising also allows you to get your Personal Branding message out to thousands or tens of thousands of people at a time—and usually more than once, since all publications give discounts for buying space in multiple issues.

Pros

- High visibility and therefore a great credibility builder
- Large target market coverage

- Small regional publications can be very cost-effective

- Allows some targeting by readership

- Publications usually have strong demographic information

Cons
- Poor direct-response tool as few people will call

- Difficult to gauge results

- Your ad competes with many others in the same publication

- Large publications can be costly, or require buys in multiple issues

- Requires hiring an ad agency or design firm

Radio

Many people assume radio is beyond their budget, but that's not always correct. There are many radio stations—small local stations, college stations, public radio—that accept either advertising or underwriting of programming for fees that are very reasonable. You won't be hitting 500,000 listeners at drive time, but you can establish a presence on radio—and the instant credibility that goes with it—for a lot less than you've probably imagined.

Pros
- Covers even larger target market than print, at times when they have little to do but listen

- Confers a sense of success and legitimacy to your business

- Can use scripts, actors and music to drive home your Personal Brand in a more powerful way

- Target market cannot listen to another ad while yours is running

Cons
- Poor direct-response tool

- Sometimes requires professional production and performance talent, which can be expensive

- Can become audio "wallpaper," easily ignored by listeners

- Doesn't generally allow easy targeting because anyone can listen

Television

Advertising on TV is something most small business owners don't even consider; they assume it's too expensive by far. For some, it is. But with the profusion of cable stations and local channels, TV advertising has become much more accessible to businesses without massive budgets and in-house production studios. Most cable systems have one or more community channels on which they air local news, interviews with area personalities, and so on. These are perfect outlets for your advertising. Also, your area cable operator may be able to sell you advertising time for a very specific, limited segment of your city or county. Rather than paying to reach a million people, you pay to reach 10,000. It's possible.

Pros

- Best visibility- and credibility-building tool available

- Extensive target market coverage possible

- Region-specific buys can target geographic areas

- Gives you even greater credibility than radio

- Allows you to communicate your Personal Brand even more strongly

Cons

- Very difficult direct-response tool; hard to recoup your investment

- Also requires professional production and talent, which can get very expensive

- Local channels may have odd hours or little viewing target market

- Producing TV commercials can be very time-consuming

Outdoor

Billboards, bus-stop shelters, the sides of buses—these are some of the common places you'll find outdoor advertising. There's a fine line between commerce and civic blight, so we urge you to be judicious in how you advertise outdoors. But it can be very useful in making your presence known and establishing your Personal Brand over the long term. Much like Yellow Pages ads, outdoor ads are frequently something you buy and leave alone, so after six months you "own" (in the public's mind at least) the billboard at the corner of First and Main.

Don't forget the most important piece of outdoor advertising you'll ever have: your signage. Whether you have a curbside sign or a sign on your building, great signage should be your first investment in outdoor advertising. Make sure you check with your city to find out what kind of signage is allowable.

Pros

- Highly visible

- Up 24/7 for maximum Personal Brand exposure

- Usually cost-effective

- You can buy multiple locations around town for savings

Cons

- Difficult to gauge results

- Can lose impact over time, and fail to be noticed

- Subject to vandalism

Online

- Traditional online advertising is a waste of time. Banners simply don't work. If you want to advertise online, consider purchasing search keywords from a Web site like Google or Overture. For a fee, you can be among the top search results returned when a Web user searches using one of the words you've purchased.

Pros

- Most users find what they need via search

- Targeted

- You pay only for search results

Cons

- Not all clients use search engines

- Some users distrust paid search results

Step-By-Step

- Contact whatever media you're thinking about advertising with and get a media kit. It's a package of information about advertising—costs, demographics, sample ads, etc. It will tell you what you'll spend and what you'll get.

- Once you decide where you'll advertise, contact an ad sales rep and start negotiating. Much of the time, ad rates are negotiable, though it really depends on how prosperous the medium is. On the Web, you can almost set your own price, and on local radio, it may be the same. If there's a public radio or TV station in your area, consider underwriting. These public outlets don't accept commercials, but they do allow companies to pay for all or part of a program in return for an on-air mention. It's very prestigious, so depending on your target market, check it out.

- After you've set a rate and signed your contract, you'll need to contract with one or more professionals to create your ads. For print and outdoor, you'll need a writer and designer. For radio and TV, you'll need a writer, a production studio (which will usually be able to recommend directors and producers), and talent such as voice-over actors or on-camera actors. For online ads, you'll need a Web designer.

- Write your ad with your goal in mind. Is it to create awareness? Generate phone calls? Publicize an event? No matter what you do, make sure you prominently place your phone number and Web address in print and outdoor ads, and repeat that information at least twice in radio and TV.

- Keep it simple. You don't have a big budget, especially for radio or TV. So keep the ads straightforward: who you are, what you do, how you create value.

- Don't do your own voice-over work. Appearing on camera, if you're relatively comfortable, can work. It's worked for millions of local businesses. But most people on radio sound like they're reading a script. Hire professionals.

Catalogs

Back to something not quite so scary: the ever-popular product or service catalog. It's surprising how many companies forget about this humble yet useful tool for selling their services. Admittedly, it's not appropriate for some businesses; can you see an attorney mailing out a catalog of "Fine Imported Criminal-Defense Motions"? But for retailers, craftsmen, contractors, clothing or interior designers, caterers—anyone with an extensive line of products or services—an all-encompassing catalog can be a wonderful complement to a Personal Brochure.

Step-by-Step

- What will go in your catalog? The essentials: a compelling cover, a personal letter from you as an introduction, a table of contents, detailed descriptions of your products/services, prices, an order form. Your design should include your phone number and Web address on every page, and you should come up with five or six special promotional offers to place throughout the catalog. Also, some businesses bind in a Business Reply Card, to allow recipients to send back a survey or special request.

• Design your catalog to coordinate with your Personal Brochure. This helps reinforce your Personal Brand.

• How many pages will your catalog have? It should have at least eight, but try to get 16 if you can.

• Print on thinner paper than you would use for your brochure, 80 or 100 lb. book stock, full color. Make sure your designer formats the piece so it can be mailed without an envelope.

• Use the front and back covers to promote special offers and savings in bold type with powerful graphics.

• Mail catalogs once a year, unless your offerings change dramatically.

CD-ROMs

Corporations still use CD-ROMs for presentations, press kits, demos, and interactive brochures. There are many uses for a CD-ROM, but is this tool for your business? More often than not, the answer is yes. Conservative professions like law, accounting, corporate consulting, and banking can use a professionally produced CD-ROM for presentations, while creative businesses like writing, design, and Web development often use them as creative portfolios. Contractors, architects, and interior designers use them as part-portfolio, part-instructional manual for their clients, and real estate agents use them to showcase properties. A quality CD-ROM can be a powerful complement to your Personal Brochure or Web site.

By far the biggest challenge with a CD-ROM is getting the recipient to use it. Studies show only 5 percent to 10 percent of promotional CD-ROMs are ever loaded, a very poor return on your investment. More often, you're paying for the "wow" factor that comes with the "look" of the CD and its fancy packaging. If you do want your CD-ROM to be used, they tend to work best with people in tech-savvy businesses: computers, the Internet, automotive, etc.

Step-by-Step

• What kind of CD-ROM do you want to create? There are four basic categories: presentations, such as PowerPoint slide shows; demos, which use video or animation to show how products or factory machinery works; portfolios, which are electronic samples of your work; and manuals, which tell your clients how to do something, from appraising their home to hiring a contractor. You can also use a CD-ROM to create an Electronic Press Kit (EPK), which contains your press releases, photos and other information in a format any journalist can access.

- You need to hire a multimedia developer, and possibly a writer, to create your CD-ROM. Your developer will work with you to create a content map and do the design and programming that bring your CD to life. Once the work is done, you'll get a gold master CD-ROM.

- Take your gold master to a CD replication service. A reputable company will do three things for you: duplicate as many copies of your CD as you need, design and print an attractive sleeve or booklet insert (which can also be designed by your brochure designer), and deliver the whole thing in an audio CD-style jewel case.

Personal Brand Case Study

Marty Rodriguez
Century 21 Marty Rodriguez Real Estate

Position: The world's most successful REALTOR®
Location: Glendora, CA
Business: Real estate agent
Online: cmarty21.com

Is Marty Rodriguez the world's greatest REALTOR®? By many yardsticks, yes. She's the No. 1 agent for the nation's top residential realty firm, Century 21, which has recognized her not only as its top producer in America, but worldwide. Marty's name has become "top of mind" to home sellers in California's San Gabriel Valley.

In a bad year, Rodriguez sells a home a day. In a hot market, she'll close 450 (or more) transactions annually. It's an astonishing pace, and you might think Rodriguez's life is all real estate. It is, and she loves it.

Century 21 certainly appreciates Rodriguez. In 1996, they created a franchise for her when she mulled leaving the company. In the last few years, she's been honored by *Hispanic Business* as one of America's 100 Most Influential Latino Businesspersons, has co-authored *The Complete Idiot's Guide to Online Buying and Selling a Home*, and has been profiled in *Fast Company*.

How It Started:

One of 11 children raised in a two-bedroom, one-bath home, Rodriguez discovered her zest for sales in Catholic school, selling more candy and Christmas cards than her classmates. When her husband Ed began building spec homes in the late 1970s, she got her real estate license, so she could sell them.

Her first six years in the business amounted to a learning curve. She and her husband were building a custom home, her children were young, and her business partner was carrying a sack of personal problems. As the crash of the late 1980s weeded out dilettantes and hobbyists from the profession, she asked herself, "What do I have to do to stay in business when everybody is going out of business?"

Rodriguez quickly learned the answer: The successful REALTORS® were not always the best salespeople, but they were the best at building their Personal Brands.

Most Important Steps in Building a Personal Brand:

What is Personal Branding to Rodriguez? "I think it's just a matter of being everywhere," she says. And everywhere she is. Rodriguez and her agents practice rigorous warm calling, because keeping in touch with past and present clients means protecting leads. That personal contact complements steady direct mail: regular "just listed/just sold" cards drip to past and future clients.

Advertising keeps her in the public eye, and so do public relations and networking. In addition to ongoing newspaper and magazine stories, she sponsors the Marty Rodriguez Scholarship Fund for San Gabriel Valley students, and networks nationally among leading Hispanic entrepreneurs.

Biggest Success:

Rodriguez has built her franchise, Century 21 Marty Rodriguez Real Estate, around one concept: Everybody does only what he or she does best. Each employee makes the most of a single focused attribute. Her buyers' agents don't prospect for listings, her marketing manager doesn't troubleshoot computers, and her listing coordinator doesn't perform inspections or run around removing lock boxes. Marty herself just sells properties. In simplicity is performance.

This business structure wasn't the product of any coaching session, but of Rodriguez's own vision. "There was nobody in this area that thought what I thought," she explains. After seeing her colleagues burn out from trying to do everything at once, she took a different tack.

"I learned to delegate," she notes. "I don't cook, I don't do housework, I don't open the mail, I don't manage my own money. I focus on real estate."

On Personal Branding and Generating Referrals:

"I get calls from people I don't even know," Rodriguez says, citing a mortgage broker who brought her a ready buyer out of the blue. "She just sold my reputation," she notes. For that favor, the mortgage broker will get either a gift certificate or a check in appreciation.

Advice:

"Interview people who really do well in the business so you know what you're really supposed to do. Learn what they don't teach you in real estate school; learn about the real effort and commitment necessary to stand out."

Brandstorming Other Tools:
6 Great Things You Can Do Right Now

1. If you have your new Personal Logo, design your new signage.

2. Contact local publications to see if any are willing to barter services for advertising.

3. Survey your city for ideal locations for outdoor advertising.

4. Look at other non-traditional marketing tools your competitors are using.

5. If you're interested in making a CD-ROM, purchase a CD burner.

6. If you're interested in doing a catalog, look into the cost of an in-house binding system such as coil binding. If you run many catalogs regularly, this can save you time and money.

Bottom Line No. 16: How Personal Branding Equals More Business
Turning a product catalog into new business

Situation: You're a fashion designer in Seattle, working on your own to design funky footwear for local boutiques, but you want to grow. You know there's more money to be made by selling your shoes to boutiques and distributors all down the West Coast, but you don't have the budget to advertise, and so far phone calls have been a waste of your time.

Solution: You hire a friend who's a professional graphic designer to design a 16-page catalog to promote your footwear line. In it, you talk about your background, the genesis of your design ideas, and you shoot tons of great digital photos of your shoes worn by models that you pick off the street—real people, not professionals. For your design, you put the emphasis on "real," creative and daring, hoping to catch the attention of buyers and store owners. You've already got a good Web site, so you offer a 20 percent discount on orders placed online. You print, compile your own mailing list of about 300 shops and distributors, and mail.

Result: The combination of ultra-cool catalog, real-world models, and convenient Web site increases orders by 300 percent in just eight weeks. Better still, you're getting orders from San Francisco, San Diego and Beverly Hills, and you've got meetings with several major retailers in Southern California. You use some of the incoming revenue to enhance your Web site, do another mailing, and you're off and running (no pun intended).

Brand Surgery: Avoiding Tragic Branding Mistakes
The Patient: Using Other Marketing Tools

- Be wary of "group" advertising deals, where a bunch of similar businesses pool their money to buy ad space. All this will do is tell readers you're just like the others.

- When considering Web advertising or sponsorship, don't rely on the total number of users the site owners say they have. You need to know *unique* visitors.

- If you do advertise, don't get too clever. Clever ads might win awards, but people will remember the ad, not your business. Focus on clearly telling people how they can benefit from choosing you, and make it easy for them to contact you.

- Don't go cheap on your catalog design or printing. It makes your products look cheap.

- Make sure the majority of your prospects are computer users before you produce an expensive CD-ROM.

the brand called YOU

Part Five:
Establishing Your Personal Brand in 12 Months

Write Your One-Year Branding and Marketing Plan

Now that you have a basic understanding of Personal Branding, including the tools and forces that make it work, we're going to walk you through the development of your actual Personal Brand with the step-by-step writing of your One-Year Branding and Marketing Plan.

This can be a complex process, filled with detailed interviews, charting of people's responses, and analysis of where your public image falls on a curve. But we've tried to keep it simple, because Personal Branding isn't an exact science. There is a specific process you'll need to follow, but it's something you can do in a day if you dedicate the time, or in a week if you take it piecemeal.

Writing Your One-Year Marketing and Branding Plan Step-By-Step

Part I: Determine Your Personal Brand

1. Brand Assessment: What is your Personal Identity today?

2. Goal Setting: What are your personal and professional goals?

3. Brand Objective: What do you want your Personal Brand to accomplish?

Part II: Refine Your Personal Brand

1. Select your target market

2. Determine your specialization

3. Write your positioning and Personal Branding Statement

4. Determine your Leading Attribute

Part III: Launch Your Personal Brand
1. Branding Strategy
    - Target markets
    - Branding channels
    - Message
    - Tools and timing
    - Strategy document

2. Budget

3. Action Plan/Marketing Timetable

PART I: DETERMINE YOUR PERSONAL BRAND

Your Personal Brand must reflect four ideas:

1. **Your brand objective**
2. **Your personal and professional goals**
3. **Your message**
4. **Your methods**

1. Brand Assessment: What is your Personal Identity today?

You already have a Personal Brand. Your customers and prospects already have an image of you, perceive your abilities in a certain way, and have a few words that come to mind when your name comes up. So you're not working in a vacuum.

This can be a mixed blessing. On one hand, clients may hold a strong, positive perception that's in line with what you would like your Personal Brand to be. On the other, some parts of your target market may hold misperceptions about you that are damaging to your career. Before you set out to create your Personal Brand, you need to know what kind of "brand baggage" you're hauling.

Talk to people. Interview folks in your professional sphere: clients, colleagues, prospects, business leaders you may know, members of the media, and so on. Ask them what comes to mind when they hear your name, what values they associate with you, what they *think* your strengths are. Ask them to describe the work you do in five words or less. What you should get from this process:

- Which words or phrases come up repeatedly?

- What do people tell you about yourself that you didn't know?

- How does the way people say you create value differ from the way you think you create value?

How much does the perception of others—your current personal image—deviate from how you think you're perceived, and from how you want to be perceived? Track this information by creating three columns on a sheet of paper like so:

A. How I think I'm perceived	B. How I am perceived	C. How I want to be perceived

Fill in columns A and C before you start interviewing, and fill in B when you're finished with your interviews. Then look at the difference between the three. Is there not much difference? Then you don't have to work very hard to change perceptions with your Personal Brand, you just need to reinforce them.

If there's a big difference, then you must build a Personal Brand that closes the gap—especially between B and C. And the bigger the difference, the harder your brand needs to work.

Changing People's Perceptions

Most likely, you'll be somewhere in the middle. You'll end up with a list of three or four strong ideas from your interviews, and two will be right on with how you want to be perceived, one will be slightly off, and one will be way off. Ninety percent of business owners and professionals fall into that category, and if you do, you don't need to do anything extraordinary. Just create your Personal Brand with care and market it with originality and persistence.

How We Evaluate Personal Brands

When we're contracted to evaluate and strategize for Personal Brands, here is how we conduct a Personal Brand evaluation.

1. **Icon Status**—Does the person represent a concept larger than himself or herself? If so, how clear is that representation, and does anyone else share it?

2. **Reach**—How large is the Personal Brand's sphere of influence, and how well-known is the person within it?

3. **Influence**—Within his or her sphere, how much influence does the Personal Brand wield?

4. **Revenue**—How much revenue was the Personal Brand responsible for, directly or indirectly, in the last calendar year?.

5. **Goodwill**—What is the level of goodwill toward the Personal Brand? Goodwill is the difference between a *great* and a *powerful* Personal Brand.

2. Goal Setting: What are your personal and professional goals?

Your brand needs to take you where you want to be as a person and as a professional. It's important to create a brand that fits with your lifestyle, the type of people you like to work with, how you want to manage your time, and so on. So determine what you want from your business or professional life in two areas:

Your Goals:
• How much money do you want to make in a year?

• In five years?

• Do you want to hire employees?

• If you have employees, do you want to grow further?

• How many hours per week are you prepared to spend working?

• Do you eventually want to sell your business?

• What would you like your lifestyle to be in five years?

• Would you like to retire, and when?

Your Methods:
• Do you want to work closely with others or in solitude?

• Do you want to work at home or in an office?

• Will you interact with clients in person, or by phone and e-mail?

• Are you candid and critical, conservative and discrete, or in between?

• Must you be the leader, or would you rather take direction?

• Are you fast, or do you take your time?

Does the brand you desire have room for growth, so you can reach your financial goals? Or does it have the potential for too much growth, making it impossible for you to remain a one-person operation? Does your brand of choice tie you too closely to the business, so if you choose to sell in the future, the business won't have any value unless you go with it? Will your brand require you to travel half the year when you'd rather work at home by e-mail? Consider all your answers carefully as you hone your Personal Brand.

3. Brand Objective: What do you want your Personal Brand to accomplish?

A brand objective is different from a goal. Goals usually center on income, accomplishments and lifestyle, whereas your brand objective determines how you will be known as your Personal Brand takes shape.

Your Brand Objective:

- Which word or phrase would you like your target market to use when describing you?

- What do you want to be known for in your profession?

- What emotions would you like your brand to produce in people?

- Which major accomplishment do you most want to share?

- How do you want to be remembered?

PART II: REFINE YOUR PERSONAL BRAND

At this stage, you're got the basics written down. Next, we figure out the main elements of your brand. At the end, you should have a single Personal Brand Statement, a target market, and a Leading Attribute written down; then you'll be ready to look at launching your brand. This process includes all the key components of any Personal Brand:

- Target market—Who your customers are

- Specialization—How you work with them

- Leading Attribute—The single idea you want to be known for in your market

- Positioning—How they label you

1. Select Your Target Market

Refinement starts here because you can't finish your brand until you know the target market. Take a close look at the types of customers you've been working with over the past year or two and answer these questions:

- Which clients produce the highest hourly earnings?
- Which clients generate the most referrals?
- Which prospects seem most receptive to my work style?
- Which prospects have the potential to make me the most money?
- Which prospects have the most growth potential?
- Which people do I enjoy working with most?
- Which prospects do I have the most in common with, in terms of lifestyle and personality?

You'll have several groups of existing clients and prospects written down. Pick the one that offers the most opportunity and pose these four questions:

- Does it have the potential to increase my income?
- Do its members need what I can provide?
- Based on their culture, values and background, will they perceive the value in my Personal Brand?
- Can I afford to market to this group?

If the answers are all "yes," you've got your target market. If not, set that group aside for later and choose another that passes the test. Examples of target markets:

- Divorced men
- Boat owners
- Southwestern advertising agencies
- Residents of a certain gated community
- Long-distance commuters
- Educators
- Pacific Islanders
- Retired professional athletes

2. Determine your specialization

As we've said, specialization is the key to people attaching unique value to what you offer. In a world where too many people try to be all things to every consumer, being a specialist gives you much greater credibility, and makes your Unique Value Proposition, or UVP, that much stronger.

Follow the steps laid out in Chapter 6:

1. Choose your target market. See above.

2. Figure out how to tailor your service to that market.

3. Establish your business model to fit your market.

3. Write Your Positioning and Personal Branding Statement

Unlike specialization, which deals with how you work with clients and the services you provide, positioning deals with the mind and how you're perceived. This is where you define the way you want clients, prospects, and your sphere of influence to think of you.

As discussed in Chapter 7, positioning involves determining who you are, what you do, and your Unique Value Proposition, with a touch of lifestyle or personality thrown in for flavor.

Who You Are

"An architect" is not a good answer. "A designer of eco-friendly residences" is. Why? Because it takes the professional out of a generic realm occupied by thousands of other architects, and makes him or her into a specialist, a purveyor of a service offered by a much smaller group. There's less competition, and more room to grab market share. Plus, it instantly tells the prospect, to some degree, what the architect does.

Figuring out who you are:

• Look at your profession and all the things you do as part of it.

• Look at the aspect of your work at which you excel.

• Look at the area where you generate most of your income.

• Figure out the service you could provide that's in the highest demand.

Then write it all out. If you're a graphic designer, and you love logo design, get 70 percent of your income from working with ad agencies, and know the big demand in your area is for packaging design, you could write your "who you are" statement this way:

"An experienced designer of consumer marketing..."

The idea is to hint at your core skill without limiting you too much. You don't want some prospect to stick you in a narrow niche and only consider you for a small range of work when you can do more.

What You Do

This describes how you approach your work and how you want prospects to view the services you provide. Here, focus only on your target market, and be sure to take into account your specialization.

Factors to look at:

• The three or four specific, high-value services you provide

• For whom you provide them (we're not looking for a target market statement, but a descriptive statement that paints a picture of the people or companies who are your ideal customers)

• How you work with customers—fast, personal, casual, etc.

Write it out and play with combinations. You're looking for a verbal picture of the most important, most valued things you do for your most lucrative, most enjoyable clients. If you were our packaging designer, you'd fill in the blanks this way:

• Services: innovative packaging concepts; bold, creative logo design; merchandising consulting

• Customers: Creative advertising agencies and consumer-goods companies

• Work style: intensely creative, collaborative, fast-paced

The result for our fictional designer:

> "...specializing in product packaging and logos for innovative ad agencies and design shops..."

The "innovative" description tells prospects whether they're right for this designer, and also says he is innovative.

Unique Value Proposition

What do your clients gain from working with you? Be specific. It does our tree-hugging architect no good to tell prospects he gives them "the house of their dreams." But if his value statement is, "Creating homes designed for simplicity, sustainable living, and spiritual beauty," that's strong stuff to the right target market. Value is emotional as well as intellectual.

What do you do for your clients or customers? What problems do you help them solve? How do you improve their lives or businesses? How do you make things easier or more rewarding for them, or prevent or help them through a crisis? That's the information you need.

Now our designer might write this:

> "...who want to look like geniuses by transforming how their clients merchandise their products."

The statement addresses both the desire of the ad agencies (emotion and ego) and what they aspire to do for their clients. The designer suggests he can make it happen. That's value.

Lifestyle or Personality

Finally, this is a Personal Brand we're positioning. So we can't finish without adding appropriate elements of you as a person. These can be your education, your family background, your religion, your lifestyle, your hobbies—whatever is genuine and stands the best chance of appealing to your target market. Some lifestyle/personality components we've seen in Personal Brands:

- Beach bum

- Harvard graduate

- Classic-car collector

- Former Air Force pilot

- Native of Paraguay

For our fictional graphic designer, we'll choose beach bum, or for something more polished, "coast-loving."

Your Personal Brand Statement

Time to pull everything together. Write down the components of your position:

- Who you are

- What you do

- Unique Value Proposition

- Lifestyle or personality

The ultimate product of all this work is your *Personal Brand Statement*, or PBS. That's a single, concise statement of your position, summing you up in a few words. Essentially, your PBS *is* your Personal Brand.

Our designer's rough Personal Branding Statement:

> "An experienced, coast-loving designer of consumer marketing, specializing in product packaging and logos for innovative ad agencies and design shops who want to look like geniuses by transforming how their clients merchandise and sell their products."

Too long, but we'll edit. Remember, your PBS is not a marketing slogan. Few people other than you and your team will ever see it. Instead, the PBS is a compass to guide you as you launch and market your Personal Brand. It should remind you of the identity you're working to build and the perceptions you're trying to create. Check all the branding work you do against it. If any idea, no matter how cherished, doesn't fit your PBS, dump it and start over.

Let's pare down our designer's rather lengthy statement:

> "A coast-loving designer specializing in product packaging and logos for daring creative agencies seeking to transform how clients merchandise products."

This PBS tells you what this person does, whom he does it for, his specialty, work style, personal passion, and how he creates value for his clients. Not bad for 22 words.

Work with your PBS over a few days, and show it to friends and colleagues. Incorporate changes, polish and tweak. Once you have something you can look at without wanting to change every week, carve it in stone. That's your Personal Brand. Get to love it; you're going to be together a long time.

4. Determine Your Leading Attribute

As we discussed in an earlier chapter, your Leading Attribute is the single clear idea that should come to people's minds instantly when you have a strong Personal Brand, as in "John Wayne = All-American Movie Tough Guy."

But since you already have your PBS and have established your Personal Brand, why worry about your Leading Attribute? First, it's useful to have a way to communicate your brand quickly and clearly in a few seconds; this is your "elevator pitch," because in theory, you could use it to tell a prospect about you during a brief ride to the 18th floor. It's ideal for business cards, outdoor advertising, photo captions, for broadcast interviewers giving listeners a quick description of you, and for you when meeting new contacts.

Second, it's a wonderful way to gauge how well your Personal Brand is catching on in your market, and how clear your message is. Remember, the Leading Attribute is how you want prospects and key influencers to think about you and describe you to others. So by listening, reading trade publications and monitoring your "buzz," you can quickly discover whether or not people are talking about you in the right way. If not, you can take appropriate action.

To find your Leading Attribute, simply look at your PBS and pull out the single powerful idea you want to be known for, the thing you'd like to appear in the first line of your obituary. For our now-familiar designer, his Leading Attribute would be:

"Audacious consumer packaging and logo designer"

Simple, quick and a little descriptive, his Leading Attribute tells people exactly who he is and what he does without wasting anyone's time. These days, that's grounds for sainthood.

PART III: LAUNCH YOUR PERSONAL BRAND

1. Branding Strategy

This is where Personal Branding turns into Personal Marketing. You've got your brand; now you've gotta sell it. If you've never thought about marketing strategy before, this may seem intimidating. It isn't. Despite what you hear from big branding agencies trying to pump up their fees, the strategy is very simple at its core. You need to decide four things:

1. Which target market to pursue

2. Which channels to use to deliver your Personal Brand message

3. What message to deliver

4. The tools and the timing

Target markets

You probably have more than one, grouped by geographic area, industry, or just the fact you don't want to deal with more than 500 prospects at a time (good move). Figure out which ones you want to market to now, as you launch your Personal Brand. We recommend choosing no more than three, and prioritizing them, with your most important and potentially lucrative target market being the first to get your branding message.

Branding channels

The channels you use will depend on your budget, but also on what's likely to work for your target market. Busy corporate executives generally don't read their own mail, so direct mail is probably a waste for them, while it's ideal if you're marketing to households.

Regardless of your target market, you should always use these channels:

• Brand identity (Personal Logo, stationery, signage, etc.)

• Personal Brochure

• Direct mail

• Web site

Beyond those, it's your call, based on available money and time. We recommend PR and networking for everyone, since they're low-cost. Remember, you can always add or change channels as you go. Your available channels:

1. Client Referrals
2. Direct Mail
3. Networking
4. Professional Referrals
5. Seminars
6. Public Relations and Sponsorships
7. Warm Calling
8. World Wide Web
9. Advertising
10. Outdoor Advertising
11. Radio Advertising
12. Television Advertising
13. Tradeshows and Special Events

Message

At brand launch, keep your message straightforward and simple: This is who I am, this is what I do, this is how I can help you, this is how to contact me. How you say that is entirely up to you, and that's where the choices come. Working with your writer and designer, you need to decide how you'll convey those ideas. Will it be with strong graphics and little text? With a lengthy story? With a short, punchy slogan and edgy photographs?

Your decision depends on your profession and the prospects you're pursuing. But a good general guideline is: Launch your Personal Brand with a broad, simple message you can build on in coming months. For example, if you're a personal trainer, you might launch your brand with a direct mailer that has this hook: "10 Things the Diet Companies Don't Want You to Know About Losing Weight," revealing No. 1 in this mailing, and so on. You've just introduced your Personal Brand and set the recipient up for nine other deep, dark dieting secrets to be revealed in future mailings.

Remember, the most important things your message can do are differentiate you from your competition, convey how you create value, and make an intellectual or emotional connection with your target market.

Tools and Timing

The channels you choose will dictate the marketing tools to use. For instance, if you're going to use direct mail, you'll likely use Personal Postcards. Personal contact and networking will require business cards and a Personal Brochure, while using PR will mean creating a media kit. Identify your channels and choose the tools you'll need to leverage each channel, focusing on balance and available resources.

Tools Checklist

- Personal Brochure
- Personal Postcard
- Direct-mail cards, letters, and newsletters
- Personal Logo
- Personal Web Site
- Business card
- Stationery system
- Signage
- Press releases
- Publishing articles or books

- Publishing "special reports"
- Speaking
- Audio tapes and CDs
- Direct e-mail
- Print advertising
- Broadcast advertising
- Outdoor advertising
- Search engine keywords
- Catalog
- CD-ROM

Put an automatic schedule in place for your entire Personal Brand marketing program: press-release mailings, thank-you cards, awards entries, travel plans to conferences, and so on. It's best to plan things monthly.

When is the best time to launch your brand? Certainly, you don't want to launch at a busy time of year, unless your business is geared to that time of year (gift baskets during the Christmas season, for instance). You should also avoid times of chaos or change in your industry, such as scandals or major stock market downturns, unless you're in business to address these problems.

Most important, don't launch when a competitor is busting out a major marketing push of his or her own. That's why it's crucial to keep track of what your competition is doing. When they zig, you zag. Let them exhaust the novelty of what they're doing, and evaluate their marketing for weaknesses. Then make your move.

Strategy document

Now write down all four categories. An example for a fictional corporate sales trainer:

- Target markets: 1) West Coast insurance firms, 2) Texas insurance firms, 3) Mortgage lenders over 500 employees

- Branding channels: Company identity, direct mail, direct e-mail, Web, publishing, and networking

- Message: I'm a specialist in organization and lead management for sales professionals who want to maximize their per-hour compensation.

- Tools and timing: Personal Brochure, Personal Postcard, e-mail messages, ghostwritten articles published quarterly in two trade publications, at least six networking events per month (where I'll hand out brochures). Mailings will be monthly, and I'll launch my brand campaign after the summer national sales meetings, when most of my prospects will set their new sales goals.

2. Budget

How much should you spend marketing your Personal Brand? Successful brands usually spend between 15 percent and 25 percent of their total income on marketing their Personal Brand. If that seems like a lot, you're right. But it's necessary. You're dropping your brand into a crowded pool and hoping it swims. That takes high-quality marketing tools and consistency. That means money.

What you spend to develop your Personal Brand is the most important business investment you'll ever make, so if you can, spend aggressively. Make two budgets:

1. A launch budget to cover the high initial costs—printing; paying writers, designers and Web developers; buying mailing lists; new signage; etc.

2. A monthly budget to cover your monthly marketing costs—staff, postage, photocopies, overprinting on Personal Postcards, travel, etc.

Costs to consider and where to find the numbers:

Expense	Info Source
Printing	Shop same job to 3+ printers
Photography	Get quotes from 3+ photographers
Creative fees (writing, design, etc.)	Get estimates from creative pros
Postage	Post office
Photocopying	Local copy shop
Mailing-fulfillment house fees	Quotes from mailing houses
Direct-mail lists	Talk to mailing-list companies
Web hosting	Web developer, Web magazines
Web programming	Get quotes from 3+ programmers
Advertising space	Media kits
Travel	Airlines, hotels, travel Web sites
Memberships (for networking)	Individual organizations
CD-ROM duplication	Get quotes from duplication services
Awards entry fees	Awards organizations
Space rental (for seminars, events)	Space managers
Gifts, meals, rewards	Case-by-case basis

Set your budget, but be flexible. If your earnings increase, bump up spending. If they go down temporarily, cut back by no more than 5 percent. Remember, your Personal Branding is your growth fuel, and you don't want to drain the tank.

3. Action Plan/Marketing Timetable

Once you've made all your decisions, create a master schedule and action plan you can print in large format, and put it on your office wall. Give a copy to each member of your staff. Then create a Personal Branding handbook that details every aspect of your brand marketing: what you're mailing and when, where you're networking, costs of everything, key contacts, etc.

Most important, create a month-to-month calendar for every aspect of your plan. This master calendar should list the following for each month:

1. Your branding channels

2. Direct-mail deadlines: printing, labeling, bundling, and mailing

3. What type of Personal Postcard goes out each month

4. Dates of all conferences and other events for 12 months, and your travel dates

5. Networking events and locations

6. Dates for mailing press releases

7. Dates for sending direct e-mail

8. Dates for Web site content updates

9. Deadlines for delivery of columns

10. Dates for networking and direct-mail follow-up

11. Ad sales closure dates for publications in which you advertise

12. Who's responsible for each of the above

13. Your monthly marketing budget

14. A running total of your monthly marketing expenditures

If possible, don't make yourself responsible for anything you don't have to do. That way, if you're traveling or buried in work, your branding machine keeps running.

Build "triggers" into your Master Schedule. These are pre-set conditions that, when they occur, set certain events in motion. For example, when you gain a new client by referral, a trigger goes off to send a thank-you gift to the person who gave you the referral.

What to Do in the First 30 Days:

1. Get your Personal Logo designed and print your new business cards.

2. Print new stationery, mailing labels and envelopes with your new logo and slogan.

3. Change signage, apparel or anything else that should have your new logo and slogan.

4. Complete your Master Schedule.

5. Finish and print your Personal Brochure.

6. Design and launch a Phase One version of your Personal Web site: home page, bio page, services page, portfolio or case studies page, and contact information. You can complete the whole site after launch.

7. Send out your initial press kit.

8. Take out a phone directory ad, if appropriate to your business.

9. Send a personal letter to your current base of clients, prospects, colleagues and professional contacts explaining your Personal Brand launch, your reasons behind it, and what you hope to do for them in the future.

What to Say to People You Work with Now

As we said under "What to Do First," it's important you let current clients and prospects know why you're making this change and what it means to them. Direct mail is fine; personal contact by phone or face-to-face is better. Either way, explain you're launching this new identity to help grow your business, to focus on the areas where you provide the greatest value, and this will in no way change your availability for them.

It's reassurance, it's courtesy, and it's good business sense. Who knows? If your clients or colleagues understand marketing, they might help you spread the word.

Brand Consistency

Consistency in the timing of your branding and in the message is critical to the healthy growth of your Personal Brand. Prospects and key influencers must see the same visuals, the same value points, and the same emotional message over and over before it makes an impression. If you change your message on a whim, deliver direct-mail cards whenever you feel like it, or show up at networking mixers whenever the mood strikes you, you'll appear unprofessional.

Some tips for keeping your Personal Brand marketing consistent:

- Always check your latest message against your PBS and position.

- Follow your Master Schedule.

- Update your Web site content monthly, at least.

- Use your logo and slogan everywhere.

- Train your staff to support the values in your Personal Brand.

- Ignore trends.

- Give your marketing six months to generate results before you consider changes.

- Assemble a team of skilled contractors—writers, Web developers, printers, etc.—and use them for everything.

Living Your Brand

It's not enough to market your Personal Brand. You've got to live it. This is why it's so important to choose a brand that reflects who you really are and what you really care about. If your Personal Brand reflects your true passions, lifestyle and personality, it's going to be easy and fun for you to build, and you'll do a better job as a result.

If your Personal Brand says you run marathons, run marathons. If it tells people you're a serious jazz fan, know your Stan Kenton from your Dave Brubeck, and so on. Make this process foolproof by simply building your brand around what you do well, what you love and how you live, including your flaws and foibles. That way, you don't have to change a thing.

Personal Brand Case Study:

Mike Parker
Mike Parker Landscape

Position: Landscape design with an artistic flair
Location: Laguna Beach, CA
Business: Landscape design
Online: mikeparkerlandscape.com

You can't miss the trucks with "Mike Parker Landscape" emblazoned on their sides. They wind their way through some of Southern California's most idyllic, expensive neighborhoods—Laguna Beach, Newport Coast, Dana Point, Laguna Niguel and San Clemente. Follow them through the hills and you're likely to wind up parked in front of a home straight out of *Architectural Digest* with a knockout lawn, terrace, or xeriscape. That's the work that's made Mike Parker the leading name in landscape design in this status-obsessed corner of the Southland.

Since 1976, Parker has presided over an empire built on landscape design, construction, and maintenance—and a strong Personal Brand. The Laguna Beach entrepreneur has corralled award-winning architects and landscape designers under the umbrella of Mike Parker Landscape—and maintained a powerful Personal Brand through consistency, quality, and a multichannel strategy.

How It Started:

In 1976, Mike Parker Landscape was just one truck, one man, and a dream to make art and make a little money. The company began as more or less a landscape maintenance business, one of hundreds in suburban

Southern California. But Parker brought a touch of artistry to his work, and that artistry became a leading attribute of his Personal Brand.

"I'd always been interested and involved in various artistic endeavors: ceramics, drawing and painting," he says. "My clients recognized I was doing more than just gardening, and began having me renovate their garden spaces. This allowed me an artistic outlet, and a way to pay the bills."

Parker used his leading attribute—his artistic ability—to change the perceptions of his target audience and position himself not as a glorified gardener, but a Picasso of the hedgerow and paving stone. His differentiator was in place, and he ran with it.

Most Important Steps in Building a Personal Brand:

Parker uses public relations and consistent direct mailing to stimulate referrals from colleagues and clients. He has also used direct mail to pitch a premium or special service, or to boost business in anticipation of economic downturns.

Mike Parker Landscape is also a very visible company. Besides free plugs on its ever-present trucks, Parker maintains an attractive, highly visible headquarters alongside bucolic, winding Laguna Canyon Road. His company runs consistent image advertising in high-end lifestyle publications, each ad dominated by a splashy photo showcasing a current project or a seasonal design idea. What's more, Parker's firm has engaged in some high-end PR: designing several gardens for the Philharmonic Houses of Design, a program sponsored by the Philharmonic Society of Orange County and the American Society of Interior Designers (ASID). These efforts have made it far easier to attract builders, architects and vendors.

Biggest Success:

From a "solo act" bringing in less than $100,000 in annual revenue, Mike Parker Landscape has grown to a staff of 90 and gross revenues of $6 million per year. Referrals account for 90 percent of the company's business.

The referrals have grown organically, appropriate for a company specializing in soil, plants and flowers. Parker has broadened the firm's reach—and encouraged referrals—by scouting for landscape designers and architects who have built their reputations around a particular talent or style. "This helps keep our product fresh, and [it] has resulted in the networking of talents and projects," Parker says.

On Personal Branding and Naming:

"It never occurred to me *not* to put my name on what I do. Contractors in general face a challenge of overcoming the bad experiences people have often had with a contractor. Putting your name on what you do in conjunction with a good reputation makes the process of proving oneself that much easier."

Advice:

"If you wait to do your mailings when you've slowed down, you've waited too long. In the landscape business, it works better when your company has a strong local presence and reputation."

Brandstorming Your Brand Launch:
6 Great Things You Can Do Right Now

1. Tell everyone in your sphere of influence about your plan to launch a Personal Brand.

2. Change your working environment to fit your Personal Brand.

3. Look at how you dress and change your style to suit your brand.

4. Discuss the meaning of your Personal Branding strategy with your staff.

5. Take this a step further and talk to each of your employees about how they can develop their own Personal Brand within your business.

6. Plan a launch party to inaugurate your new brand.

Bottom Line No. 17: How Personal Branding Equals More Business
Remaking your brand to resonate with customers

Situation: You're the owner and operator of an auto shop that does good business in the local community, but you're prevented from expanding and opening new locations by the marketing punch of the big auto-repair chains like Midas and Aamco. You're not experienced in marketing, but you know what's been bringing customers back to you for over 25 years: personal service and attention, little things like driving their car home, asking about their kids, and giving them cards on their birthdays. But how can that turn into more business?

Solution: You decide to take that personal service and build it into a Personal Brand. You talk to dozens of customers and discover not only are you primarily working with families, you're working with family cars: minivans, SUVs, wagons. The light bulb goes on and you zero in on the things parents care about when they have their car serviced: reliability, safety, getting it back in time to meet a busy schedule. Then you craft a Personal

Brand: the smart mechanic grandfather who specializes in the family car, not just repairing it but giving customers ideas for making it safer and more reliable, and helping it last longer. You launch a direct-mail campaign and a new name on your shop sign: "Grandpa's Auto Repairs: Personal Care for the Family Car."

Result: A little hokey? Maybe, but it works. Within six months, your business on BMWs and the like is down 80 percent, but your business for vans, SUVs and wagons has jumped over 200 percent. You "own" this segment of your market now, and because you love kids and see more of them than ever, you're enjoying your work more as well as making more money. Best of all, a new location looks likely.

Brand Surgery: Avoiding Tragic Branding Mistakes
The Patient: Your Brand Launch

- Don't promote your "individuality" to the exclusion of all else. Prospects don't care about your quirks. They want value.

- Don't create a brand that promises public behavior you can't continue in private. If you brand yourself as a paragon of virtue but run with hookers after hours, you'll alienate many clients.

- Don't over-promise. If you're inexperienced, focus on something else. Once you get more experience you can re-brand, but if you promise too much and can't deliver, those bridges are just waiting for a match to go up in flames.

- Don't be shy. If you're hesitant about telling people how good you are at your specialty, get over it. Personal Branding isn't for the timid.

- Do be specific and aggressive in setting yourself apart from your competition. More than one branding campaign has been over before it began because the business owner lost his nerve and become "just another insert-profession-here."

- Don't interview good friends about how you're currently perceived. They won't be honest with you. Talk to clients who know you well, ask them to be honest, and if they hurt your feelings, take it. Like medicine that tastes bad, it's good for you.

CHAPTER 18

Maintaining and Defending Your Brand

So you're sending out direct mail, going to networking events, and handing out Personal Brochures at a delirious pace. But is your brand really doing what you want? How do you control its growth, your spending, and the brand you're building?

You do it by managing your Personal Brand and following some simple, effective maintenance procedures that will keep your brand fine-tuned... and clue you in to problems before they harm your business. The first step is to manage your Personal Brand's growth by letting it evolve in phases.

The Phases of Your Brand

Why phases? Because when you're launching your Personal Brand and making such a substantial investment, it's smart to keep things under control and monitor your market for unintended consequences, such as an influential person being terribly offended by your brand message. Our phased plan:

Phase One: Building Your Identity (launch 3 months out)

- Relying mostly on your Personal Postcard, begin your Six-Week Marketing Blitz of new prospects and your 12-Month Branding Campaign to current clients, prospects and contacts.

- Send two copies of your Personal Brochure to all your current clients and contacts, along with a letter explaining your new brand launch and asking them for referrals.

- Begin networking, and hand out business cards and Personal Brochures whenever possible. Begin a contact database.

- Develop a system for tracking the results of your direct mail, and a follow-up system for responses.

- Launch your Web site with the minimum sections if necessary, and quickly complete it with all value-added features.

- Purchase any local advertising you want to use.

- Mail your initial press kits.

Phase Two: Leveraging Your New Visibility (3-6 months out)

- Evaluate your brand and marketing for the last three months. Adjust accordingly.

- Evaluate the success of your first direct-mail campaign by responses, new clients, and referrals generated. Adjust your messaging if necessary.

- Begin your direct-mail campaign to other target markets.

- Ask new Phase One clients for referrals.

- Begin submitting article and column ideas to the local and trade press.

- Sponsor local events or sports teams.

- Seek out public speaking or panel opportunities.

- Increase your advertising presence with outdoor or larger print ads.

Phase Three: Seizing Increased Market Share (6-9 months out)

- Evaluate your brand and marketing for the last three months. Adjust accordingly.

- Continue your direct-mail and referral campaigns to your current clients and contacts.

- Research and identify new potential target markets.

- Design a special direct-mail program for the most desirable 20 percent of your prospects, using tools such as personal sales letters printed on fine stationery or newsletters.

- Launch a bold new advertising campaign with new messaging, using whatever combination of print, online, outdoor, and broadcast you can afford.

- Review your total prospect pool and discard the bottom 20 percent.

- Review your client/customer roster and cut loose the 20 percent that produces the least revenue or referrals (preferably by referring them to someone else).

- Add new features to your Web site.

Phase Four: Prepare New Strategies [9-12 months out]

- Evaluate your brand and marketing for the last three months. Adjust accordingly.

- Begin looking for strategic partners.

- Investigate the feasibility of doing instructional seminars.

- Begin a redesign of your Web site.

- Explore expansion into new locations.

- Up your media presence by landing a regular column or radio hosting assignment.

- Brainstorm with your creative team on new visuals and messages for your branding.

- Examine your overall marketing results for return on investment.

- Chart your income growth.

- Chart how well you and your team have followed your Master Schedule.

- Survey your clients and contacts and learn what you've done well and what needs improvement.

- Discard what hasn't worked in the past year.

- Take a vacation.

Phase Five: Reinvest and Reinvent [Year Two]

- Evaluate your brand and marketing for the last three months. Adjust accordingly.

- Establish new goals for the next 12 months.

- Create a new Master Schedule and budget.

- Launch your redesigned Web site.

- Send your redesigned, rewritten Personal Postcards to your current contacts and your new target markets.

- Launch and promote ventures like new locations or seminars.

- Further increase your advertising presence in print and broadcast.

- Create something big: a charity event, a contest or a foundation.

- Investigate publishing a book or magazine.

- Apply for membership in the influential leadership groups for your profession.

- Continue to network and maximize personal contact.

Tracking and Constant Re-Evaluation

One of the biggest mistakes we see in novice Personal Branders is they try something once, track the results halfheartedly, receive poor returns, and give up. That's not the way. Great Personal Branders create a long-term strategy, attempt new marketing, track everything, reassess, make modifications, and perform again. Before you launch any marketing initiative, create a system for tracking what works and what doesn't.

One of our favorite ways to make tracking pay off is "data mining." That's where you track and record every aspect of your brand marketing, from addresses of prospects who respond to mailers to how fast each client pays you. After a few months, turn this raw data over to a firm that mines data as a business. Quality data mining will reveal hidden patterns in your business—who makes you the most money, which geographic regions respond most often to your first mailings, and so on. Such data can really boost your ROI.

Is Your Brand Working?

A Personal Brand is like an exotic foreign sports car. You can't just let it run at top speed without regular maintenance, or it will burn itself up. You've got to constantly monitor your brand to keep it relevant, focused, emotionally connected with your target market, and different from your competition. Fail to do that and you'll find yourself by the side of the road kicking your tires.

Maintenance of your Personal Brand demands continual vigilance in three areas of evaluation:

1. **Short-Term Results**

Is your brand bringing in new business or increasing your influence? You can assess this very simply, by looking at your bottom line. Are you making more money? Getting more inquiries? Getting more referrals? Also, look at your circle of contacts. Are you a familiar face to more influential people, or a regular at important networking events? Are you getting more face time with those who can further your career? Focus on the rate of change from month to month and over a six-month period. At the end of six months, your income should be on a steady rise, and your sphere of influential contacts should be markedly larger.

2. **Brand Awareness**

How well-known are you in your target market, your marketplace, and your industry? Get into the world of your prospects and start listening. Ask friends to tell you what they hear. Save articles. Are you being talked about? Are opinions about your work stronger? Are you having an effect on decisions even when you're not around (the "proxy self" effect)? Do more people know who you are, what you do, and what you stand for personally and professionally?

This is hard to turn into numbers, but you should be able to gauge the awareness of your Personal Brand in a few weeks. Then, over six months, follow the changes. Is awareness increasing? Are you being considered for more work, or asked your opinion on professional issues more often? Do more people know what you do without being told?

3. **Reaching Goals**

This is why you created a Personal Brand in the first place. Is your Personal Brand helping you get to your goals? Look at both short-term goals—landing a column in the financial section of a prominent local newspaper—and long-term goals, such as buying the house of your dreams. If you're not there, are you at least making progress? Write down all your goals and mark them as "reached," "approaching," "in progress," or "distant."

Strategic Awareness: Take Your Brand's Temperature

With Personal Branding, the best defense is, well, a good defense. That is, rather than launch a Personal Brand and let the chips fall where they may only to do damage control when problems arise, prevent the problems from occurring. That's what strategic awareness is about.

Look at today's monster Personal Brands: Tiger Woods, Oprah Winfrey, Madonna. These superstars are all intimately aware of everything that affects their Personal Brands, whether it's a story in a tabloid or the sales figures for their latest endorsed product. Of course, they have massive publicity machines to help them be aware and manage their brands, but what matters is they constantly take their brand's temperature. They're tied to the culture of their brands, allowing them to evolve as the culture evolves. This way, they don't make wrenching changes, and they can head off problems before they develop.

Cultivating awareness of your Personal Brand should become part of your everyday routine. You should constantly be aware of the shifts within your target market and industry—through networking, conversations, the media, and stories you hear from others. Some of the keys to making your strategic awareness as effective as possible:

- Take notes. After meetings, projects, networking events and the like, note important conversations and observations in writing.

- Take note of people whose names or faces surface repeatedly. They may be part of a powerful cultural shift.

- Talk and listen. Get in conversation with people in your target market and your industry. Listen to the stories, the gossip, and the speculation.

- Read everything. The trades, the local paper, internal company newsletters if you can get your hands on them, industry and corporate Web sites.

Fine-Tuning Your Brand

Let's say you practice strategic awareness, absorb stories and rumors from your prospect pool like a sponge, and realize there are problems with your Personal Brand. It's not connecting emotionally with key influencers, it lacks credibility, or it's just too similar to someone else's. Don't panic. Huge, wholesale changes to a Personal Brand usually do more harm than good. Some basic fine-tuning can usually give your brand the boost it needs.

1. **Relevance Check**. Does your Personal Brand still resonate with your target market? Perhaps the culture has changed and you're now out of touch. Example: During the dot-com boom of the late 1990s, the arrogant slacker computer programmer was the icon of the age. It didn't matter what a slob he was or how bad he interviewed; he got six figures and all the glory. He fit the culture. But with the tech free-fall, those mercenary code cowboys have either had to shape up and learn to wear ties or they're flipping burgers.

2. **Authenticity Check.** We've said it again and again: Your Personal Brand must reflect who you really are—passions, attitudes, talents and flaws. Yet some people still insist on crafting a false persona for themselves. Have you done that? If your Personal Brand is less than authentic, it will not only make you look like a phony, but it will make your work less pleasurable. Take a hard look at who you are and who your brand says you are. If the two don't match, make some changes.

3. **Goal Check.** Maybe your brand is doing fine, but you're not getting closer to your goals, or perhaps your goals have changed. Take a step back. Do you need to alter your brand to better reach your goals, or do you need to set new goals?

4. **Competition Check.** Copying someone else's successful business idea may as well be our national sport. It happens all the time. But there's a risk: your brand can be diluted and you can lose business. You might even be seen as the copycat! By constantly watching for imitators, you can catch them early and make aggressive moves to consolidate your position. Always follow this rule: When confronted by a potential imitator, always act fast and aggressively. Take the initiative.

5. **Brand Check.** Perhaps you misjudged the value or unmet need your target market was seeking. If you did, your Leading Attribute is off-target. When prospects think of you, they're dismissing you from consideration for an opportunity. You need to make a ground-level adjustment to your Personal Brand, to the "who you are" and "what you do" information.

6. **Message Check.** In some cases you'll find your brand is great but your expression of it is wrong. You're using humor in your direct mail and it's falling flat, or your designs are too conservative for a creative, hip target market. Talk to your clients and prospects to get a better idea of what drew them to you. Then sit down with your creative team and develop new messaging.

Dealing with Brand Disasters

Every once in a while, the *Titanic* hits an iceberg. You launch what seems like an effective Personal Brand and it bombs. You're hemorrhaging cash and you've got to stop the bleeding. It's not a fun place to be, so it's best to catch big problems before they become disasters. The three warning signs your Personal Brand may be about to go down:

• Someone does it better than you. If somebody comes along and copies your Personal Brand but then kicks your butt in a fair fight, you might need to find a different brand.

• No one knows who you are. After six months of tireless brand marketing, you're still anonymous in your field. That can mean you've promoted your Personal Brand poorly, but more likely your brand is out of touch with your target market.

• People react negatively. Some negative reaction to your Personal Brand is desirable. After all, you don't want to be neutral and boring, but to attract the right prospects and repel the wrong ones. But anger, resentment and outrage are definitely not healthy for your future.

Making Radical Changes

At some point, you may need to forgo fine-tuning and make big changes to your Personal Brand and your brand marketing. If that ever becomes the case, the first thing you should do is take a step back and make sure the danger signs are real, not just fleeting trends.

If they are real, and you're in danger of damaging your business, the first step is to eradicate all traces of the current brand marketing. Stop any direct mailings, pull any ads, quit going to networking events, and so on. Other than serving your current clients, adopt a bunker mentality for a short time. You need to stop, reassess, and figure out what to do.

Next, accept the fact you may have to launch a completely new Personal Brand. As we've said in the past, people's minds are very hard to change. A new logo or postcard ain't gonna do it. To erase damaging brand baggage, you must do one of three things:

1. Re-launch to a completely new target market

2. Re-launch a new Personal Brand totally unlike your old one (not just a slight variation on the theme)

3. Re-launch in a new profession or specialty

Not easy choices, but there you are. Once you've decided how to re-launch, follow all the steps we've outlined for creating and marketing your Personal Brand. Make sure to do it BIG. There's no room for subtlety when you launch after a disastrous Personal Brand experience. Forget the old brand ever existed and re-launch as if you're shiny and new. You want the force of your new Personal Brand to completely erase the bad aftertaste of your last one.

Repeat all the management steps and hope for better luck this time.

The Care and Feeding of Your Personal Brand

• Form a "feedback circle" among friends and colleagues. These are people you can count on to tell you how your Personal Brand and marketing are working in the real world. Take them out for dinner or coffee once a month and pick their brains.

- Survey your entire sphere of influence—clients, prospects, colleagues, key contacts—at least twice a year. Find out if you're living up to your promises, if there's anything you can do better, and so on.

- Get your face familiar, not just your name. Remember, we do business with people we like. Those are people we know. Become a familiar face at events of all kinds, and make sure all photos of you are the best they can be.

- Take on a leadership role in your profession. If there's room on a governing board, an awards committee or a debate panel, get on it.

- Dress and drive the part. Sad but true, people do judge us by what we wear and the car we drive. So it's up to you to make those things fit with your Personal Brand. If you're trying to sell yourself as a financial planner to millionaires, invest in the handmade Prada suit. If you're positioned as the beach bum fashion photographer, driving a vintage Woody is going to help your image. Just don't confuse the two.

- Contract with a clipping service. These companies will track every mention of you in the print media and send you copies of every word written about you. Web sites like www.plumbriefings.com and www.clipgenius.com are especially useful in helping you keep track of how your brand is being covered in the media.

Following "The Way of the Personal Brander"

These days, Personal Branding is so woven into the fabric of business and society, you really must do more than practice Personal Branding's strategies. You must train yourself to think like a Personal Brander 24/7.

How? By always being conscious of how everything you do, publicly and privately, affects your brand. We strongly recommend our clients and readers follow the way of the Personal Brander by regularly doing the following:

- **Planning**—Personal Branders are constantly reviewing, revising, and planning their future marketing and branding strategies and activities.

- **Networking**—Many people attend industry conferences to hear the big speakers, but the best reason is to network with fellow professionals. You've heard of using "other people's money" to leverage your success? We believe in leveraging "other people's experience" and learning from their mistakes. Master these two questions, young Jedi:

- What is the biggest branding/marketing success you've had this last year?

- What is the biggest branding/marketing failure you have had this last year?

- **Execution**—Spend an equal percentage of your time and your money on your Personal Branding. If you spend 20 percent of your revenue on brand building and business development, spend 20 percent of your time overseeing those activities. A "just write a check" mentality sets you up for failure. You must be personally involved in every branding decision your company makes.

- **Continuing Education**—Even though we feel this book is the final word in Personal Branding, please do not stop here. Please continuously attend marketing and branding seminars, and read books and articles. Refer to our Recommended Reading section for more suggestions.

Personal Brand Case Study

Wylie Aitken
Aitken Law Offices

Position: Defending the rights of the little guy
Location: Santa Ana, CA
Business: Major Personal Injury Law & Insurance Bad Faith
Online: aitkenlaw.com

Wylie Aitken has always considered the legal profession a higher calling, a mission to protect the interests of people who need help. Perhaps that's why in 36 years he's become one of the most respected personal-injury litigators in California. In fact, in the last three years he's been honored as one of the 100 most influential lawyers in a state of 143,000 lawyers.

"It's a combination of multilevel involvement," Aitken says. "Number one, it's because I love it, and therefore I put the effort into my profession. Number two, because I do a great job for my clients, I've been able to establish a good professional reputation among my peers (i.e., other lawyers). Number three, I am very involved in professional activities. Number four, I do a good deal of work out in the non-legal community. It's multi-tiered involvement that I do because I want to."

How It Started:

A plaintiff tort lawyer since 1966, Aitken prosecutes on behalf of those who suffer injury due to an unsafe product, an unsafe highway or a careless act—a profession that routinely pits him against large municipal and corporate entities and the large law firms that represent them. His upbringing, he states, made ending up defending the rights of the common man an inevitable career direction.

"I was a son of New Deal Democrats," he says, "so representing the little guy seemed natural. I identified with workers, so representing the little guy was consistent with what I considered to be part of being a lawyer, and I was able to bring my personal passion to it."

Most Important Steps in Building a Personal Brand:

At age 35, Aitken was the youngest president in the history of the California Trial Lawyers Association, and he began to get substantial media coverage—radio, Sunday morning newsmaker shows, and so on. He realized that the media exposure was a valid tool to get his name out at a time when he considered advertising by an attorney to be neither proper nor ethical.

"I realized how my practice benefited when people said, 'I saw you on television,'" he says. "So I utilized the contacts in the media that I had developed."

Aitken also realized the fleeting nature of media visibility. "It's an ongoing process, an ongoing commitment to merit which then led to continued media coverage," he says. "I had a mentor who had decided to take time off, and I couldn't believe how quickly you could have your Andy Warhol moment of fame. People were saying about him, 'Is he still practicing?'" Aitken ensures he remains in the consciousness of the legal profession and the community by sending a newsletter to past clients, and when his notoriety turns into features in the local business magazines, he sends those articles to contacts and clients.

"Lawyers call me and say, 'Who is your press agent?' I tell them, 'I don't have a press agent!' You don't necessarily need a press agent. I have found the real key to be hard work and focus."

Biggest Success:

The media event that made Aitken most famous arose out of a tragic accident. "I had a case in Orange County in which a young girl, Laura Small, was attacked by a mountain lion. The case captured the public's imagination, and we started getting gavel-to-gavel publicity. When the trial ended successfully, we ended up with a photo on the front page of the *Los Angeles Times*. A friend called me up and said, 'Do you have any idea what just happened? Do you have an idea what the cost of putting a full-page ad in the *Times* would be?' They put it on the front page of every edition. That kind of exposure is unique and some would credit it to dumb luck, but I there was a lot of hard work and drudgery put in to make the case a success before that publicity came."

On Personal Branding and Politics:

"A young lady came into my office and asked if I would help her run for city council in Anaheim. I was very impressed with her. So I became a mentor for Loretta Sanchez, and later we took on Bob Dornan [the bombastic, far-to-the-right congressman whose antics had become an embarrassment even to the GOP]. Dornan decided to challenge the election, so I was also Sanchez's attorney for 15 months. The election and the contest of the results generated a good deal of publicity."

Advice:

"Don't lose sight of your own limitations and what got you where you are in the first place. Don't believe your own publicity. Continue to identify what made you unique in the first place, and stick with it. That comes from a client who told me, 'What makes you unique is you're so approachable and easy to talk to.' Don't lose sight of that, keep perspective, and maintain your focus. There are plenty of people who get full of themselves and are gone a short while later."

Brandstorming Brand Maintenance:
8 Great Things You Can Do Right Now

1. Contact candidates for your feedback circle.

2. Begin hashing out a brand-crisis management plan.

3. Select a brand-crisis manager from your employees.

4. Determine the channels for your brand awareness—rumors from friends, newspaper articles, chat rooms, industry events, and so on.

5. Check the competitive landscape for people who have copied you in the past. Might they copy your Personal Branding?

6. Contact a clipping service. A great place to start is at About.com at websearch.about.com/library/weekly/aa031901a.htm.

7. Let your staff know it's OK to critique your branding or marketing ideas and suggest their own.

8. Make detailed lists of secondary target markets, once your first market is under control.

Bottom Line No. 18: How Personal Branding Equals More Business
Repositioning to appeal to your target market

Situation: You're a tutor for the children of the upper-income families of your area. For some time, you've done quite well with your Personal Brand: a conservative, Yale-educated scholar with a background in literature and the arts. You've positioned yourself, printed a very nice Personal Brochure, and have a strong client base. But lately, you've noticed clients drifting away. A little investigation shows you're losing some of your best pupils to a rival who also claims a classical education and continental sophistication, with one exception: She also has a strong background in computers and the Internet, and she wows parents with promises to teach their offspring about technology, and wows kids with fun computer- and Web-based learning.

Solution: You're not a technical whiz, so you can't compete with your rival on the same playing field...but you need to redefine your Personal Brand to regain your relevance. So you look at your other field of expertise: your fluency in French, Italian and Russian. You decide that will be your new Personal Brand: the classically trained tutor who will teach your son or daughter to be conversant, if not fluent, in one of those languages in one year, as well as teaching them about the history and culture of the country. You print a new brochure and do a direct mailing to your former clients as well as new prospects.

Result: As you thought, your foreign language positioning strikes a chord with upper-crust parents who want their child to speak a foreign language. You have long conversations with former clients and their children, and you start to retake some of the ground you lost to your competitor. After a year, you own a whole new segment of the market, and you have as many students as you can handle.

Brand Surgery: Avoiding Tragic Branding Mistakes
The Patient: Brand Maintenance

- Don't ignore warning signs.

- Don't flout the distaste or anger of some segments of your target market.

- Don't automatically assume other people just "don't get it."

- Don't get so busy you fail to notice changes in culture, tastes or values.

- Don't play to the lowest common denominator.

- Don't talk down to your target market.

- Don't play it too cool and detached.

- Don't hoard your increased profits. Reinvest them in better marketing.

- Don't feel any sense of entitlement. There's no such thing.

- Don't forget all the marketing in the world is no substitute for treating people with courtesy, connecting with them, and giving them more than they expect.

CHAPTER 19

Things to Know, Mistakes to Avoid

No more pep talks. No more drills. You know the material, you've got all the tips and recommendations you can stomach. Now get out there, create your own winning Personal Brand, and let it carry you to your goals. But like any good coach, we're not going to let you hit the field without some good, final advice.

Things to Know and Do

Imitation is inevitable. If you're successful in your Personal Branding, someone will try and copy what you've done. Of course, they won't have this book, so they'll be at a disadvantage. But you'll have another big edge: You were first. The "first-mover advantage" we spoke about in Chapter 7 is very powerful, making anyone who tries to copy you look like a follower, not a leader. Make sure, though, that the people in your target market know the newcomer is an imitation, and you're the original.

Everyone has weaknesses. You might find yourself gunning for an entrenched leader in a very desirable market, or facing a well-financed imitator intent on replacing you in your niche. Either is a threat to your Personal Brand, your market share and your business, but remember: Every business has weaknesses. You just need to find them. Study your foe and you'll find the weakness: a lack of market knowledge, arrogance, poor creative work, a past scandal, something. It's there. When you find it, exploit the daylights out of it. Remember, this isn't friendship. It's your career and livelihood.

People will scoff. Some clients, prospects and especially professional colleagues will look at your Personal Branding with scorn. "That's not how this business works!" is a common objection, along with "Marketing doesn't work for what we do!" Most of the time, this is pure ignorance; occasionally it's envy from someone without the guts to take a risk. Don't let the doubts of the unenlightened discourage you. Most professionals are in the business of selling products or services, rather than themselves. Let them. It makes it easier for you to grab their customers.

Good printing is worth every penny. For the folks in the back row: The look and feel of your branding materials, the gloss and weight of the paper, and the richness of the color photos says as much about you as the design and writing. Do not skimp on printing costs, even if you have to cut back elsewhere. If a printer or anyone else tries to sell you on "saving money" by using cheap paper, politely slam the phone in his or her ear. You'll thank me when you get boxes of gorgeous brochures while your competitors hand out glorified facial tissues.

Under-promise and over-deliver. Don't pitch yourself as the greatest efficiency consultant in Western history. Just tell your prospects you're good at what you do. Then deliver like you're the best ever. This is *managing client expectations,* and it's one of the most powerful ways you can build a database of clients who are in love with you. Promise good work on a reasonable deadline, then deliver astonishing work ahead of schedule. Maybe you could have done brilliant work in a short time anyway, but by promising less, you set your client up to expect "good." Then you gave him "great."

Updated materials keep people interested. Make moderate changes to your Personal Brochure, Personal Postcard and other materials every year to keep them fresh, and completely redesign your branding tools every three years. This keeps things fresh and catches the attention of some people who hadn't noticed you before. With your Web site, frequent updates are mandatory, at least monthly.

Don't chase too many prospects. At the start of your Personal Branding campaign, we recommend marketing to one target market. Any more and you may overspend, find yourself with too many prospects to service, or simply lose track of to whom you're marketing. If you have a strong Personal Brand and you've chosen the right market, this should bury you in business.

People love a good cause. There's no downside to getting involved—as a sponsor, organizer or even founder—of charity or civic events like golf tournaments, 10K runs, tree plantings or Habitat for Humanity. Getting involved—and making sure your target markets know of your involvement—creates goodwill and helps you feel like you're working for more than a paycheck.

Don't stop being a salesperson. Remember, Personal Branding doesn't close anyone. Its purpose is to get the right prospects into your office, 90 percent ready to sign on the dotted line. Selling them is your job. So polish your pitch and your sales skills, and make sure you're ready to treat prospects like gold when they walk through your door.

Think about how you can add value. When we talked about Personal Postcards, we made the point that effective direct mail offers the recipient some benefit. What benefits can you offer your prospects to call you? What can you promise a client who gives you a great referral? Think about things that provide information of value like "special reports," discounts on special services you can provide, free subscriptions to targeted publications, free software, free seminars, even fun things like gift certificates to local restaurants and movie theaters. Know your target market and match each offer to the target.

Your staff members are the most important people in your business. If you take care of your staff and treat them right, they'll treat your clients and prospects like royalty. Hire your people with care, and reward them for helping make your Personal Branding campaign successful—bonuses for sticking to the Master Schedule, for reaching new business milestones, and so on. Make them a team, listen to their ideas, and encourage feedback. A great staff will take care of you and make your work a thousand times easier.

Growth means spending money. Sure, you can pick up new clients cheaply by networking and the like, but if you want to expand, open new offices, and build a business you can sell for millions, you've got to spend. So don't be shy about it. When your profits increase, reinvest 50 percent into your Personal Brand marketing. Then give the rest to your staff.

Mistakes to Avoid

Don't show your branding materials to your colleagues before you print them. Spare yourself the lame advice and negative talk, and print your materials when you're happy with them. Then show them around all you want with the temptation to change them removed.

Don't hand out tacky items with your Personal Logo on them. Coffee mugs, memo pads, flyswatters and refrigerator magnets don't do much to burnish your brand identity. They just make you look cheap and tacky. Leave them to the other guys. If you must create items with your logo on them, go high-class: tiepins, money clips, high-quality pens, polo shirts.

Don't ignore the Internet. You must have e-mail and a Web site to do business today. Period. Get it. Beyond that, don't forget the Web is a fantastic source of research and information. A few hours online can yield a new list of prospects, a host of new online and print publications for your PR efforts, information about competitors, hot news about your industry, and a lot more.

Don't copy someone else. After all we've said about the perils of copycatting, you wouldn't go out and imitate someone else's brand, would you? You'd be surprised how tempting it is. When you've been hammering away with your Personal Branding campaign for three months and the new business is just trickling in, copying that successful guy across town can looking awfully appealing. Don't. You gain nothing except a reputation as being lazy and unoriginal.

Don't panic. Don't freak out and change your strategy or decide Personal Branding doesn't work. It always takes time. This is a busy world, and no matter how strong your brand and compelling your message, people will take time to notice you. When they do, they'll call you, tell others, and your business will start growing. Give Personal Branding at least six months of steady effort before you consider giving up.

Stop thinking like a sole proprietor and start thinking like a business. If you're going to engage in Personal Branding, you've got to run like a business. First of all, it makes you more efficient, and as your marketing gets more intense, efficiency will keep you going smoothly. Second, if your brand marketing works, you'll be dealing with a lot more clients, and running like a business helps you service them efficiently.

Don't be afraid of new ideas. Just because we haven't mentioned a Personal Branding or marketing tool in this book doesn't mean it doesn't work. It just means we didn't want to throw the kitchen sink at you. So if a wild idea catches your eye, from launching your own Internet radio station to a little subversive "guerilla" marketing, go for it. Just make sure it adheres to the basics: it suits your target market, it communicates your Personal Brand essentials, and it's not being done by anyone else.

Don't hesitate to ask us. We wrote this book as a resource for growing businesses of all types, but every Personal Branding challenge is different, from how to be your own publisher to when to mix public and private life. So if a question comes up this book doesn't answer—or if you have a question or gripe about something in the book—let me know about it. You can contact me at:

Peter Montoya

Peter Montoya Inc.
1540 South Lyon Street
Santa Ana, CA 92705

888-730-5300
info@petermontoya.com

I'd love to hear your questions, debate our conclusions, or give you feedback on your creative ideas. Personal Branding is fluid; it's always moving and changing. By plugging into your energy and your ideas, we all become better Personal Branders. Please don't expect a reply back from me personally. I receive over 100 e-mails a day (and rising) and if I can't personally respond one of my qualified staff members will.

Index

A

Aamco   252

Adebayo Ogunlesi   16

Adobe   159, 170

Advice   21, 32, 41, 46, 47, 55 – 57,
69 – 70, 85, 100, 122, 133, 147, 163,
176 – 177, 184, 193, 206, 218, 229,
252, 266, 269, 271

Airport Signage   105

Al Ries & Laura Ries   96

America Online (AOL)   37, 174

American Airlines   156

Ancle Hsu   15

AOL Time Warner   37

Apple   156

Architectural Digest   250

Arnold Schwarzenegger   154

Associated Press   199

Attitude   39, 64, 127, 177, 260

Attributes   29, 51 – 52, 61, 97

B

Banners   105, 224

Bayer   192

Ben Cohen   37

Bill Gates   16

Billboards   47, 105, 160, 223

BMW   90, 97, 156, 209, 253

Bob Dornan   266

Bob Dylan   42

Bob Vila   3, 13, 75 -76

Bob Vila's Home Again   76

Britney Spears   42

Bus Benches   105

Business Card   2 – 3, 20, 29 – 30, 36,
46, 58, 66, 68, 71, 104, 111, 113, 139,
144, 146, 151, 153, 159, 164 – 165,
168, 171, 177, 181, 200, 203, 205, 209,
212, 219, 242, 245, 248, 256

C

Calvin Klein   82, 90

Carla Cico   15

Catalog   104, 179, 221, 225 – 226,
229 – 230, 245

CD-ROM   221, 226 – 227, 229 – 230,
245, 247

Century 21   227 – 228

Characteristics   2, 12, 14, 51 – 52, 54,
63, 67, 92

Charles Schwab   2, 13, 19, 90,
153 – 154

Chief Branding Officer (CBO)   29

Cisco Systems   217

Classified Advertising   105

Client Referrals   28, 48, 104, 112, 244

CNBC   32, 193

CNN   15, 32, 193

Colin Powell   13, 16

Commercials   25, 105, 223, 225

Company Brand   1, 4, 5, 22

Complete Idiot's Guide to Online Buying, The   227

CoolList   192

D

Dale Carnegie   3, 154 – 155

Dana Point   250

Daniel Will Harris   174

David Bach   31

David Deal   20

David Ji   15

DeBeers   38, 156

Dee Mellor   16

Direct Mail   22, 25, 28 – 30, 33 – 34, 43, 47, 58, 68, 80 – 81, 96, 98 – 100, 104, 106, 108, 111, 113 – 117, 119, 122 – 123, 145, 156, 160, 171, 179 – 182, 184 – 185, 189 – 190, 192, 194 – 195, 198, 204, 213 – 215, 228, 244 – 249, 251, 253, 255 – 256, 261 – 262, 267, 271

Display Advertising   105

Donald Trump   97

Donna Karan (DKNY)   151

Donna Maria Coles Johnson   120

Dr. Barry Friedberg   83

Dr. Todd Walkow   132

DSL (Digital Subscriber's Line)   102, 174, 176 – 177

E

E-Mail   20, 71, 85, 101, 103 – 104, 106, 108, 110, 127, 133 – 134, 166, 169 – 171, 173 – 174, 176 – 177, 183 – 185, 190 – 192, 194, 204, 213, 215 – 216, 236 – 237, 245 – 246, 248, 272 – 273

E-Newsletter   104, 175

Editor Relationship Program   104

Elle   70

Endorsement Letter   104

Enron   37, 61

Equifax

Eric Kim   15

Ernst & Young   209

Exclusive Channels   107, 114

Exhibit Booths   105, 112, 113, 146

F

Famous Amos   3

Farmer's Insurance   192

Fast Company   227

Federal Reserve Chairman Alan Greenspan   17

Ford   10, 98, 153, 172

G

Gestalt   38

Gillette   156

Ginni Rometty   16

Google   172, 224

Guerrino de Luca   15

Gwyneth Paltrow   69

H

Hamlet   41

Hebert Demel   15

Holiday Inn   97

Honda   38, 192

Horse Sense   96 – 97

Host-Paid Radio Show   105

Host-Paid TV Show   105

Howard Schultz   97

I

Incentive Program   104, 115, 215, 218

Inclusive Channels   107

Infomercials   105

J

Jack Welch   16

Jerry Greenfield (Ben & Jerry's)   37

Jim Bakker   19

Jimmy Buffett   13, 90, 163

Jimmy Swaggart   41

Joe Montana   19

Johnnie Cochran   43

Jonice Padilha   69

K

K-Mart   18, 76

Kenny Fisher   44

Kyle Boschen   146

L

Laguna Beach   161, 162, 250

Laguna Niguel   250

Larry Ellison   16

Larry King   3

Leading Attribute   52, 53, 234, 237, 242,
    243, 251, 261

Lifestyle Market Analyst   56, 85

Louis Barajas   56

Lucille Ball (I Love Lucy)   40

M

Madonna   13, 43, 259

Mailing Calendar   104

Mandy Moore   42

Martha Stewart   3, 76, 90, 97

Marty Rodriguez   227, 228

Mary Kay (Ash)   3, 54, 90, 154

Media Kit   104, 224, 245

Meg Ryan   19

Mercedes   90

Michael Jordan   13, 51 – 52, 198

Microsoft   170

Midas   252

Mike Parker   250 – 251

Monica Lewinsky   154

Myrtle Potter   16

N

Naina Lal Kidwai   15

Networking   8, 28, 46, 104, 109,
    112 – 113, 116 – 119, 122, 146, 148,
    165, 209 – 220, 228, 244 – 249, 251,
    255 – 256, 259 – 260, 262 – 263, 271

Newport Coast   250

Newsweek   193

Nike   18, 99, 206

O

O.J. Simpson   38, 43

Oprah Winfrey   2, 15, 18, 64, 259

Orville Redenbacher   90

Outdoor Advertising   28, 105, 160, 223,
    229, 242, 244

Overture   224

Oxygen network   206

P

Pacific Gas & Electric   217

Patti Glick   216

Paul Viti   209, 211

Pay-for-Guest TV Show   105

PDFs   170

People vs. Larry Flynt, The   205

Personal Brand Statement (PBS)   95,
    100 – 101, 237, 241 – 242

Personal Brander   33, 106, 112, 125,
    209, 258, 263, 273

Personal Postcard   104, 116, 133, 179,
    181 – 189, 191 – 195, 214, 245 – 247,
    255, 257, 270 – 271

Phone Script   104

Polonius   41

PowerPoint Presentation   104, 160

Premiums   34, 98, 105

Press Releases   39, 104, 109 – 110, 119,
    197, 199, 201, 203 – 204, 208, 227,
    245, 248

Print Advertising   105, 245

Product   3 – 4, 13, 17, 19, 25 – 27, 34,
    39, 40, 43, 51, 53, 55, 81 – 83, 89, 90,
    94, 97, 99, 104 – 105, 112 – 113, 117,
    121 – 122, 141 – 142, 154, 156,
    166 – 167, 169 – 170, 186, 188 – 189,
    197, 222 – 223, 225 – 229, 240 – 242,
    251, 259, 264, 270

Professional Referrals   104, 114, 188,
    244

Public Relations   29, 104, 109 – 110,
    165, 197, 199, 201, 203, 205, 207, 228,
    244, 251

R

Radio Advertising   105, 244

Rainbeau Mars   205

REALTOR®   95, 227

Referral Request   104, 214 – 215

Reward   30, 82, 104, 110, 114 – 116, 129, 213, 218, 241, 247, 271

Richard Barton   15

Rob Lawes   15

Robert Bly   83

Robert Kazutomo Hori   15

Rosie O'Donnell   64

S

Sales Letter   104, 179, 182, 256

Sallie Krawcheck   15

Salomon Brothers   155

San Clemente   250

Selling a Home   227

Selling/Sales   2-3, 17, 23 – 29, 33, 44 – 45, 47 – 48, 54, 63, 77, 90 – 91, 95, 104, 107 – 108, 117, 126, 139 – 142, 148, 151, 165, 179 – 180, 182, 184 – 185, 187, 209, 211, 225, 228, 246, 248, 256, 259, 271

Seminar Manuals   104

Seminars   6, 28, 31, 104, 107 – 111, 117 – 119, 121, 123, 134, 146, 166 – 167, 170, 211, 244, 247, 257 – 258, 264, 271

Service Literature   105

Service Offers   104

SmithBarney Citigroup   155

Special Events   105, 112, 146, 160, 166, 244

Sponsorships   104, 109, 110, 112, 204, 244

SRDS (Standard Rate Data Service)   85

Starbucks   97

Stephen Covey   19

Steve Jobs   16

Strive Masiyiwa   16

SUVs   252 – 253

Suzanne Somers   97

T

Television Advertising   105, 223, 244

Tiger Woods   2, 15, 198, 259

Times Square   210

Todd Eckelman   99

Tom Hanks   13

Topica   192

22 Immutable Laws of Branding, The   159

Tradeshows   105, 112 – 113, 146, 211, 244

U

Unique Selling Proposition (USP)   94

Unique Value Proposition (UVP)   94, 239, 240, 241

UPS   156

USPS (United States Postal Service)   213

V

Vanessa Williams   69

Volvo   97

W

Wall Street Journal   193

Wally Bock   192 – 193

Walt Disney   13, 90, 153 – 154

Walt Disney Company   3

Walter Cronkite   13

Warm Calling   104, 108, 118 – 119, 122, 189, 228, 244

Web Site   6, 29, 34, 40, 53, 68, 81, 84 – 85, 99, 101, 103 – 104, 106, 109 – 110, 112 – 118, 121, 123, 160, 165 – 169, 171 – 178, 181, 182, 183, 185, 187, 191, 195, 198, 200, 204 – 206, 208, 212, 215, 218 – 219, 224, 226, 230, 244 – 245, 248, 249, 256, 257, 268, 272

Wieden + Kennedy   18

Will Rogers   40

William Shakespeare   41

Wyland   161 – 163

Wylie Aitken   264

Y

Yahoo!   192

Yellow Page Advertising   105

Yoga Journal   205 – 206

Glossary

Attitude: A powerful, very personal interpretation, by each person you meet, of whether you are "good" or "bad."

Attribute: A distinctive, compelling characteristic that communicates an intellectual or emotional benefit to a Personal Brand's domain. Most Personal Brands have 3 to 6 attributes.

Audience: Everyone exposed to the Personal Brand, targeted or not.

Brand Equity: Having "ownership" of a portion of a domain's perceptions by driving home a Personal Brand message until that message is part of the domain's culture.

Characteristic: Any basic human trait, from eye color and accent to sense of humor and eating habits.

Great Personal Brand: A Powerful Personal Brand (see below) with the added dimension of being regarded as a purveyor of goodwill or positive values. Example: Oprah Winfrey.

Influence: The power of a Personal Brand to motivate others to think or act in a way beneficial to its source.

Leading Attribute: The single most potent attribute, the one thing the Personal Brand will be known for above all others. Example: Michael Jordan's leading attribute is "greatest basketball player of all time."

Personal Brand: A personal identity that stimulates precise, meaningful perceptions in its audience about the values and qualities that person stands for, personally and professionally.

Personal Brander: Someone who runs his or her business by the Personal Branding philosophy and has made a lifelong commitment to build his or her Personal Brand.

Personal Branding (verb): The process of crafting a Personal Brand by linking who you are, what you do, and how you're different or create value for your target market.

Personal Branding (noun): All tactical tools that create or reinforce a brand—brochures, direct mail, catalogs, Web sites, signage, etc.

Personal Image: The identity you've passively created for yourself—your name, your profession, a description of how you do your work. Example: "He's that temperamental photographer." When you apply active branding techniques to this, you get a Personal Brand.

Personal Marketing: Using your Personal Brand in such business-building activities as advertising, direct mail and public relations.

Position: A statement that defines the niche you occupy in your chosen field, and the "space" you occupy in the perceptions of your target audience.

Powerful Personal Brand: A highly influential Personal Brand that elevates its source to the pinnacle of his profession, yet has no image of inherent good-will or public welfare. Example: Bill Gates.

Professional: A skilled individual who works for someone else in a corporate or small business environment.

Proxy Self: A brand "presence" that is known to the people in a domain, and influences their behavior and decisions on the source's behalf even when the source is not present.

Response Cue: Individual bits of information, often expressed through marketing or identity materials, designed to evoke an emotional response in a Personal Brand's domain.

Slogan: A statement that explains what you do, who you do it for, and/or the benefit.

Source: The human being behind the Personal Brand—the originator of the carefully packaged, projected persona that's the public face for the person beneath.

Sphere of Influence: A group of individuals, a company, and influential people to which your Personal Brand is focused. Through your domain you gain access to the overall audience.

Target Market: The precise group of individuals or companies who are on the receiving end of your Personal Branding message; the parties you want to turn into clients.

Peter Montoya: From Personal Branding to Personal Triumph

This isn't the typical author biography, but this isn't your typical book. In the definitive guide to Personal Branding, it seemed right to use one of the most powerful Personal Marketing tools, the Personal Brochure, to tell you a little about myself. So off we go.

>>>

Start With Good People

Many times I've been asked the secret of a strong company, and I always give the same answer: "Great people." Of course, I was lucky enough to learn about people in the best way imaginable: growing up in a big, crazy Southern California family.

An after-hours creative session with some of the team.

There were a few jokes about the Biblical names of us five boys—John, Matthew, Mark, Luke and Peter—but mostly there was fun, laughter and love. In this time I learned an important lesson: it's not talent or education that determine a person's value, but integrity, compassion and hard work. As I got older, I knew I wanted to associate with those kinds of people.

A Journey of Enlightenment

Fascinated with the concepts of personal image and individual marketing, I was determined to absorb it all. I spent two-and-a-half years working for the country's largest sales and personal development trainer. Here I discovered that while step-by-step instruction is the key to success, a turnkey approach doesn't work; every pupil has different needs.

Me and two of my best friends—Maxine and Molly dressed up for Halloween.

My next stop, a personal marketing firm, was an inspiration more for what they were missing than for what they were doing. Here I began to understand and develop the core principles of Personal Branding, as well as its organic nature. My next move would be my own.

A Risk Worth Taking

Founding Peter Montoya Inc. in 1997 was the boldest move I had ever made—and the riskiest. In the early days, when I was broke, I sold my house to keep the company afloat.

Me with some of my family: Mom (Denise), John, Matt, Mark and Luke.

But I never doubted what I was doing. I've always believed that Personal Branding was a fundamental business force just waiting to be understood. I was determined to be the one who revealed its power to the world.

That mission has led me to innovate—launching the magazine *Peter Montoya's Personal Branding* and creating my unique "What's Your Brand?" seminar, for example.

But the success I've had so far—including this book—has ultimately been the result of exhaustive work fueled by an absolute dedication to an idea I passionately believe in.

Full Circle

Today, I've come back to family, by creating two families of my own. First, on New Year's Eve 2001, I married Lynn, the love of my life and my true inspiration. Second, I'm fortunate enough to have populated Peter Montoya, Inc. with some of the most extraordinary

The love of my life and I at our big night, December 31, 2001.

people I've ever had the privilege to know. They're my family, too.

So it really does come down to people. Find good ones who match your dedication and turn them loose. Stay true to the mission and your passion, and don't be afraid to risk something new.

It's sure worked for me.

Get the magazine that picks up where the book leaves off.

Subscribe to **Peter Montoya's Personal Branding**—the only publication dedicated to Personal Branding!

Peter Montoya's Personal Branding is the only place you'll find the critical secrets you need to become a Personal Branding scholar and develop the skills to achieve the success you crave.

Each full color issue is a power-packed user's manual of insights, how-to tips and real-world branding stories:

> Profiles of some of today's hottest Personal Brands

> Personal Branding basics and what makes them great

> Practical brand strategies for entrepreneurs

> Career advancement tactics for corporate professionals

> Ideas on using Personal Branding in sales, negotiation, financial services and more

Get the most potent professional success tool ever devised. Get branded...or get eaten. Call or click today!

Here's What You'll Learn...

Personal Brochures

My writers and designers have created hundreds of stunning Personal Brochures for clients of all types—conservative, wild, urban, rural, you name it—in every industry. Use our knowledge to create the most important Personal Branding tool you'll ever have.

Personal Postcards

Personal Branding demands continual communication, and direct mail makes it happen. Learn what top branding strategists do to develop a direct response schedule—a schedule that can work with your market, and within your budget.

Brand Identity:
Logos & Stationery

"Identity" means logo, slogan, business cards and letterhead. These elements are often a prospect's first point of contact, so they need to be impressive and professional. Your personality and style must be encapsulated in a logo that reflects who you are and instantly communicates to your audience what makes you unique.

Web Sites

A Web site is no longer optional; it's essential. You'll learn how to design a site that's not about fancy graphics, but about meeting your strategic goals. Whether you need online applications and functionality or a powerful lead-gathering tool, you'll learn how to use the Internet as a resource that works.

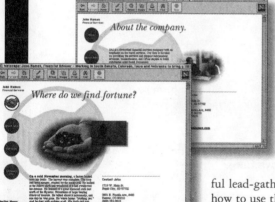

Custom One-Year Marketing & Branding Plans

How do you get your brand message out? What tactics do you use? What are your goals? Every Personal Brand begins with these questions—and we'll show you the answers.

Register today: (888) 730-5300 or www.petermontoya.com

At The Brand Called You,® you'll learn the branding techniques of billion-dollar Personal Brands.

> How to control your client's perception of you by creating and instilling your position.

> How to select a precise target market that will earn you far more money than marketing to everyone.

> How to tap into the incredible power of marketing channels, including networking and professional referrals.

> Direct mail mistakes to avoid, and how to use direct mail correctly to attract clients and generate referrals.

> How to name your practice, and create a slogan to help your Personal Brand grow into a market-moving force.

> Master the Web site secrets that will transform your portal into a client-servicing, business-generating power-port.

Sign up today!

For pricing, locations and upcoming dates call **(888) 730-5300** or go to **www.petermontoya.com.**

PeterMontoya Inc.
The Leaders in Personal Branding

Register today: (888) 730-5300 or www.petermontoya.com

Quick Order Form

Fax orders: 714-285-0929. Send this form.

Telephone orders: Call 888-730-5300 toll free. Have credit card ready.

E-Mail Orders: orders@petermontoya.com

Postal Orders: Peter Montoya Inc., 1540 South Lyon Street,
Santa Ana, CA 92660 USA

PLEASE SEND THE FOLLOWING BOOKS.

*I understand that I may return any of them for a full refund –
for any reason, no questions asked.*

	Qty	Price	Total
The Brand Called You		$24.95	
The Brand Called You for Financial Advisors		$29.95	
The Personal Branding Phenomenon		$24.95	

(Sales tax: Please add 7.75% for products shipped in California)   **Sales Tax** _____

Subtotal _____

Grand Total _____

Appropriate shipping charges will apply

PLEASE SEND ME MORE *FREE* INFORMATION ON:

☐ Other Books   ☐ Speaking/Seminars   ☐ Mailing Lists   ☐ Coaching

NAME: _____

ADDRESS: _____

CITY: _____ STATE: _____ ZIP: _____

TELEPHONE: _____

E-MAIL ADDRESS: _____

Payment:

☐ MasterCard   ☐ Visa   ☐ AMEX   ☐ Discover   ☐ Check (Payable to Peter Montoya Inc.)

CARD NUMBER: _____

NAME ON CARD: _____ EXP. DATE _____